# Praise for *The Disney Way*

"I've been obsessed with the enchantment of the Disney empire ever since I was a little girl. As an adult entrepreneur and CEO, studying Walt Disney's magical culture is beyond inspiring and motivating. *The Disney Way* has become a business handbook for me and my entire team."

—Tyra Banks, Founder and CEO, **TYRA** *Beauty*

"This book is about the real magic: stimulating and harmonizing the collective energy of your people."

—Ken Blanchard, bestselling author of *The One Minute Manager*

"So useful you may whistle while you work."

—*Fortune*

"It was the Disney standard of imagination and engagement that inspired me so many years ago. . . . Now, Bill and Lynn bring these ideals and practices into practical use, with something for any dreamer to use."

—From the new foreword by John Christensen, coauthor of the bestselling book *FISH!*

"Do buy this book. Dare to bring its principles to life. Believe there's a better way. What you'll discover in *The Disney Way* is that the world's most successful leaders do not leave their fortunes to chance."

"The powerful message of *The Disney Way* is that you can and must push the boundaries, invent and reinvent, but that creativity is not the beginning and end of the story. You cannot build an enduring enterprise without impeccable attention to detail and devotion to executing your plan."

—Suzanne Bates, Founder and CEO, Bates Communications and author, *All the Leader You Can Be: The Science of Achieving Extraordinary Executive Presence*

Walt Disney's "Dream, Believe, Dare, Do" principles will help any organization build a long-standing culture defined by dedicated and passionate people who take pride in delivering excellent quality and like Disney, never forget why the guest is standing out there in line."

—David Overton, Founder, Chairman and & CEO

"In *The Disney Way*, you will read how Walt's Dream, Believe, Dare, Do principles enabled Ottawa County, Michigan to become a true role model for twenty-first century governance. Ottawa County Administrator Al Vander-berg and his team are exceptional leaders who understand how the world and peoples' needs are changing. Together they have built a culture that treats every resident and organization in a courteous and responsive manner as a valued customer. As a seasoned public servant, Al was inspired by *The Disney Way* and has led Ottawa County in building trusting relationships with other government, business and nonprofit organizations, then collaborating to innovate new ways to enhance the value of services they provide their communities."

—James W.F. Brooks, retired CEO, Beverage America,
Chairman, Brooks Capital Management, LLC

"Getting large numbers of people who are working in disparate functions, to volunteer their passion and their finest individual and collective efforts toward delivering on the critical few objectives that will have the biggest impact on their organization's success is the single most impactful thing a leader can do. To be able to do so, consistently, throughout an entire orga-nization requires a winning culture—the most durable of competitive advan-tages. *The Disney Way* is not only a compelling read, it provides leaders at every level with the principles, actionable best practices, and inspiration to go out and create a winning culture in their team, division, or company. You will be glad you took the time to read it yourself, and will want to get a copy for your leaders at every level!"

—Bob Whitman, Chairman and CEO, FranklinCovey

"'The employee is the company' is the sentiment at the center of both Zappos' and Disney's experience. Moving your business toward that level of engagement is at the heart of *The Disney Way*."

—Tony Hsieh, author of *Delivering Happiness*

# The
# Disney
# Way

# The Disney Way

• • •

## Harnessing the Management Secrets of Disney in Your Company

Bill Capodagli
and
Lynn Jackson

New York   Chicago   San Francisco   Athens   London
Madrid   Mexico City   Milan   New Delhi
Singapore   Sydney   Toronto

2 3 4 5 6 7 8 9 10   LCR   21 20 19 18 17

ISBN: 978-1-259-58387-2
MHID: 1-259-58387-2

e-ISBN: 978-1-259-58388-9
e-MHID: 1-259-58388-0

**Library of Congress Cataloging-in-Publication Data**

Names: Capodagli, Bill, 1948– author. | Jackson, Lynn, 1955– author.
Title: The Disney way : harnessing the management secrets of Disney in your
   company / by Bill Capodagli and Lynn Jackson.
Description: Third edition. | New York : McGraw-Hill, 2016.
Identifiers: LCCN 2015051020| ISBN 9781259583872 (hardback) | ISBN 1259583872
   ()
Subjects: LCSH: Walt Disney Company—Management. | BISAC: BUSINESS &
   ECONOMICS / Management.
Classification: LCC PN1999.W27 C37 2016 | DDC 384/.80979494—dc23 LC record available at http://lccn.
loc.gov/2015051020

McGraw-Hill Education books are available at special quantity discounts to use as premiums and sales promotions, or for use in corporate training programs. To contact a representative, please visit the Contact Us page at www.mhprofessional.com.

This work is based upon the author's experience and research at The Walt Disney Company and elsewhere and is not sponsored or approved by Disney or any other firm. This book does not include any confidential or proprietary information from Disney or any such other firm.

For the late Grace Capodagli—Bill's loving mother—
whose Dream, Believe, Dare, Do journey made her life
and the lives of many others worth living

# Contents

Foreword to the Third Edition, by John Christensen     ix

Preface to the Third Edition     xi

**Chapter 1.** Walt's Way     1

## DREAM

**Chapter 2.** Make Everyone's Dreams Come True     15

## BELIEVE

**Chapter 3.** You Better Believe It     31

**Chapter 4.** Never a Customer, Always a Guest     53

**Chapter 5.** All for One and One for All     75

**Chapter 6.** Share the Spotlight     101

## DARE

**Chapter 7.** Dare to Dare     125

## DO

**Chapter 8.** Practice, Practice, Practice     143

**Chapter 9.** Make Your Elephant Fly—Plan     163

**Chapter 10.** Capture the Magic with Storyboards     179

**Chapter 11.** Give Details Top Billing                              203

**Chapter 12.** Love: The Real Pixie Dust                             215

## PUTTING IT TOGETHER

**Chapter 13.** Ottawa County, Michigan: Disney's Success Credo
Transforms County Government                                          233

**Chapter 14.** Producing a Customer-Centric Culture:
An Implementation Strategy                                            253


**Epilogue. The Magic Continues**                                    263

**Acknowledgments**                                                  270

**Index**                                                            273

**About the Authors**                                                285

# Foreword

I can still remember the feeling of excitement that came over me every Sunday evening . . . the great anticipation of getting my grilled cheese sandwich and tomato soup on a TV tray and awaiting the start of my favorite show.

Then, on the screen it would appear. The beautiful castle, and Tinker Bell would wave her wand, and the pixie dust would drop, and *The Wonderful World of Disney* would begin. Wow! All those feelings come back as if it were just last night. For me, that was over 50 years ago, but that feeling still excites me every time I have a Disney experience.

What is the *magic*? Part of me wants to know, while the other part of me just wants to keep on experiencing it, like wanting and not wanting to know how a magic trick is performed. Bill and Lynn have cracked open the curtain so we can all have access to some of the insights into The Wonderful World of Disney.

It was the Disney standard of imagination and engagement that inspired me so many years ago, and with that pixie dust in my heart, I discovered the *FISH!* Philosophy, a group of daily practices that reflect the ideals Walt Disney shared with the world. Now, Bill and Lynn bring these ideals and practices into practical use, with something for any dreamer to use.

We have all heard of the Disney secrets: customers are called "Guests," Theme Parks are called the "shows," and behind the scenes is called the "backstage." But the real magic that Bill and Lynn share with us is Walt's underlying philosophy of "I dream, I test my dreams against my beliefs, I dare to take risks, and I execute my vision to make those dreams come true: Dream, Believe, Dare, Do."

The Walt Disney Company has seen many changes over the years, and it is going through change now, but what keeps on guiding this great big Dream is Walt's values and beliefs. Few people have had the chance to see the true magic behind the curtain, but learning about these guiding principles, as readers will do with this book, opens the magic for so many of us.

In this book, Bill and Lynn reveal how the Dream, Believe, Dare, Do principles are lived in organizations of all types, from startups to nonprofits to healthcare facilities. Among these exciting organizations are **TYRA** *Beauty*, Ottawa County, Michigan, and Rainbow Babies & Children's Hospital.

Walt gave the world so many gifts—the gift of Dreaming big, Believing in your Dreams, Daring to take risks, and Doing it (executing it), and you can share in those Dreams too.

Make your Dreams come true.

John Christensen
Playground Director, Coauthor of *FISH!*
Charthouse Learning—Home of the *FISH!* Philosophy

# Preface to the Third Edition

The late legendary management consultant Peter Drucker once said, "When you see a successful business, someone once made a courageous decision." Those who have prospered despite a pathway of obstacles have done so with an inner compass that steers their course . . . deeply held values that have crystallized and led them to achieve tangible results. Walt Disney, the great storyteller and innovator, had such a compass that defined his enviable empire. His four steps were simple:

> **Dream beyond the boundaries of today, believe in sound values, dare to make a difference, and then just go out and do it: Dream, Believe, Dare, Do.**

For over two decades, Capodagli Jackson Consulting has inspired and led thousands of leaders, employees, and conference attendees to embrace these four principles, the success formula that worked for Walt. *The Disney Way* was named as a "best business book" and deemed "so useful, you may whistle while you work" by *Fortune* magazine. *The Disney Way* is still a popular choice among readers, evidenced by the *Los Angeles Times* in the quote, "There is still magic in Disney's words."

In the 2007 edition of this book, Capodagli and Jackson shared a collection of unique stories of triumph. Most of these organizations, from The Cheesecake Factory to Ernst & Young, had both global reputations and stellar achievements.

In this edition, the authors feature organizations that are predominantly in start-up mode or have revamped their strategies to become more customer-centric. The lineup includes six entities that have recently launched their businesses or have reinvented their cultures: **TYRA** *Beauty*, zTailors, Science Center of Iowa, Joe C. Davis YMCA Outdoor Center/Camp Widjiwagan, the Grand Lake Center of Grand County, Colorado, and McLean County, Illinois, Unit (School) District No. 5. There are also three well-established organizations that are striving to continuously improve: ACTS Retirement-Life Communities, University Hospitals Rainbow Babies & Children's Hospital, and California State University Channel Islands. Two additional organizations, Flanagin's Bulk Mail Service and The Village Toy Center, demonstrate how the Dream, Believe, Dare, Do principles apply in a small community business. And, finally, how Ottawa County, Michigan, one of the most progressive state administrative divisions in the United States, has used each element of *The Disney Way* as a starting point to create an amazing culture over a period of three years.

At the end of Chapters 2 through 12 are riveting examples of how one of the featured organizations has put into action the lessons of the chapter. Chapters 12, 13, and 14 are brand new chapters that showcase the following: Chapter 12, "Love: The Real Pixie Dust," which explains the importance of love for employees, customers, products, and yourself; Chapter 13, "Ottawa County, Michigan: Disney's Success Credo Transforms County Government," is the detailed account of the county's phenomenally successful customer-centric journey; and Chapter 14, "Producing a Customer-Centric Culture: An Implementation Strategy," is a roadmap for implementing the Dream, Believe, Dare, Do principles in any organization.

Throughout the book, you will also find Questions to Ask and Actions to Take chalkboards. These will provide you with ideas for living the Dream, Believe, Dare, Do principles and sustain outstanding rewards in doing so. At the end of each chapter, an Internet link to Chapter Chats with Bill is provided in which coauthor Bill Capodagli discusses additional insights regarding the content.

This book tells the story of how passion for employees, customers, and products has translated into immeasurable success for Walt Disney and other great leaders, past and present. Their stories come to life through examples of real drive, courage, humanity, and a compelling thirst to make a difference within their own organizations. These leaders possess a charismatic quality that naturally inspires others to challenge themselves. In the same vein, they rely on the power of everyone on the entire team to journey together and unlock the future possibilities that they believe are endless.

The inspirational stories in this updated and expanded third edition of *The Disney Way* will challenge the original readers to examine their Dream, Believe, Dare, Do results, and they will provide new readers with a framework that will enable them to soar beyond the limits of traditional management through these four powerful principles. From entry-level recruits to CEOs, from private companies to public agencies, Walt Disney's principles continue to redefine the nature of business in our age and revolutionize the art of management.

# Chapter 1

# Walt's Way

*I only hope that we don't lose sight of one thing . . . that it was all started by a mouse.*

Walt Disney

When a young Midwestern artist was struggling to get his first filmmaking business off the ground in 1923, he borrowed $500 from his Uncle Robert. Uncle Robert insisted on repayment in cash rather than taking an ownership interest in the venture. That young artist, Walter Elias Disney, went on to advance the demanding art of animation to new heights and founded a company based on such sound business principles that it has survived for nearly a century and has influenced virtually every aspect of American culture.

Hindsight, of course, has a well-deserved reputation for startling clarity, and we don't know if Uncle Robert lived long enough to feel a full measure of regret. But, had he opted for stock in The Walt Disney Company instead of a cash repayment, the return on his $500 would have amounted to almost a billion dollars from 1923 to the present.

How did a boy who was born into rather modest circumstances in turn-of-the-century Chicago accomplish so much? Legend has it that Walt Disney explained his success this way: "I dream, I test my dreams against my beliefs, I dare to take risks, and I execute my vision to make those dreams come true."

Dream, Believe, Dare, Do: These words reverberate across the decades of Disney achievement. Everything Walt did—every choice he made, every strategy he pursued—evolved from these four principles. And as the bedrock upon which his life and work rested, they naturally formed the basic values that dictated how he ran his Company. Thus, the ways in which The Walt Disney Company trained and enabled its employees, managed creativity and innovation, and provided service to its customers were all influenced by this four-pillared credo.

## Why Disney?

The more we learn about this legendary figure and his achievements, both as an artist and as a creative business leader, the more certain it becomes that the Disney story embodies valuable lessons for every organization.

Like nearly everyone else alive today, we, the authors, grew up being almost as familiar with the Disney name as we were with our own. Many childhood hours were spent sitting on the floor before the TV set watching *The Wonderful World of Disney* and being transported to the Magic Kingdom. And neither of us has been able to forget the thrill of seeing *Peter Pan* for the first time.

### Bill

As a young father introducing my own children to *Peter Pan*, I marveled at its ability to rekindle the emotions I initially felt watching them as a six-year-old. Disneyland had much of the same effect when I visited for the first time over 40 years ago. Not surprisingly, as the trip was coming to an end, my then three-year-old son didn't want to leave, and I felt a little bit that way myself.

On this trip, though, I was captivated by much more than the fabulous attractions. Viewing the Park through the eyes of an industrial engineer, I was thoroughly intrigued by the processes. How did Disney manage all those crowds? How did they train their employees? How did they run their customer service? What was the secret of the success of their complex technology? I came away from that first visit deeply impressed by the organization—and with a lot of questions.

### Lynn

As for me, *The Wonderful World of Disney* television show was one of the best things about being a child. But it wasn't until many years later, when I became heavily involved in the field of training and development, that I realized the true magic of Disney's philosophy. For me, the seed for benchmarking Disney was planted when I took a copy of *Service America* by Karl Albrecht and the late Ron Zemke with me on a trip to Florida in the mid-eighties. I knew it would help me prepare for an upcoming seminar that I was to conduct for a group of salespeople from all over the country. While reading Albrecht and Zemke's book, I realized why Walt Disney believed that every employee *is* the company in the mind of the customer. From that point on, my goal in training salespeople was to inspire them to begin living that mindset. Then, on my next trip to Walt Disney World, I closely observed the best of the best in action, doing just that.

● ● ●

Years later, when we started looking around for companies that could serve as examples in our consulting business, we found ourselves coming back again and again to Disney. A great deal of scrutinizing, analyzing, and researching led us to conclude that none compared to Disney when it came to running an organization. Where one company might excel in customer relations, another might work well with its suppliers, Disney does it all. The Walt Disney Company combines consistency in direction and overall strategy, unrivaled customer service, product creativity, employee training, relatively low turnover, and impressive profitability to make it the perfect business model, at least in our eyes.

Having studied the Disney phenomenon for over four decades, we are convinced that the management techniques we call *Walt's Way* are as valid today as they were in 1937, when the very first animated feature film *Snow White and the Seven Dwarfs* captured the hearts of moviegoers. Skeptics need only look to the spectacular successes The Walt Disney Company continues to achieve year after year, decade after decade, for affirmation of *Walt's Way*.

And if you're wondering whether the Disney magic has legs, we can answer that with a resounding *yes*! Over the years, we have encouraged clients in many different industries to use Walt's Dream, Believe, Dare, Do credo to improve their customer service, leadership, and innovation, while at the same time creating an atmosphere of fun. The Company that Walt founded has, in effect, served as a laboratory for us and, in turn, our clients.

## A Legend in the Making

Like many other young men of his time and place, Walt Disney held a succession of jobs punctuated by stints of formal education. In 1923, his skill as an artist and his interest in cartoons took him to California where he and his brother, Roy, founded the company that was originally known as the Disney Brothers Cartoon Studio. Five years later, they introduced the character of Mickey Mouse in the synchronized sound cartoon *Steamboat Willie*. The cartoon and the mouse were an instant hit.

By the 1930s, this endearing little scamp had captured the hearts of audiences worldwide. Known as *Michael Maus* in Germany, *Miki Kuchi* in Japan, and *Miquel Ratonocito* in Spain, he even had a car named after him! When Fiat, the Italian automobile company, produced its first small car shortly after World War II, it was christened *Topolino*, Mickey's Italian nickname. Even though Mickey became a senior citizen a few years back, his ageless persona continues to be recognized and loved by young and old on every continent.

Mickey may have led the parade, but Disney was not a one-mouse band by a long shot. No other company in the notoriously chancy entertainment business has ever achieved the stability, phenomenal growth, and multidirectional expansion of Disney.

In spite of its ever-increasing reach, The Walt Disney Company has consistently kept to the central course described by its founder at the outset: to provide the finest in family entertainment. Firmly grounded in Walt's innate sense of principle and his Midwestern values, this mission has, over the years, become clearly associated with the Disney brand. Audiences expect it, and they are seldom disappointed. Whatever form the family entertainment might take—a Theme Park ride, a Broadway musical, an Ice Capades production—it has to be a good show in every regard. When Walt talked about delivering "the good show," he didn't mean simply a glittering spectacle relying on superficial bells and whistles. He meant an entirely original, perfectly executed production with substance, created to delight a wide audience. He believed that this was what customers wanted and expected from him, and he was fanatical about providing it.

What's more, the concept of a good show encompasses far more than the on-stage action in a single production. Because Walt insisted that customers be treated like Guests, great customer service has become a standard feature of the total package The Walt Disney Company offers. And wrapped up in that package is a gift of creativity—in product, service, and process—that makes even jaded adults smile with childlike delight.

Accomplishing such magic requires the talent and dedication of loyal staff as well as an army of suppliers and other partners. Extensive training, constant reinforcement of the Disney culture and its values, and recognition of the valuable contributions that employees and partners make continue to enable them to turn out one fantastic show after another as they strive to meet the exacting standards Walt established.

It is this consistency of direction, obsession with customer service, commitment to people, and creative excellence that make The Walt Disney Company a standard by which others might be judged and an exemplary enterprise from which others can learn.

## A Consummate Dreamer

Walt Disney was a businessman and a lifelong dreamer who started out as a commercial artist. But it was precisely his unfettered imagination, coupled with a bent for experimentation that propelled him to the pinnacle of success. Dreaming was the wellspring of Disney's creativity.

The story is told that as a schoolboy in art class, Walt was assigned to draw flowers. In what might now be seen as a quintessential touch, and, indeed, the precursor to many of Disney's animated characters, young Walt embellished his work by sketching a face in the center of each flower. His teacher was less than impressed by the boy's deviation from the norm, and, lacking a magic mirror like the one the Wicked Queen had in *Snow White*, she failed to recognize the creative genius whose dream world would make him one of the most famous people in history.

Perhaps because he himself was the greatest of dreamers, Walt encouraged both his artisans and his hundreds of other employees to unleash their imaginations too. He knew that a reservoir of creative power often languishes within a company's ranks simply because no one ever bothers to tap it. Rather than hire someone for one specific purpose and forever pigeonhole that person—which is the norm in too many companies—Walt not only welcomed ideas from all of his employees but also actively sought to turn those ideas into reality.

From dreams spring ideas, and from ideas come innovations, the lifeblood of any company. Walt Disney instinctively knew, however, that an unshakable belief—in one's principles, in one's associates and employees, and in one's customers—is necessary for dreams to become reality.

No matter how ingenious an idea was, no matter what kind of financial interests were at stake, Walt demanded that the Company adhere to his belief in and commitment to honesty, reliability, loyalty, and respect for people *as individuals*. Whether he was producing a cartoon or building a Theme Park, he refused to sell a shoddy product to his audience.

When *Pinocchio* was released in February 1940, the *New York Times* hailed it as "the best cartoon ever made." But *Pinocchio* had a difficult birth. The story of the puppet-maker Geppetto and his "son" Pinocchio, the all-but-human puppet he created, was six months into production, and the team of animation artists was almost halfway through its meticulous, time-consuming drawings for the full-length feature when Walt Disney called a halt. Pinocchio was altogether too wooden, he said, and the character proposed for Jiminy Cricket made him look too much like, well, a cricket. Never mind that $500,000 had already been spent, Walt was not deterred. Previous efforts were tossed aside, and he called Ward Kimball, one of his talented young animators, into his office.

Ward, who was upset because his labors on *Snow White* had ended up on the cutting-room floor, was planning to use the occasion to resign when Walt summoned him, but the animator never had a chance. He got so excited listening to Walt talk about his dreams for the film and his ideas about Jiminy Cricket that Ward entirely forgot his own intentions of leaving. Instead, he stayed at the Company and went on to create a cricket that was more human than insect, one that embodied the spirit of hope that children of all ages possess, but that sometimes needs reinforcing.

The decision to halt the production of *Pinocchio* was made because the movie was failing to live up to one of Walt Disney's values: his insistence on excellence. At the time, Disney already had won worldwide acclaim. Walt probably could have let the film go as it was without doing any serious damage to his Company or his reputation—and with substantial savings. But he recognized the difference between mediocre and excellent, and he would not compromise.

That's not to say that Walt was a spendthrift. Quite the contrary: He was always acutely aware of the bottom line, but he simply refused to let it dictate every decision he made. "Why should we let a few dollars jeopardize our chances?" Walt once wrote to his brother, Roy. Before it was finished, *Pinocchio* cost $3 million. Although high priced for its day, this film classic long ago paid for itself in the degree of sophisticated animation, craftsmanship, and artwork it achieved.

Walt Disney's strength as an imaginative and principled creative force grew from his willingness to take risks, to experiment, and to invest his resources and his time in new ventures. From the beginning, he searched for innovative ways to give his audiences the best of all possible entertainment fare. He pioneered a new art form in making *Snow White*, and he did it in the face of nearly unanimous ridicule.

"No one will sit through a 90-minute cartoon," Walt's advisors told him. But Walt ignored the naysayers and clung tenaciously to his dream, confident that he could produce a film that would appeal to both adults and children. His willingness to challenge accepted wisdom and take a risk wound up paying handsome dividends. For example, *Snow White and the Seven Dwarfs*, which was released in 1937, grossed $8 million, an astonishing amount when you consider that at the time movie tickets cost only pennies. It received a special Academy Award, and some consider it to be one of the greatest films ever made. *Snow White* has also been equally popular in reissue, and it has earned itself a place in the top 50 all-time highest-grossing films.

From 1930 through 1942, Walt Disney managed to transform animation from a marginal segment of the entertainment industry to a new art form. He used technical innovations to create a seamless mixture of story, color, and sound. Knowing that great visions require great, but calculated, risks, Walt dared to follow his instincts.

## Turning Dreams into Reality

Walt Disney's remarkable accomplishments might suggest that he had no difficulty in taking whatever action was needed to fulfill his dreams. It was not always easy, however, particularly when a lot of skeptics stood in the way, but Walt knew that dreams lie dormant unless the dreamer can do what it takes to make them come true.

When his fertile mind produced an idea, he set about transforming that idea into a concrete product, service, or process. If his methods of executing his vision were sometimes unconventional or broke the accepted rules, so be it. The point was to put on the good show.

For example, when Disneyland was being built in the early 1950s, Walt himself was often on site checking every detail. He spent countless hours with the creative and knowledgeable staff he had hired, putting his personal stamp on everything from landscape design to attractions to music.

But then he did something rather unusual: he asked everyone who was working on Disneyland, from electricians to executives, to test each attraction as it was completed. There was nothing new about Disney's reaching for perfection, but the Park was on a tight schedule with opening day near at hand, and this idea clearly seemed to be a waste of time and money. Imagine asking your staff for critical input about a new product or service just before you're ready to launch it. Walt's request was a bit farfetched. Or was it?

Although a great deal of what he did is foreign to many leaders, this was Walt's way of doing whatever needed to be done to achieve his vision. It was another way of making absolutely sure that everything was the best that it could be and that nothing was missing.

And Walt's unusual request proved to be vital when a Cast Member (Disney's language for employees) realized that something was missing from a swashbuckling Disneyland attraction called Pirates of the Caribbean (the last attraction Walt supervised before his death in 1966). A construction worker, or Cast Member, who happened to hail from Louisiana bayou country, approached Walt after taking the ride and told him, "Something's missing, but I can't figure out what it is."

"Ride it again, and keep on riding until you've figured it out," Walt told him.

Finally, after repeated trips through Disney's Caribbean, the Cast Member realized what was wrong: in tropical climates, the night should be alive with fireflies, but there were none on this attraction. In short order, Walt Disney saw to it that his version of a Caribbean fantasy had fireflies blinking in the dark.

Whether it was fireflies in a Theme Park attraction, the portrayal of a wise and lovable cricket, the treatment of a Disney Guest (Disney's language for "customers"), or the removal of a candy wrapper threatening to litter Disneyland's landscape, Walt was a perfectionist down to the last detail. As for those candy wrappers, it isn't just the staff of street cleaners who are charged with litter removal at Disney Parks. Instead, any Cast Member who spots a bit of trash tries to sweep it up before even it flutters to the ground. That is part of the Disney culture that is ingrained in everyone—it becomes part of their DNA. It is everyone's job to keep the Parks clean. Cast Members are trained extensively and the culture is reinforced because Walt considered this approach essential to executing his Dream.

He also knew that creating magical moments was impossible without a framework within which ideas could be effectively implemented while controlling costs. To that end, the Company follows a rigorous process of project management. And to solve problems that arise in planning and communicating project ideas, it has adapted the storyboarding technique originally used to keep track of the thousands of drawings needed for the animation of cartoon features.

Execution of ideas is never left to chance in the Disney universe. It is a well-planned process.

## Embracing the Disney Spirit

Dream. Believe. Dare. Do. Just as Walt Disney never wavered from his four-pillared credo, history is replete with examples of great accomplishments derived from the same commitment. We are reminded, for example, of President John F. Kennedy's challenge to America in 1961 to put the first man on the moon in the ensuing decade. Kennedy had a dream that he firmly believed could become a reality because he saw that it fit perfectly with the can-do spirit that has driven the United States from its outset. To make such a commitment and to embark on this monumental space project was daring, to be sure, but in the doing, America saw a man set foot on the moon's surface, and the entire world reaped scientific benefits that had far-reaching significance (Figure 1-1).

So, too, have Walt Disney's Dream, Believe, Dare, Do principles led to unimagined glories as the empire he established continues to grow and thrive. Back in 1923, it's doubtful that even Walt himself could have foreseen that the Disney interests would one day extend to movies, television, Broadway

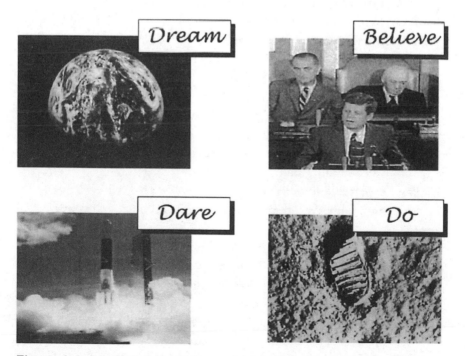

**Figure 1-1**. President John F. Kennedy's challenge to America in 1961 to put the first man on the moon.

theater, worldwide theme parks, a vacation club, and a cruise line (not to mention the nation's largest laundry facility at Walt Disney World).

Disneyland (which recently marked its sixtieth anniversary) and Walt Disney World draw ever more Guests from the far reaches of the world. *Walt's Way* has made such an impression on these Guests that over 70 percent of them are repeat visitors!

Disney's financial record is equally impressive. It continually proves to be a solid investment. For example, if you invested $1,000 in Disney stock in 1984, it would be worth nearly $96,000 today, while a similar investment in Standard & Poor's Index of 500 stocks would be worth a little over $11,000.

Such is the power of *Walt's Way*: Dream. Believe. Dare. Do. You too can incorporate those words into your business vocabulary by following the 11 fundamentals (we added one more to the original 10 cited in the earlier editions) that are at the heart of the Disney methodology:

1. Give every member of your organization a chance to dream, and tap into the creativity those dreams embody.
2. Stand firm on your beliefs and principles.
3. Treat your customers like guests.
4. Support, enable, and reward employees.
5. Build long-term relationships with key suppliers and partners.
6. Dare to take calculated risks in order to bring innovative ideas to fruition.
7. Train extensively and constantly reinforce your organization's culture.
8. Align long-term vision with short-term execution.
9. Use the storyboarding technique to solve problems, plan projects, and improve communication.
10. Pay close attention to detail.
11. Love your employees, your customers, your product, and yourself!

In the chapters that follow, you will see how the Dream, Believe, Dare, Do principles are being put into action on a daily basis by organizations from healthcare to manufacturing. We will share our insights as to how even Disney stumbled along the way, and we will present our recommendations for re-creating the magic. Throughout the book, we have capitalized the words "Company," "Cast Member," and "Guest" (as they refer to The Walt Disney Company) to honor the tradition of treating these important entities as proper nouns. In keeping with Walt's tradition of referring to people by their first names, we also refer to ourselves as "Bill" and/or "Lynn."

We would also like to point out that we are not suggesting that leaders merely imitate Disney. Obviously, each organization and individual situation is different, and the wholesale adoption of another's methods is neither wise nor practical. But more importantly, Disney itself has won continued success by constantly reinventing its own products to maintain superb quality. To imitate another and adopt a particular method lock, stock, and barrel implies contentment with the status quo that flies in the face of everything Walt stood for.

---

**Remember: Innovate, don't imitate.**

---

## Parting Thoughts

We believe that gaining an understanding of the hows and whys of Walt Disney's Dream, Believe, Dare, Do principles will enable you to innovate, make changes, and find your own unique pathway to continued success. In the next chapter, you will learn why we always say, "It all begins with a Dream." And, finally, we hope that you will enjoy "Chapter Chats with Bill"—additional insights available through an Internet link at the end of each chapter.

---

**Chapter Chats with Bill: http://capojac.com/disneyway/1/**

---

# Dream

DREAM

# Chapter 2

# Make Everyone's Dreams Come True

*A dream is a wish your heart makes.*

Jiminy Cricket

I t is no easy matter to convey a dream. Dreams, by nature, are deeply personal experiences. But true to his imaginative genius, Walt Disney was able to transform his dreams into stories that effectively articulated his vision to others. More importantly, the stories served to draw others into his fantasies, thereby marshaling the power of their collective creativity for the benefit of his dream.

In the early days when his Company was small, Walt used to call the animators into his office to discuss an idea for a new film project. With dramatic effect, he would embark upon a story—not a literal narrative account of his idea but an ancient myth, perhaps, or some other related tale that conveyed the feelings and emotions behind his dream and his hope for the project's success. In short order, the master would capture the imaginations of his Cast Members and in the process, stimulate the kind of excitement and commitment of minds and hearts that he knew would be necessary to turn Disney-size dreams into reality. For example, he insisted that the castle at Disneyland be built first—before anything else—so that this visual structure could help shape the vision and rally everyone around the dream he was trying to create (Figure 2-1).

**Figure 2-1.** Coauthor Bill Capodagli at the Castle That Helped Shape Walt Disney's Dream for His Sleeping Beauty Castle in Disneyland— "Mad King" Ludwig's Neuschwanstein Castle in Bavaria.

He was such a vivid and persuasive storyteller that his listeners usually found themselves swept up—like Ward Kimball on the *Pinocchio* project— in a passionate endorsement of Walt's vision. Long before solid plans were in place for the next movie or cartoon, before any budgets were prepared, and prior to any administrative and engineering problems being ironed out, Walt had established a team atmosphere around the forthcoming venture. Thus, he began nearly every new project with eager and enthusiastic participants, an enormous advantage in a process that often involved long hours of work, seven days a week.

Among the most important projects that Walt began near the end of his life was the California Institute of the Arts, now known as CalArts. His artistic legacy is perhaps best preserved in this college-level professional school that encompasses all the creative and performing arts. Walt once said, "It's the principal thing I hope to leave when I move on to greener pastures. If I can help provide a place to develop the talent of the future, I think I will have accomplished something."

One of those "future talents" was John Lasseter, who now holds a string of titles including Chief Creative Officer of Walt Disney Studios, Pixar Animation Studios, and DisneyToon Studios; and Principal Creative Advisor at Walt Disney Imagineering. The story of John Lasseter's long journey to landing his current role in Disney Studios is an inspiring one, and it sparked us in writing *Innovate the Pixar Way: Business Lessons from the World's Most Creative Corporate Playground.* When it comes to his life's work, John speaks with raw emotion and refreshing candor: "I do what I do because of Walt Disney—his films and his Theme Parks and his characters and his joy in entertaining." After the Disney organization purchased Pixar in 2006, John and Ed Catmull (Co-founder of Pixar Animation Studios and President of Walt Disney and Pixar Animation Studios) began to propel the Walt Disney Studios' reascension to greatness.

Keeping Walt Disney's dream alive within Disney itself was critically important to John and Ed. When the duo came aboard to lead animation at Disney in 2006, they endured pressure to close down Disney Animation and replace it with their brainchild—the box-office hit maker, Pixar. But, since John and Ed both credit Walt Disney as being an inspirational force in their lives since childhood, they would not let this happen. John said, "Ed and I absolutely could not do that." With the last decade's string of Disney hits that included *Tangled, Frozen*, and *Big Hero 6*, they have realized their dream of a luminescent Disney Studios as a fitting tribute to their beloved founding father.

## Storytelling: How Dreams Come Alive

Disney is arguably the most successful entertainment conglomerate of all time. In 2014, Disney's Parks and Resorts claimed record attendance, even though the Magic Kingdom's daily admission prices increased for the twenty-seventh consecutive year. During the same fiscal year, the Parks and Resorts operating profit was a whopping $2.66 billion, a 20 percent increase! When you peel back the economists' facts and figures, you find the root cause of Disney's timeless success: the art of telling the "story."

Stories are part and parcel of our lives, regardless of our uniqueness or value systems. They document our histories, educate us, entertain us, and often inspire us to act, or do. With only 23 percent of consumers trusting ads on TV and only 20 percent trusting ads in magazines or on the radio, it's more important than ever to engage your customers with storytelling.

Stories capture our imaginations and produce experiences. They also create a unique image, one that can be forever embedded in our memories. These stories are one of the main reasons Disney has Guests who return year after year!

Universal Studios in Orlando, Florida, is just about seven miles away from Walt Disney World, and yet it has less than *one-third* of the attendance of just the Magic Kingdom Park alone. While Universal Studios is the home of attractions that may be just as innovative or unique as Disney's, they do not seem to be able to match Disney in terms of the results that its brand and stories produce. For most of us, the inspiring tales of Disney's heroes and heroines have captured our hearts since childhood.

Disney stories are told over and over, from generation to generation, and many of them are best remembered through music. "Bibbidi-Bobbidi-Boo" (Academy Award nominee for Best Original Song), from the 1950 Disney classic *Cinderella*, is still being sung by children today. And who hasn't heard Idena Menzel sing the Academy Award winner "Let It Go" from the 2013 animated feature film *Frozen*? Born with the magical ability to create and control ice, her character Princess Elsa is feared and ultimately ostracized by her kingdom of Arendelle. Alone, she trods up a steep mountain shedding her glove, then her cape, and begins to fearlessly unleash her magical powers. The majesty of her voice and her declaration of freedom seem to bring the whole movie together in what has become one of Disney's most familiar songs. We can't imagine the story without it.

It doesn't matter if you are writing the next Disney song, developing a line of cosmetics, or preparing to open a new long-term-care center. A story must be told in a fresh and engaging way. And, like Disney, everyone in the organization must tell it over and over again.

## Imagineers: Learning from the Master Storytellers

The use of storytelling to rally all project members around a vision is still an important element of the Disney approach, thanks to Walt's formation in the early 1950s of a creative group called Imagineering. Organized during the building of Disneyland, the group's purpose is to carry on the Disney tradition by dreaming up new creative venues, such as the Theme Park attractions.

Today, there are hundreds of Imagineers all over the world who attest to the fact that frivolous blue-sky notions can lead to realistic, yet innovative, outcomes.

Let's look at an example. When The Walt Disney Company set out to build an additional waterpark at Walt Disney World, a small team met in the office of the team leader, a Senior Vice President. They wanted to create a story about the theme of the waterpark and get the project underway. The office was decorated with all manner of personal memorabilia, including those little glass snow globes that, when shaken, produced a flurry of swirling snowflakes. As the team was struggling to come up with an idea for a theme, the executive picked up one of the snow domes and said, "Too bad we can't make a waterpark out of one of these." After a general pause, a team member asked, "Why can't we?" From that simple question, the team took off on the apparently impossible notion of building a ski resort in the sunshine of central Florida.

The creative team went to work. One artist sketched a picture of an alligator wearing earmuffs and careening down a slope on skis. Another drew a fanciful rendition of a winter resort enclosed in a snow dome. While everyone agreed this idea wasn't exactly suitable for Florida, they refused to discard the dream. Instead, they turned to the well-established Disney storytelling method and devised a tale based on a blizzard:

> One cold winter day, a capricious winter storm brought a heavy load of snow to Florida. An entrepreneur came along and built a ski resort. He did well until the weather returned to normal, melting the snow and turning the ski runs into rushing waterfalls. Luckily, the waterfalls were then turned into . . . what else but water rides for adventurous athletes!

Using this fantasy story as their inspiration, Disney Imagineers built the new waterpark and gave it the name Blizzard Beach.

Another example of this tried-and-true approach proved itself when the Imagineers constructed a story about the theme of the shopping and nightclub complex that eventually became Pleasure Island. To set the stage for the envisioned experience, they wove an entirely fictitious tale about Merryweather Pleasure, a sailor who had numerous adventures sailing the seven seas. One day, Merryweather decided to settle down and raise a family in Orlando, Florida, where he built a canvas and sail-making company. The business flourished, and sailors from all over the world would come to buy Merryweather's sails. They would stay up to the wee small hours of the morning sharing their tales of adventure. Finally, Merryweather's passion for the sea became so great that he sailed off into the sunset forever, leaving his company in the hands of his two sons. They were lazy and indifferent to their father's legacy, however, and gradually the factory fell into disrepair and was forced to close. Then one day, the Imagineers discovered the run-down warehouses and turned them into exciting restaurants and nightclubs where once again, people came from all corners of the world to share their stories of travel and adventure.

Both of these stories are ludicrous! Sailing off into the sunset from Orlando, Florida, is impossible—it's 90 miles from the sea. And a blizzard in central Florida? But the real importance of these examples is that they united team members around whimsical notions that piqued their creative playfulness and drew them completely into the visions for the projects. Repeating and embellishing these fantastical stories engaged team members in a way that discussion of budgets and staffing problems could never have done.

As we are writing this book, Imagineers have been crafting and bringing to life a new story about the mammoth and magical Disney Springs that is replacing the entire Downtown Disney area that included Pleasure Island. This is the largest expansion in the over 40-year history of the entertainment complex. Executive Creative Director Theron Skees worked with his Imagineering team to produce a "historic timeline." He said, "Everything at Disney starts with the story. Disney Springs was about bringing a story to this venue that has been around for three decades. . . . Like many waterfront towns throughout Florida, . . . the settlement grew into a full-sized town. . . . That's how Disney Springs was born." From the Cast Member costumes to the choices of architecture, all the pieces of the "story" are in perfect harmony with the Florida town that grew over time. Once the story is complete, Guests will enjoy more than 150 shopping, dining, and entertainment experiences. So once again, the district will bustle with activity of world travelers who come together in the spirit of fun and adventure.

You might say, "Well, that's fine for Disney, but how can we bring our creative energies together to produce something special and create results for our company?" Now, let us introduce the Dream Retreat.

## Dream Retreats: Sparking Teamwork and Creativity

Disney Imagineers are the inspiration for an event that we call a Dream Retreat. In the retreat atmosphere, people begin believing, "If you can *Dream It*, you can *Do It*." For over two decades, we have been amazed by the levels of teamwork and creativity produced in many of our clients' Dream Retreats. This is where the development of a new culture of Dream, Believe, Dare, Do begins to take form.

Walt Disney instinctively knew that participation by Cast Members in the development of a new show gave them a sense of commitment, both to the project in question and to the organization itself. Judging from the extremely low turnover rates at his namesake Company, we can say that Walt's instincts were, as always, right on target. While the norm at most theme parks is a 150 percent turnover rate, the rank-and-file turnover rate at Disney Parks is *less than 30 percent.* Within the Company's management ranks, turnover is even lower—less than 6 percent.

What's more, everything we have learned in working with organizations worldwide lends support to the validity of Walt's inclusive approach. From working with multinational teams, we have discovered that employees all over the world, from China to India to Italy, mostly agree on what is important and what is offensive in a corporate culture. They dislike arrogance on the part of management, and they desperately want real, two-way communication that includes them in planning and resolving critical issues.

A Dream Retreat has proven to be an ideal way of helping organizations initiate needed change. Besides involving employees in strategy and facilitating their understanding of the vision and direction they are pursuing, a Dream Retreat environment propels participants into a world of new ideas that often spark innovative solutions to the problems at hand.

The retreats, which can last anywhere from three to five days, are typically conducted away from company premises. We have found that off-site gatherings are a great way to break down barriers and begin the planning process for the kind of change that ultimately revolutionizes a culture. When people are removed from daily routines and placed in an atmosphere that encourages free expression of their dreams, amazing ideas begin to emerge and flourish. Dreaming in this context is not a solitary occupation. Instead, participants bat around project ideas, argue, laugh, and brainstorm solutions as a team.

We have found that most people tend to be open-minded and willing to experiment once they understand that communicating their long-term plan is pivotal to innovation and project success. If leaders want employees to embrace the organization's plan, they have to let them know what that plan is. We often think of a former client organization that literally kept its strategic plan under lock and key. Employees cannot possibly help advance specific goals if they aren't privy to the overall plan.

Some leaders have difficulty in understanding the basic value of Dream Retreats. "What will my company gain from such an idea?" we are asked. "It sounds like some kind of a vacation to me." A Dream Retreat is *only* a vacation from operating in the old, less-than-optimal style. In reality, a Dream Retreat involves a lot of hard work and grappling with tough decisions. Employees are removed from the administrative details that hamper their creativity at the office so that they can focus on strategy and planning in a fresh, innovative way.

## Tracking Good Ideas

When Walt Disney was at the helm of his Company, everyone was invited to voice their opinions and to make suggestions—in fact, this wasn't just encouraged, it was required. The corporate hierarchy dissolved when it came to offering ideas for improving a movie script, a Theme Park ride, or an animated sequence. Even for the 1940 Disney classic *Fantasia* in which animation was set to classical music, the Company held a contest to choose the title of the film. After tallying over 2,000 entries, the word *fantasia* received the most votes. (In terms of music, dictionary.com defines *fantasia* as "a composition in fanciful or irregular form or style" and "a potpourri of well-known arias arranged with interludes and florid embellishments." Both definitions apply to the film that marked its seventy-fifth anniversary in 2015.) Today, there are still numerous opportunities to harvest good ideas from all corners of the organization.

When Michael Eisner was CEO of The Walt Disney Company, he instituted a thrice-yearly event known as The Gong Show, named after a television program popular in the 1970s and 1980s. Animators, secretaries, and anyone else who thought he or she had a good idea could formally make a pitch to a panel of top executives, including Peter Schneider, the first President of Walt Disney Feature Animation.

At each event, an average of 40 ideas were presented as succinctly as possible. It was a tough milieu because the listeners at the table provided immediate and honest reactions. "You must have immediate communication and not worry about people's egos and feelings," Peter said about these meetings. "If you do that enough and people do not get fired or demoted, they begin to understand that no matter how good, bad, or indifferent the idea, it can be expressed, accepted, and considered."

The Gong Show was a valuable learning experience for many employees, helping them to see why one idea works and another doesn't. It was also an experience that enhanced the atmosphere of freedom—freedom both to dream and to share those dreams with the Company's highest authorities. And, by creating an environment in which people felt safe to express their creativity, The Walt Disney Company opened itself up to literally thousands of good ideas—ideas so good that they have sewn the seeds for many of Disney's animated features. *Hercules*, for example, is a result of The Gong Show and grew from an animator's idea that a man is judged by his inner strength and not his outer strength. Though the storyline ended up changing, the basic premise stood and the movie went on to be a commercial success.

In more recent years, Disney CEO Bob Iger, who is a bit of a technology "wizard" himself, has become intimately involved with the Digital Immersive Showroom—a state-of-the-art way of testing and tracking the best ideas from the Imagineers. With some of the most expensive graphics and audio capabilities in the industry, The Dish is a 10,000-cubic-foot virtual reality room at Disney's Imagineering Labs where some of their best Theme Park ideas come to life. This mammoth windowless curved-wall sanctuary is the domain of chemical engineers, software developers, and roboticists in five research divisions—in short, the perfect place to pitch their wackiest dreams to Bob. After a project such as Shanghai Disneyland's Enchanted Storybook Castle receives Bob's blessing and before the actual construction begins, The Dish comes alive with Imagineers who work through the critical design issues, special effects, and timing and audio cues. With the new castle's claim as the largest and most elaborate of any in Disney Theme Parks, The Dish was essential to allowing the Imagineers to explore the environment virtually. Imagine having to create a 196.8-foot castle with a grand staircase, a restaurant, a boat ride, a salon, and an impressive array of other attractions, all without a way to ensure that the technical design work would flow well with the artistic design. When Walt Disney introduced Imagineering back in the 1950s, virtual reality rooms would have seemed as foreign as the aliens in that decade's "golden age of sci-fi" movies.

Companies don't have to have slick and swanky technology or a department called Imagineering to take inspiration from Disney's constant quest for new ideas. Innovation can be as simple as creating pleasant smells like the popcorn on Main Street or sounds that enhance the visual experience like the whistle of the Liberty Square Riverboat or the eerie sounds emerging from the Haunted Mansion.

## Cultural Transformation

In short, leaders must give themselves and their team members permission to dream. The simple act of letting imaginations run free will increase creativity and innovation—two values that organizations cannot afford to live without.

Of course, any kind of cultural change comes slowly, and the powerful transformation to be fueled by adoption of the Dream principle is no exception. If your company is large and old attitudes and methods are firmly entrenched, it may take three to five years for the new culture to take permanent root. However, we have worked with organizations that began realizing improvements in customer service and productivity within a few months.

In spite of visible short-term gains, however, some leaders will still voice concern over the slowness of the overall transformation process, at which point we relate the story of the hundredth monkey.

In the 1950s, on the Japanese island of Koshima, scientists studying macaque monkeys dropped sweet potatoes in the sand. The monkeys liked the taste of the potatoes, but they found the sand to be unpleasant. One young, innovative monkey discovered that washing the potatoes in seawater eliminated the grit and made the potatoes taste better. She quickly taught this to her mother and several of her playmates, and the playmates began teaching the technique to their own families.

As one would expect, other young monkeys in the troop were soon imitating this monkey's intelligent behavior. After several years had passed, the last lines of resistance were finally eroded after one particular incident. Legend states that one morning, a large number of monkeys were washing their potatoes. The exact number is not known, but for the sake of the story, we'll say that it was 99. Later that morning, 1 more monkey learned to wash his potato. As the day progressed, each of the remaining dirty-potato-eating monkeys began washing his potato until every monkey in the troop had developed a taste for clean potatoes!

A similar transference of learned behavior also occurs in organizations that are undergoing change. Although the exact number may vary, a point is reached where, if only one more person adopts a new set of values, the synergy is so great that nearly everyone else will internalize the new culture too.

Whether or not this story is legend or fact, there are several lessons that we can learn from the hundredth monkey story:

- First, total transformation takes time. In the case of the Koshima monkeys, it took several years.
- Second, the benefits of transformation must be real. Just as the monkeys enjoyed the benefits of eating clean potatoes, employees must be able to experience real gains as they adopt cultural change.
- Third, management must consistently model the desired behavior. The innovative monkeys continued to exhibit the potato-washing method before other members of the troop. Be persistent.
- Fourth, there must be top management commitment at the outset. When the first monkey learned to wash her food, she taught the skill to her mother and a handful of others. The converts provided positive feedback by embracing and using the newly learned skill. Without their early commitment, it's unlikely that the entire troop transformation would ever have taken place.

Time, persistence, and commitment are the keys to long-term benefits. And remember, as we always say, "The first 99 are the hardest!"

## Parting Thoughts

The Dream principle is first and foremost a visionary undertaking, but both leaders and their teams must keep the overall organizational values firmly in mind as they plan new strategies and set about implementing cultural change. In other words, if innovation is to be successful over the long term, it's imperative that an organization remain true to itself. In the next chapter, we explore what Walt Disney did to ensure that his dreams and those of his Company remained firmly grounded in a set of basic core beliefs. And we examine how a Disney-like adherence to a values-based approach is helping other organizations to achieve bottom-line success.

---

### Our Featured Organization: zTailors

**A DREAMER WHO NEVER GIVES UP**

The late poet and lyricist Rod McKuen once wrote, "You have to make the good times yourself, . . . take the little times and make them into big times." It seems that this has always been the kind of dreamer that George Zimmer is, from opening his first Men's Wearhouse store in Houston in 1973 to launching his new venture zTailors—the "on-demand personal tailoring service that gives everyone an opportunity to look their best with just a tap of their smartphone."

Over a decade ago, George Zimmer told us, "Although all four of Walt Disney's principles are important, it begins with the Dream. Because, ultimately, what makes businesses successful is their ability to do something that in effect has not been done before." That is classic George Zimmer. He is a long-range thinker whose creativity and patience to reap the "big" reward have propelled him to become one of the entrepreneurial giants of our time.

zTailors is a new way of life for the man who famously announced to the world in that unmistakable gravelly voice, "You're going to like the way you look. . . . I guarantee it." George shared with us how a "little thing"—in this instance, a simple business card—helped him dream for the future: "It was not one of those 'ah-ha' moments. It started back in 2013 (the year George was released from his position as CEO of Men's Wearhouse). . . . I needed some way to give people my phone number, and I made up cards that read, 'George Zimmer, Tailor.'"

Before he had his business cards made, George was not planning to start a tailoring business. Then, some six months later, things began to fall into place. First of all, Uber Technologies—the creator of the mobile app that connects consumers who need transportation with independent Uber drivers—had generated a new business model that companies were adopting for their own applications. George would soon become one of these "Uberification" trendsetters.

Utilizing the new technology to bring tailors and customers together was one of his most innovative ideas, but for George, the deeper desire was to create a team of professionals who would actually define the company—a team of zTailors. As George laments, "Tailors are at the bottom of the retail apparel industry. . . . They feel basically insecure about their jobs."

Since the very beginning of his career, George has had a special relationship with tailors. He admits, "Some of them consider me the Godfather and some of them consider me the Pied Piper. I am happy with either moniker." For years, when he would visit his retail stores, he would intentionally walk through the front door and immediately go to the tailor shop to speak directly with the tailor. He knew that the salespeople and management considered tailors to be the lowest on the "totem pole," and George wanted to make it known that he loved his tailors. In fact, he told us that he considered tailors to be "better than anyone you will ever speak with in your life." Most tailors think of themselves as true artisans. As George remarked, "Artisans can look at a garment on you, and they almost don't have to mark it. They actually can just look at it, and then they can sit down at a machine and sew it without marking it."

Armed with a following of expert tailors from all over the country, George believes that zTailors will soon become the hub of the growing online apparel sector. Most of us in the buying public purchase articles of clothing or receive them as gifts, wear them a few times, and then end up storing and forgetting about them for years. George describes our closets as having a "good" and a "bad" side, and he says that America's cumulative "bad" side constitutes billions of dollars of clothes that could be tailored to make them wearable. Through a laptop or a cell phone, we now have the power to tap into a national network of tailors that can help transform our wardrobes, no matter where we are, and to also choose a tailor whose expertise best suits (no pun intended!) our needs. zTailors is sure to become one of our "regulars" in a stable of services that make our lives easier. (And we know that we will love our zTailors look and believe that George will guarantee it!)

"Authenticity" is one of the values to which George has aspired throughout his life. And, his authenticity with Macy's (the dominant player in the online apparel business sector at nearly $5 billion) and other future partners will likely serve as a critical behavioral cue for his tailors. George explains, "We want people who sell apparel to trust us to go to their customer's home and make it fit, and who trust us to know that we are not going to steal their customer and make them custom clothing."

Like Walt Disney did with the theme park experience, George Zimmer is reinventing the tailoring experience. (As this book goes to print, he is also launching another exciting business, Generation Tux, a tuxedo rental service.) For George, creating something that helps others make their dreams come true is as thrilling today as it was when he founded Men's Wearhouse over four decades ago. Will his passion pay off? When we add up his "little times" of charting a brand new journey, enticing others to join him along the way, and shepherding his host of beloved zTailors, we look for George to be rewarded with a "big time" in the end!

## Questions to Ask

- Does top management acknowledge that the process of Dreaming inspires creativity?

- Does top management understand that adopting new paradigms takes time and commitment? Are they willing to see the transformation through to its fruition?

- Do your teams participate in off-site retreats in which they engage in strategy and planning?

- Do you utilize the storytelling technique to communicate your vision or dream?

## Actions to Take

- Affirm that you are ready, willing, and able not just to Dream but to Believe, Dare, and Do to make your Dream come true.

- Hold off-site Dream Retreats for top management and all departmental teams.

- Write a press story that announces and details your own Dream coming true.

- Use the storytelling technique as a method to assist teams in launching projects.

Chapter Chats with Bill: http://capojac.com/disneyway/2/

# Believe

BELIEVE

# Chapter 3

# You Better Believe It

*When you believe in a thing, believe it all the way, implicitly and unquestionable.*

Walt Disney

When Walt Disney was still an infant, his family moved from Chicago to a farm in Marceline, Missouri, about 100 miles east of Kansas City. Farm life is hard and demanding, and a growing boy, then as now, always has chores to do. But after the barn was mucked out or the apples picked, young Walt would lie in the grass and gaze up at the Missouri sky or watch insects and butterflies flit overhead. These were memories that he treasured all his life.

From those early years growing up in a rural environment, Disney formed beliefs and values that stuck with him throughout his life and from which he never deviated. His love of nature, handsomely depicted in numerous animated and live action films, surely can be traced to those experiences, as can the basic foursquare family values that still guide The Walt Disney Company today.

Perfectly complementing Walt's firmly held beliefs was the philosophy expressed by his brother, Roy: "When values are clear, decisions are easy." Together, these precepts formed what is, in effect, The Walt Disney Company's mantra: "Live your beliefs"—or what we simply call Believe.

Carrying that theme a step further, we might add that if "seeing is believing," then the unparalleled success of The Walt Disney Company is convincing proof of the power inherent in the Believe principle. But as our clients know, before success can be achieved, a set of heartfelt core values must be formalized, communicated to the company at large, and actually lived day to day. Disney has shown the way.

## Built on Beliefs

Early on, Walt infused his work with the personal core values that also came to define his Company. In his initial Mickey Mouse cartoons, for example, the character of Mickey was overly rambunctious and even a bit crude at times. But Walt quickly recognized that such behavior would never do if Mickey was to be embraced by audiences young and old. The mouse would have to reflect the solid values held by his viewers. Thus, Walt saw to it that honesty, reliability, loyalty, and respect for people as individuals—the same values he would espouse within the Company—formed the essence of Mickey's character.

As we stated in the previous chapter, The Gong Show idea that grew into the 1997 movie *Hercules* was approved precisely because it fit so perfectly with The Walt Disney Company's core values. Inspired by the tale of the mythical Greek hero, the film idea was based on the premise that a person should be judged not only on his or her outer strength but by inner moral strength as well.

"The core value puts process into creativity," said Peter Schneider, former President of Walt Disney Feature Animation. That's the way The Walt Disney Company sees it. Thus, the first step in any project, movie-making or otherwise, is to determine what core value is being promoted. When it came to the making of *The Hunchback of Notre Dame*, for example, the creative team decided, after much discussion and soul-searching, that the core value of the story was self-value. They had to agree on this premise before they could go forward.

We are convinced that a refusal to compromise values is necessary if an organization is to scale the heights. What's important is not only the content of a company's core ideology, but rather how consistently that ideology is expressed and lived.

Offering your customers the best product or service means establishing certain values as Walt Disney did and also having the good sense to recognize when the situation dictates that one value takes precedence over another. Walt insisted on safety, courtesy, good show (quality of product or service), and efficiency in priority order. First and foremost, it was never permissible to jeopardize a Guest's safety in any way, at any time, no matter what the attraction or performance. That meant that if a child was in danger of falling out of a Jungle Cruise boat, for example, courtesy, show, and efficiency temporarily fell by the wayside until the situation was corrected. Or if someone was having difficulty understanding directions, courtesy to that Guest won out over show and efficiency.

By the same token, the value of a good show carried more weight than did a desire for efficient operations. Excellence at every level was, and is, the watchword at The Walt Disney Company because Walt believed that he could live up to his core values of honesty and reliability only by giving audiences the best possible entertainment. He refused to take shortcuts merely to inflate the bottom line.

Dick Nunis, retired Chairman of Walt Disney Attractions, started his career at Disneyland as a Main Street Cast Member. One of the jobs Dick had on his way up the corporate ladder was managing the Jungle Cruise attraction. Shortly after being promoted to Manager and wanting to impress top management, Dick devised a way to save money whenever the wait times became too long. Scheduling more boats meant more Cast Members, which resulted in a larger payroll expense. So, instead of adding more boats, Dick simply increased the speed so rather than taking the expected nine minutes for the attraction, it took only about six minutes. He also told his Cast Members to talk a little faster, and perhaps leave out a joke or two. In those days, Walt would frequently walk around the Park to observe the reaction of the Guests and would even ride many of the attractions. One day, Walt decided to experience the Jungle Cruise, and it happened to be on a day when the attraction had been "super-charged." Needless to say, he was not happy. When he got out of the boat, he called Dick aside and read him the riot act. He told Dick that he was responsible for the Company's most valued asset: the Guest. The majority of Disney's Guests were repeat visitors, and they expected a consistent show. So if that meant bringing on an additional crew to deliver the good show, then so be it. Walt said, "Front line equals bottom line." Deliver unforgettable frontline customer service and the bottom-line dollars will follow.

Just as Walt refused to accept a substandard *Pinocchio* even though reworking the characters significantly bumped up the cost, so too are certain details that enhance the show at a considerably greater cost. The exquisite topiaries in the Theme Parks are just another example that proves this point.

It takes 3 to 10 years to grow and shape the trees in the Parks to look like Dumbo, Mickey, and other characters. Obviously, it would be more efficient and less costly to install plastic statues instead. But since the topiaries add natural beauty that imparts a greater level of excellence to the entire show and are enjoyed and photographed by thousands of Guests, it is essential to make them as perfect as possible.

In the end, Disney's adherence to their ideologies and the Company's willingness to spend time and money to deliver excellence have been amply rewarded by the huge success of its films, Theme Parks, and other ventures.

## Formalizing the Beliefs

To ensure that Cast Members at all levels would be guided by his beliefs and his visionary sense of purpose, Walt Disney fostered what amounted to an almost cult-like atmosphere. His passionate belief in the need to instill a company culture led him to set up a formal training program that has come to be known as Disney University (commonly referred to as Disney U).

The program, which stresses the uniqueness of the Company and the importance of adhering to its values, came into being as a result of a situation Walt encountered when Disneyland opened in 1955. Initially, he hired an outside security firm and leased out the parking concession. "I soon realized my mistake," he said, explaining that with "outside help" he couldn't effectively convey his idea of hospitality. That's when the Company began recruiting and training every one of its Cast Members.

Walt wanted each and every Cast Member to embrace the basic Disney belief of courtesy to customers, of treating them like guests in their own homes. "I tell the security officers," he once said, "that they are never to consider themselves cops. They are here to help people." Setting up a security force and training the officers in the Company's values and beliefs was no doubt more expensive than outsourcing the job, but monetary considerations took a backseat to ensuring that everyone exhibited courtesy.

New Cast Members must spend several days in an experiential training program called Traditions before starting their jobs. During this orientation period, the Disney culture is communicated through powerful storytelling. The value of the program was proven several years ago when cost-cutting corporate types decided to reduce the training period by just one day. Complaints from supervisors throughout the Parks began to pour in. "The quality of Guest service is not the quality we had last season," they said.

"Have you changed the hiring policy?" Top management took a close look at the process and found out that only one thing had changed: that missing day of Traditions training. It was added back in, and the complaints stopped. Instilling the culture takes time, but anyone who has visited a Disney Theme Park is well aware of what the training program brings to the show: questions are answered courteously, crowd control is unobtrusive, and Cast Members at every turn willingly go the extra mile to make each Guest's dreams come true.

On the face of it, our advice to strictly adhere to a formalized set of beliefs and values may sound naïve and unsophisticated, if not downright impractical. It may come across as the kind of do-good counsel you read about in an inspirational pamphlet. But this is not theoretical. It is practical and proven in the stories of companies that have adopted the Believe principle.

## Long-Term Mentality

Again and again, we have witnessed how organizations are strengthened when they impart a clear understanding of their basic beliefs and core values. For one thing, a set of bedrock values gives a sense of security to all stakeholders and serves as a touchstone for company leaders. Although Walt Disney often teetered on the edge of bankruptcy, he was able to stay focused on his goals for the future because he believed so strongly in what he was trying to do and how he was trying to do it.

It is a measure of Walt Disney's certain belief in his product that he was also able to envision a continuing demand for his cartoons and movies early on. Walt's long-term planning helped him to never lose sight of his market and the family values that endure. With brilliant foresight, Walt decided on a rerelease policy that would bring his movies to a new generation of viewers at 5- and 10-year intervals. The rereleased Disney films have made as much, if not more, money on their second release then they did on the first. He intended his movies to last—and last they did, because he insisted on excellence.

Disney's cartoons and animated films look as fresh today as when Walt's animators created them. That's because he paid attention to even the smallest detail of production and combined the most skillful drawings with the best available technology. For instance, at a time when many animators were using 6 to 8 drawings per second, Disney insisted on 24 drawings.

The long-term mentality is apparent throughout the Disney empire, and its real estate transactions are just another way to prove this truth. Although Walt was never interested in real estate as a personal investment, he took a wholly different approach when it came to his Theme Parks. And his experience with Disneyland only served to harden an already instinctual tendency to take the long view.

In 1954, when Walt bought the 160-acre Anaheim, California, parcel for Disneyland, he was constrained from acquiring additional land by limited financial resources, the already heavy debt he was incurring, and estimates of what it would cost to build his Park. But Walt always regretted not buying more land, especially as his extraordinarily successful Park became hemmed in by tawdry fast-food outlets and motels. He vowed that he would not make the same mistake twice.

When it came time to plan for Disney World, Walt was not hampered by such monetary constraints. He bought 29,500 acres of Florida real estate for an average price of less than $200 an acre. Less than half of that acreage is being used today, while the remainder has risen in value to more than $1 million an acre. Selling off the undeveloped land would bring more than $10 billion into corporate coffers.

Why doesn't the Company sell the Florida acreage? Because such a sale would be at odds with the Disney long-term mentality. Still adhering to Walt's beliefs, the Company is looking ahead to expansion that will further upgrade the show. The theme park business, after all, is driven by a need to constantly offer new attractions that will entice both first-time and repeat guests.

Unfortunately, many companies do not share Disney's long-term mentality. Their satisfaction with present achievements evidences a short-term view of the world and causes them to rest on their laurels—often with disastrous results. The Xerox Corporation, for example, squandered its lead in the copying machine market to the Japanese and found itself left with only a 7 percent market share before it began a turnaround in the 1980s. Similarly, the Raytheon Company, which invented the microwave oven in 1947, barely holds a share of the microwave market now. The point is that even companies with innovative product ideas can be paralyzed by a short-term mentality that causes them to end up on the losing side.

## Believing in Innovation

For Walt Disney, innovation was second nature, which is one of the reasons he was such a strong leader. And CEO Bob Iger, with a keen sense of maintaining the continuity of Walt's leadership, continues to follow in his footsteps. In his pitch to the board to become the successor to Michael Eisner, Bob presented his three-pillar vision: investing in creative content, international expansion, and technological innovation.

Great leadership revolves around the ability to create and manage an environment for innovation. But as we've discovered over the years, too many managers find the idea of innovation downright scary, and some even react as if we were suggesting a revolution without a cause. Another common reaction is that of the CEO or Vice President who, while looking completely self-satisfied when we mention innovation, remarks, "We have one of the best R&D divisions of any company in the country. It's their job to come up with new products."

Our response to this statement is that R&D product innovations rarely change the whole culture of a company. Innovation is a three-legged animal that must encompass product, service, and process. In terms of product, innovation not only means making something entirely new but perhaps rethinking how the old works or how it is used. Process innovation leads to improvements in the way the product is produced, and service innovation changes the way the product is integrated into an entire organization.

The goal of every organization should be to encourage innovation at all levels and in all functional areas, not just R&D. But in order for everyone in a company to become an innovator, the leadership has to be committed to creating an atmosphere in which people and teams are motivated to achieve team goals while still maintaining respect for one another's personal values.

And what exactly does an innovative environment look like? For one thing, there is no such thing as "crazy." Radical departure from the old ways is often precisely what's needed if you are going to come up with solutions to customer problems. In 1937, Walt Disney sent Jake Day to the woods of Maine to take hundreds of photos and make numerous drawings in preparation for the production of *Bambi*, which would be released in 1942. "Crazy" is probably one of the kindest words that many of Walt's contemporaries in the animated film business used to describe such a radical and innovative approach to capturing the magic of the forest. But Walt let his beliefs guide his actions regardless of what the naysayers thought. And, over 70 years later, *Bambi* is as engaging to children and adults today as it was upon its original release.

The message is this: Go the extra mile yourself, and encourage your people to do the same. Let them know that it's okay to take risks and let their off-the-wall ideas take flight. Above all, encourage everyone to have fun!

Ed Catmull, Co-founder of Pixar Animation Studios and President of Walt Disney and Pixar Animation Studios, is one of the best examples of a leader who promotes innovation and risk taking. At Pixar, there's a deeply routed value of taking creative ownership that goes far beyond the fun and fanciful offices in the Company's 16-acre Emeryville, California, campus known as the Habitat. Like Walt Disney before him, Ed is a man who is famous for pioneering inventions in the motion picture industry. In 2001, he was awarded an Academy Award of Merit (along with Rob Cook and Loren Carpenter) for his work on the RenderMan rendering system, the state-of-the-art technology that produces 3D visual effects and animation. With a string of awards to his credit, you might think that Ed would be reluctant to allow his animators to try something new that might outshine his creation that has been a standard in the visual effects (VFX) industry for over 25 years.

But Ed humbly admits, "When it comes to developing new stories and technologies, we're constantly figuring it out. We don't have all the answers."

This was true in the making of *Big Hero 6*, a testimony to how Disney has learned from Pixar's collaborative culture and enlightened leadership. The movie was Disney's first to be inspired by a Marvel comic and required technology beyond the capabilities of what RenderMan could do. Even before the animators began the building of the film's high-tech city called San Fransokyo, they were experimenting with a new artistic lighting technique that would produce a more real world on-screen appearance. Developed in house as a "science project," they called it Hyperion, named after Hyperion Avenue, the location of Walt Disney Studios prior to 1939. When the production of *Big Hero 6* began, Hyperion was not ready to get rid of RenderMan or the old technique of painting by light just yet. But the animators believed in the project so much that they continued experimenting and even formed a team called a Tech Trust to expedite a demonstration of Hyperion's capability. Even so, there was a huge risk in using a brand new system that could have backfired and prohibited the film from being delivered on time.

As Disney's Animation Chief Technology Officer Andy Hendrickson explained it, "We weren't sure we could pull it off. We're constantly being challenged by 'Hey, what if we could do this in the art.' [But] it's Ed and John's [Lasseter] license and mandate to invent the future. . . . Every day of every week, trying to invent what the future is in animation and in motion picture. And it's really great to have them driving our studio." When management finally witnessed the mind-boggling photographic artistry that

Hyperion produced, they were determined to give it a try in the production. From the film's character of Baymax who looks to be made of translucent vinyl to the reflections of light playing off the buildings in the downtown scene of San Fransokyo, the special effects in *Big Hero 6* produced a "wow" factor on-screen.

Ed Catmull said, "Creativity doesn't follow titles. It just comes from where it comes from." This statement defines the culture that he and John brought to Disney.

In our research into companies that are considered to be particularly innovative, we found that certain core values repeatedly jumped out at us. One of the most common of these was respecting individuality and encouraging individual initiative. From service organizations such as Ernst & Young to manufacturing organizations such as the Whirlpool Corporation, top companies in a variety of industries all make it a point to clearly state their faith in their employees. They encourage everyone to contribute, or as Walt would say, they encourage everyone to Dream. And from those vast stores of knowledge and creativity flow the innovative ideas that consistently keep them at the pinnacle of business success.

Innovative companies define what is important to them and then communicate those values to their employees and their teams. By encouraging everyone to live those values day to day, a secure and creative atmosphere arises in which employees at every level feel comfortable breaking down traditional barriers and collaborating in a worthwhile way.

The power of the collaborative spirit at Pixar cannot be overstated. Ed Catmull said, "If you give a good idea to a mediocre team, they'll screw it up. But if you give a mediocre idea to a great team, they'll make it work."

At Disney, innovation in terms of service is much of what defines the organization, at least in the eyes of their Guests. Indeed, stories of the Company's Cast Members going to great lengths to provide extraordinary service are common. One such story concerns a family that visited Walt Disney World and stayed at a Disney hotel. The family included three young girls who traveled with their teddy bears.

At the end of the first day, the family returned to their hotel room. There, seated around the table, were the three bears with cookies and milk placed before them. The little girls were delighted, of course, and the following evening they urged their parents to hurry back to the hotel. This time, the three bears were placed sitting up in bed "reading" Mickey Mouse books. One can imagine the joy this scene evoked in the youngsters. The third evening, the girls found their bears again at the table, but this time they were arranged as though they were playing cards!

The hotel Cast Member had truly taken to heart Walt's pronouncement that "visitors are our Guests" and had come up with an innovative way to please the children and, by extension, their parents. At some shortsighted companies, management might have objected to spending extra money on cookies and milk. But at Disney, this welcoming gesture was a natural outgrowth of the Company's unshakable commitment to Guest service.

## Redefining Corporate Strategy

A number of our clients once believed that strategic planning was a necessary item on their to-do lists to be checked off upon completion. Rather than modeling strategic thinking for their workforces, many leaders are obsessed with a process that often stifles creativity and also produces high rates of staff disengagement and burnout.

To gain the most authentic buy-in to the organization as a whole, leaders need to encourage their employees to think and act like "owners." Providing employee-of-the-month parking spaces and team pizza parties might make them feel good for the moment, but they don't create the passion of ownership. You don't see most home renters treating their properties the same way they would if they were the owners, and the same principle applies to employees.

Two of the best ways to gain employee owner-style buy-in are these: First, connect the company vision or dream and strategy to the employees' roles in the show. And second, involve them in telling the company story.

More and more companies are looking to storytelling as a way to market their products and services. According to Jennifer Aaker, General Atlantic Professor of Marketing at Stanford University, "Stories are remembered up to 22 times more than facts alone."

Stories are just as important to employees as they are to customers as a way to get them to remember and internalize a key message. Some companies have developed their vision and mission statements using the storytelling method. They consider what they are trying to accomplish and how the stakeholders— the "characters" in the show—fit into the story. To simplify the difference between vision, mission, and story, we often tell our clients, "A visionary story is for Main Street; a mission or vision statement is for Wall Street."

How can you craft a compelling story that will emotionally connect you with your employees and customers? Here are five secrets from brand storytellers:

1. **Be truthful.** Even if your story's character is fictitious, you must represent your product or service in an honest manner. Think about the Aflac duck. Nobody believes that duck was actually paying bills in a customer's house. The "truth" part of the message is how the product provides extra cash to pay incidental bills when you are temporarily disabled.

2. **Infuse the story with your customers' or employees' personalities.** This is the way to engage employees and customers with an authentic spirit, not marketing hype.

3. **Build the story and characters from the perspective of the customer.** Any character in the story must be one to which the customer can relate and champion. Remember when the Aflac duck injured its beak in an accident? Not only did the Aflac duck receive 4,000 cards after the first two days of the ad run but it also acquired 18,000 Twitter followers (at that time, the Company had 750) and 348,000 Facebook fans!

4. **Create a story, not a case study.** A typical case study is all about the company—who WE are, how WE meet the customers' challenges, and how WE get results. In telling a story, the focus needs to be on the customer's journey. eBay's story is short, but effective: "Provide a global trading platform where practically anyone can trade practically anything." The power is in the hands of the customers and represents a call to action.

5. **Leave them wanting more.** If your story is enticing and inspiring, you will have the opportunity to provide a magical experience for both employees and customers, one that makes them want to come back.

Ottawa County Michigan's "Ottawa Way" customer service story is like a heart—it pumps life through its highly diverse operations on a daily basis. The following is an excerpt from their story (see also Chapter 13):

Imagine a place with miles of pristine beaches . . . with breathtaking sunsets disappearing into a seemingly endless body of water . . . with expansive wetlands . . . with hundreds of miles of hiking and bike paths . . . a place where healthy living is valued and available . . .

Imagine a team with a variety of skills—collaborating, engaging one another, and having fun . . . that work to improve, protect, and serve their citizens and the environment. This is Ottawa County, and you are the Ottawa Way!

## Vision Align: A Tool That Helps Teams Do the Right Things

A useful tool to help you to integrate short-term activities with your longer-term vision is called Vision Align. When you become engaged in the process, here are a few of the benefits you will realize:

- An established process for executing strategy
- Increased departmental cooperation
- A process by which to understand key problem areas
- Quicker, more accurate feedback

The concept of Vision Align involves setting up a structure that will allow your organization's overall objectives to cascade down through the various staff levels to the natural work group. We worked with a manufacturing team that used Vision Align and they learned a great deal from the experience. (Figure 3-1 illustrates the Vision Align process for this team.)

The organization's core strengths, values, objectives, and stakeholders are recorded on one axis. This represents a set of criteria by which the organization is measured. On the other axis, the key points of the vision or mission are recorded. The use of check marks ($\sqrt{}$), question marks (?), and exclamation points (!) designates how well the vision or mission is aligned with the measurement criteria. In this example, the preferred consumer product vision is not supported by any of the objectives. One objective, the 2 percent net material cost reduction, could even be in conflict with the mission if the cost reductions compromise customer needs. The General Manager of this organization said, "The value of Vision Align is not in the final output. It is in the process that my staff and I went through to develop the document."

## "When Values Are Clear, Decisions Are Easy" —Roy O. Disney

No company outdoes The Walt Disney Company in concern for its Guests. But even Disney has occasionally made mistakes by failing to align short-term

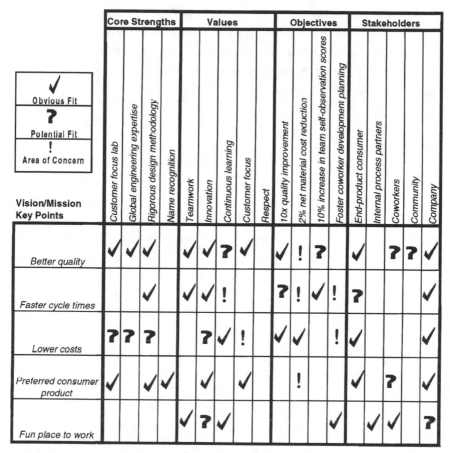

**Legend:**
- ✓ Obvious Fit
- ? Potential Fit
- ! Area of Concern

| Vision/Mission Key Points | Core Strengths | | | | Values | | | | | Objectives | | | | Stakeholders | | | | |
| --- | --- | --- | --- | --- | --- | --- | --- | --- | --- | --- | --- | --- | --- | --- | --- | --- | --- | --- |
| | Customer focus lab | Global engineering expertise | Rigorous design methodology | Name recognition | Teamwork | Innovation | Continuous learning | Customer focus | Respect | 10x quality improvement | 2% net material cost reduction | 10% increase in team self-observation scores | Foster coworker development planning | End-product consumer | Internal process partners | Coworkers | Community | Company |
| Better quality | ✓ | ✓ | ✓ | | ✓ | ✓ | ? | ✓ | | ✓ | ! | ? | | ✓ | | ? | ? | ✓ |
| Faster cycle times | | | ✓ | | ✓ | ✓ | ! | | | ? | ! | ✓ | ! | ? | | | | ✓ |
| Lower costs | ? | ? | ? | | ? | ✓ | ! | | | ✓ | ✓ | | ! | ✓ | | | | ✓ |
| Preferred consumer product | ✓ | | ✓ | ✓ | ✓ | | | ✓ | | | ! | | | ✓ | | ? | | ✓ |
| Fun place to work | | | | | ✓ | ? | ✓ | | | | | | ✓ | | ✓ | ✓ | ✓ | ? |

**Figure 3-1.** Vision Align process for a manufacturing process.

missions with their overall beliefs and values. Sometimes in the end, as was the case with the former Pleasure Island attraction at Walt Disney World, the Company has to change its approach.

When Pleasure Island opened with a jazz club, restaurants, and nightclubs, it was intended to be a place where New Year's Eve was celebrated every night. The entertainment was still geared toward the family, and the nightclub atmosphere was relatively sedate. But in a reversal of Disney's usual policy, Pleasure Island was not gated. Instead, anyone could just walk right in. Problems arose almost immediately at this new entertainment complex. In the words of the Company, "The fact that it was an 'ungated' attraction led to a number of security and Guest service issues."

Some Guests were disturbed by the entertainment offered at the nightclubs, the Company discovered, claiming it was too close to adult entertainment and not appropriate for their teenage children. It didn't take long for Disney to respond to the complaints. Within a year, new leadership entered the scene and used a similar matrix to highlight where the misalignment to the Disney measurement criteria had taken place (see Figure 3-2). Once the misalignment was identified, a new vision for Pleasure Island was created to conform to the overall measurement criteria of the Disney Theme Park. The attraction was gated to control the entrances and promote safety,

In this case, The Walt Disney Company briefly lost sight of the values that had guided it for so many years, but in typical Disney fashion, it wasn't long before the mistake was rectified. Management's swift reaction saved the attraction from failure. However, all through Pleasure Island's history (currently replaced by Disney Springs), Disney was concerned about its fit with their value of providing the finest in family entertainment.

Not everyone may share all of Walt Disney's beliefs. For example, Walt insisted that every production celebrate, nurture, and promote "wholesome American values." Cynicism was verboten at all levels. He could not and would not countenance a cynical attitude in his films, among his Cast Members, or even from potential partner companies. Whatever your particular beliefs and values are, however, they should serve as a filter through which all decisions pass in order to test their validity and worthiness. In the profound words of Isadore (Issy) Sharp, Founder and Chairman of Four Seasons Hotels and Resorts: "You can write your values on paper, but they are only words. . . . The words have significance only if behaved. Behaviors have significance only if believed."

No matter the size of the organization, leaders must devise a process that will effectively communicate beliefs and values to employees, partners, and customers. In short, we are not suggesting that you embrace *Disney's* beliefs, values, and actions wholesale but that you develop the best "show" for *your* company.

## Parting Thoughts

What we are urging is that you consider Disney's four principles Dream, Believe, Dare, Do and that you come to understand how devotion to your own core ideology can strengthen your organization. Having done that, you will be ready to enjoy the power that flows when everyone is engaged in living the same set of values and beliefs. In the next two chapters, you will

**Original Vision**

| Vision/Mission Key Points | Core Strengths | | | | Values | | | | | Objectives | | | | Stakeholders | | | | |
|---|---|---|---|---|---|---|---|---|---|---|---|---|---|---|---|---|---|---|
| | Live entertainment | Variety of entertainment | Themed experience | Guest service | Risk-taking | Diversity | Originality | Creative imagination | Finest family entertainment | 20% annual earnings/20% ROE | World's premiere entertainment company | Protect Disney name & franchise | Foster quality, imagination, & guest service | Family guest | Adult guests | Cast | Community | Company |
| Entertainment for families | ✓/! | | ✓ | ✓ | | | | ✓/! | ✓/! | ? | ✓ | ✓/! | ✓ | ✓/! | ✓ | | | |
| Provide experiences to keep guest on property | ✓ | ✓ | | ✓ | | | | ✓ | ✓/? | ? | ✓ | ✓ | ✓ | ✓ | ✓ | ✓ | | ✓ |
| Provide nightclub atmosphere in the "Disney" way | ✓ | ✓ | ✓ | ✓ | ✓ | ✓ | ✓ | ✓/! | ✓/! | | ✓ | ✓/! | ✓ | ✓ | ✓ | | ✓ | |
| Non-gated to invite people to walk in | | ✓ | ✓/! | ✓/! | ✓/! | ✓ | | ?/✓/! | | | | ! | ✓/! | | ✓ | ! | ?/! | ✓/! |

**New Vision**

| | | | | | | | | | | | | | | | | | | |
|---|---|---|---|---|---|---|---|---|---|---|---|---|---|---|---|---|---|---|
| A party for adults | ✓ | ✓ | ✓ | ✓ | ✓ | ✓ | ✓ | ✓ | ! | ? | ✓ | ! | ✓ | ? | ✓ | ? | ? | ? |
| Provide experiences to keep guest on property | ✓ | ✓ | | ✓ | | | | ✓ | ? | ? | ✓ | ✓ | ✓ | ? | ✓ | ✓ | | ✓ |
| Provide nightclub atmosphere for the 22- to 45-year-olds | ? | | ? | ✓ | ✓ | ! | | | ! | ? | | ? | ✓ | | ✓ | | | |
| Gated to promote safety and entrance controls | | | | ✓ | | | | | | | | | | | ✓ | ✓ | ✓ | ✓ |

Source: Disney University

**Figure 3-2.** Vision Align Process for realignment of Pleasure Island to the Disney Criteria.

see how Disney extended the Believe principle to encompass both Guests and partners.

---

## Our Featured Organization: ACTS Retirement-Life Communities

### A CULTURE OF LOVING-KINDNESS

Peace of mind, security, fulfillment—for most of us, these are qualities to which we aspire, and they are never more treasured than in the "golden years" of our lives. At ACTS Retirement-Life Communities (ACTS)—the largest not-for-profit owner, operator, and developer of continuing care retirement communities in the United States—all of these riches that we hold so dear on earth are possible through a culture of "loving-kindness."

From Pennsylvania to Florida, the ACTS organization has transformed the way that seniors were once cared for in our country. Jerry Grant, President and COO, told Bill, "I think of the ACTS organization and the way it was founded as a perfect example of *The Disney Way* and Walt Disney's vision of Dream, Believe, Dare, Do."

When ACTS was founded in the early 1970s, the concepts of "respect" and "dignity" were not values that most senior living establishments espoused in regards to caring for the elderly. But in a suburban Philadelphia church, a pastor and his inspired congregation led the charge to create a new model for senior care. Out of the backyard of the church—literally on an adjacent parcel—the pastor and his small group of visionaries said, "Let's build a retirement community that will lead the way in delivering compassionate care that exemplifies the honor and respect that our elderly deserve." They initially built 20 independent apartment units and a skilled nursing facility where people could move when they aged and required a greater level of care.

This new concept of retirement living was so well received by the members in the congregation that the campus began to grow, and they decided to build a sister campus, which then led to a third campus, all within the local area. After building their second community, ACTS became a nondenominational nonprofit entity, and as of 2016, it owns and operates 23 retirement communities throughout the country.

The name ACTS is derived from the Book of Acts in the Bible, which states that all of humankind shares the responsibility of caring for the elderly, particularly the widows. The ACTS founders' deeply held beliefs became the cornerstone for the organization and remain a world apart from those of the typical nursing home in America.

In the 1950s, prior to the establishment of Medicare and Medicaid, there were essentially no federal standards for nursing homes. Each state was responsible for setting its own regulations, and they varied widely. In 1987, Congress enacted legislation called the Nursing Home Reform Act, which required nursing homes participating in Medicare and Medicaid to comply with a specific set of quality standards.

Yet it wasn't enough for ACTS to provide a "compliance" mode of living. In the mid-1990s, a successful businessman and ordained minister named Reverend George R. Gunn, Jr., began to establish the culture that endures today for ACTS. He developed a simple credo—"loving-kindness"—that would soon transform the entire ACTS organization that he was destined to lead.

With loving-kindness as its foundation, ACTS offers a lifestyle that includes Disney-style service, care, and fiscal responsibility. And, for the nearly 80 million baby boomers in the United States, lifestyle choices and high standards are essential elements in their long-term retirement planning. Many of them desire the benefits of living in a residential environment with all the amenities, but they no longer desire the responsibilities of managing the family home. At ACTS, individuals who are at least 62 years old have the opportunity to live in a resort-style atmosphere in which an amazing array of on-campus activities promote the well-being of mind, body, and spirit.

When you are a member of an ACTS community, your social, nutritional, spiritual, and healthcare needs are treated as a top priority. Rather than viewing a retirement community as a place to end life, ACTS provides a way to begin life anew. Vibrant active seniors have the opportunity to live in a well-appointed apartment, carriage home, or villa with access to an array of activities and amenities to enjoy retirement life. Furthermore, when you move into an ACTS community, the cost is all-inclusive. Once you pay the entrance fee, you pay a monthly fee that will change only with an annual inflation adjustment. In other words, whether you spend 1 day or 1,000 days or more in your independent living, assisted living, or skilled care unit, your monthly fee stays at predictable rates, which provide residents with extra financial security from the increasing costs of healthcare services. And, as a resident named Ann shared with us, "Even if we run out of money, ACTS will take care of us the rest of our lives." Indeed, the ACTS Samaritan Fund—made possible by donations from residents, family members, employees, and others—is available to any residents who outlive their financial resources.

By 2050, an estimated 27 million people will be paying for long-term care services, ranging from home care to skilled nursing. In order to support seniors' living independently as long as possible, ACTS communities have a nurse practitioner available to them at no additional charge. Those who find that they need assisted living or skilled nursing services after a certain time will be able to transfer to a more appropriate campus residence such as WillowBrooke Court, an on-site health center offering state-of-the-art, personalized nursing care. The environment in Willow-Brooke Court feels very similar to an independent living arrangement except that it is smaller and has everything needed to provide the special care according to each resident's needs. What's more, when one family member requires a skilled nursing environment, visitation by a spouse or other family members is convenient because all levels of care are supported within one campus setting.

Within each of the 23 ACTS communities, the three levels of care provided require a staff of approximately 6,000 employees who embrace the culture of loving-kindness. And, with 42 different countries of origin coupled with the wide span of cultures and belief systems that are represented in the ACTS workforce, that's quite an undertaking!

For Charlie Coxson, Senior Vice President of Community Operations, immersing the entire organization in the ACTS heritage and the mission goes far beyond a responsibility. He explained, "Our culture of loving-kindness is enhanced in the way we treat our employees, and we make decisions based upon that. It may sound corny, but this is a family." Loving-kindness at ACTS does not mean there is no discipline or consequences for nonperformance. In fact, like Disney, ACTS holds its employees accountable so they always know what is expected of them.

Another connection to the Disney culture is that ACTS takes a long-term approach to developing their employees. As ACTS Chief Executive Officer Mark Vanderbeck said, "It's a daily practice of striving to create an atmosphere where every individual is valued for his or her contributions and treated with fairness, sensitivity, dignity, honesty, and respect."

From early in the organization's history, enabling employees to develop their skills and granting them the freedom to move accordingly within the organization has been deeply embedded into the culture. For example, one individual on the management team, who has nearly three decades of history with the company, began as a busboy. Employees who share the heritage and a long-term history of service at ACTS help to create a consistency of purpose and message that permeates the entire organization. When Bill visited the Indian River Estates community in Vero Beach, Florida, after delivering a keynote address to ACTS management, he was moved by the passion conveyed by every staff member with whom he met. One of the employees, Kit, described her feelings upon joining the ACTS family: "One of my first days, I received balloons and a bag of goodies, and I felt so welcome. We truly respect one another in a loving-kindness way."

ACTS employees also work together to create this spirit of unity with the residents as well. Becky is a registered nurse with a 12 year history with the organization. Becky described a heartfelt encounter: "We had a resident with no family who was having a birthday. We found out what she liked, and we went out and bought her a gift. It's the extra steps you take—that, to me, is loving-kindness." ACTS Chaplain Bill Mead agrees: "We can tell the employees you must treat someone with loving-kindness, but when employees act from their heart, there isn't anything they wouldn't do for a resident."

When Bill spoke to the residents, the spirit of loving-kindness was also evident. Connie, a resident at ACTS Indian River Estates, told him, "It means to me that the people here go beyond whatever their job description is and that they are my friends. Beyond the immediate staff, we all know the executives as well. I think it's all a part of being a family."

Following its first several decades of successfully creating this special brand of senior living, ACTS continued to grow by affiliating with other like organizations that once operated independently. Now these organizations are under the ACTS umbrella, and look, behave, and feel like any ACTS community. The corporate team inspires and entrusts their affiliate leaders to carefully educate their employees as to the power and benefits of adopting the loving-kindness culture.

Perhaps the true "test" of any set of beliefs like that of ACTS is how their team members are perceived by mere casual observers. Several years ago, during an ACTS management team conference in Orlando, a gentleman observed the interaction between several of the ACTS team members and asked Charlie Coxson, "Are you with these folks?" Charlie replied, "Yes, I am." The gentleman continued, "Who are they? I have been watching these folks all day. They interact, laugh, and have a great time together." Charlie explained, "We all work together, and we truly like and care very much about each other. That's part of ACTS culture of loving-kindness, and it's not something you can orchestrate."

The ACTS culture and set of core values have driven the company to reach the upper echelon of senior living organizations in America. CEO Mark Vanderbeck reflected, "Much like *The Disney Way*, we believe the ACTS loving-kindness model sets a standard for excellence that can be easily understood, striven for in daily behavior and decision making, and used to lift our entire organization to greater achievements."

## Questions to Ask

- What are the values your company lives by? How do all stakeholders influence those values?
- Are the actions and behaviors of your leaders consistent with the company's values?
- Do you encourage employees to think and act like owners?
- Is every departmental story and mission aligned with the overall company vision and values?

## Actions to Take

- Formalize your story and values in a written statement to be used as the constitution.

- Encourage each department to prepare a Vision Align exercise that aligns their story and mission with the organization's vision, values, core strengths, objectives, and stakeholder needs.

- Conduct regular companywide meetings to reinforce the organizational vision and values.

**Chapter Chats with Bill: http://capojac.com/disneyway/3/**

# Chapter 4

# Never a Customer, Always a Guest

*You don't build the product for yourself. You need to know what the people want and build it for them.*

Walt Disney

In an age when consumers all across the country bemoan the state of customer service, The Walt Disney Company is repeatedly hailed as a superior service provider and perhaps the best in the world. On the day Disneyland opened, Walt himself proclaimed: "Visitors are our Guests." Since then, the bar has continually been raised to new heights in the Company's desire to delight its Guests.

The theme of visitors being treated as Guests also emerges in nearly every movie Walt Disney made. The dwarfs welcome Snow White into their cottage, forest animals care for Bambi after his mother dies, the Banks family invites Mary Poppins into their home, and, of course, "Be Our Guest" is the title of one of the best-known songs from the 1991 film *Beauty and the Beast.* The Guest motif is present in every corner of Disney, from Disneyland to Walt Disney World to the Shanghai Disney Resort.

Walt Disney knew instinctively what his Guests wanted. He didn't need to do expensive research into customer tastes because, as he once put it, his audience was "made up of my neighbors, people I know and meet every day: folks I trade with, go to church with, vote with, compete in business with, help build and preserve a nation with." Disney's understanding of his customer base coupled with his innate drive for perfection meant that audiences got more than they ever knew they wanted, whether in watching his films or visiting his Theme Park.

## How Important Are Your Customers Really?

You're probably wondering what organizations do not try to please their customers. In reality, the answer is plenty. Oh, they may say otherwise, but they don't deliver. If the road to hell is paved with good intentions, then the road to business failure is littered with placards proclaiming "the customer is always right."

A cavalier attitude toward customers is shortsighted in the extreme. The hard truth is that it costs *five times* more to attract a new customer than it does to keep an old one. According to Frederick F. Reichheld, Director Emeritus of Bain & Company and author of *Loyalty Rules! How Leaders Build Lasting Relationships*, a 5 percent increase in customer retention results in a 25 to 95 percent increase in profits. The healthcare consulting firm Press Ganey reports that it costs 90 percent less to get a current patient to return for future care than it does to attract a new one.

So if the payoffs are so great, why do companies fail when it comes to dealing with customers? The answer is lack of leadership. Without question, the CEO is the primary role model for every company value, and service is no exception. In an example of a leader who just didn't understand his responsibility, the CEO of a well-known rental car company was quoted as saying, "There's nothing more irritating than having the person next to you on a plane say, 'And what do you do for a living?' I used to be polite and tell them about my company, only to have my ear bent about the story of the dirty car in Chicago. Now when people tell me that story, I empathize with them and say, 'I know it's a lousy company. That's why I'm quitting.'" What happened to the customer focus of this CEO? Maybe he never had it.

Nearly three decades ago, Tom Peters told it like it is in his revolutionary book *Thriving on Chaos*:

> Each of us carries around a crippling disadvantage: we know and probably cherish our product. After all, we live with it day in and day out. But that blinds us to why the customer may hate it—or love it. Our customers see the product through an entirely different set of lenses. Education is not the answer; listening and adapting is.

The accuracy of Peters's words is borne out by an example with which we are particularly familiar. Bill's late uncle, Shorty, the former owner of a newspaper distributorship in a Chicago suburb, had only an eighth-grade education and knew nothing about return on investment, asset turnover, or market segmentation analysis. Shorty built his business on the simple premise that his customers paid him to deliver the paper at a reasonable time in readable condition. The customers' happiness was his primary concern. For three decades, he never forgot the customers' perspective, even if that meant leaving the dinner table to attend to a complaint, which he did on many nights.

After 30 successful years as the owner and operator, Shorty sold the distributorship to people who wound up putting the company out of business within 10 years. How could this happen when they had been handed a long-standing and thriving business? It's very simple: they did not attend to customer needs, solve customer problems, and unlike Disney, they didn't produce a good show. They made the mistake of operating the business like the monopoly it was, neglecting their home-delivery customers and allowing service to the local retail stores to deteriorate.

The retailers' anger over shoddy service was compounded by the fact that they had no other choice but to buy from this distributor. Eventually, the growing number of complaints made directly to the Chicago newspaper publishers caused the distributor to lose the franchise.

All too many owners and CEOs are like the rental car executive or the newspaper distributor; they feel it is beneath them to concern themselves with everyday real issues like the dirty-car story or late deliveries from their docks. Although a "customers-first" policy usually makes its way into many of the mission statements we've read, painfully few organizations really live those words.

The results of a recent customer service study conducted by Coldwell Banker indicated "a strong correlation between the quality of a company's customer service and its long-term success." The findings also revealed that a typical consumer had switched businesses they were dealing with twice in the past three years due to "bad service." When asked to define the differences between great and poor service, consumers ranked the top characteristics of companies with "great service" as follows:

- Resolving questions and problems (66 percent)
- Knowledge of the product or service (49 percent)

- Being easy to reach (35 percent)
- Understanding requirements (35 percent)

The Walt Disney Company values each of these characteristics, and we have been wowed many times by the Company's exceptional attention to Guest problems and complaints. One example occurred when we were visiting Walt Disney World with a group of clients.

After we had all checked into our villas, we quickly departed for dinner. As we were riding along in one of the buses that shuttle visitors to and from Disney properties, the driver asked us about the condition of our rooms. One of our clients mentioned that the faucet in his sink had an annoying drip and that he hadn't had time to report it to maintenance.

"Sir, give me your villa number, and I'll take care of it for you," the driver assured him.

We didn't give it another thought, but when we returned from dinner, the faucet was fixed. And then, more impressive yet, shortly thereafter the driver showed up on his own time to make sure that the problem had been taken care of. This is the level of service you should aim for when you ask your employees to treat every customer like a guest in their own homes. The bus driver was truly committed to making the Guest experience the best it could possibly be. That is service with a capital S. The bus driver story is a great example of a Code of Conduct: "Treat your customers as you would a guest in your own home."

In Bill's work with the city of Royal Oak, Michigan, he assisted the Steering Team (leaders of the key departments) in creating Codes of Conduct that will guide the behaviors of all city employees. Their customer-centric cultural implementation is directed by Don Johnson, City Manager, and facilitated by Kayla Barber-Perrotta, Customer Service Champion. (See the sidebar City of Royal Oak, Michigan's Codes of Conduct.)

## *City of Royal Oak, Michigan's Codes of Conduct*

- Live the Golden Rule.
- Embody honesty.
- Act with patience.
- Take responsibility.

- Listen attentively.
- Communicate effectively.
- Lead by example.
- Be proactive.

In our Dream Retreats, we tell our clients that effective Codes of Conduct recognize that everyone in the organization has a stake in its success. Though Codes of Conduct cannot be a top-down decree, top management needs to be involved in the process of instilling them in their culture. During Bill's work with the Science Center of Iowa (SCI), their staff renamed the term, "Codes of Excellence." There was real ownership about their work as it was much more than just words on paper. The staff expressed their enthusiasm for being a part of a new direction for SCI, for producing the best show possible for their visitors and members, and for moving the organization forward with a single shared vision.

One of the most outstanding examples of a company that creates a good show is Nordstrom, the Seattle-based department store chain that prides itself on making customers happy. And Lynn happens to be one of the happiest Nordstrom customers around. She has been a long-time Nordstrom shopper, and one of the reasons for this is her favorite salesperson, Evita Munansangu, from the Chicago Michigan Avenue store. One summer several years ago, Lynn called the store and was connected with Evita, who assisted her over the phone and immediately impressed her. Evita was a special blend of sales consultant and friend who facilitated a truly magical shopping experience. She spent a great deal of time working to find several items for Lynn's summer wardrobe and did a beautiful job learning her customer's special style. Since then, Evita has been helping Lynn select items over the phone and by email for more than six years, which is not an easy task for any salesperson or customer. But Evita was a skilled listener and also kept track of specific customer information that would help her provide the finest service and build a trusting relationship. The Nordstorm "touch" worked for Lynn. A few years ago, Nordstrom management decided to promote Evita and move her to a department manager position, but she never fails to contact Lynn on a regular basis and continues to be her "go-to person" for anything she needs from Nordstrom.

Companies such as Disney and Nordstrom realize that good show experiences foster long-lasting relationships with their Guests. At Disney, Cast

Members don't have a job. They have a role in the show. There are on-stage roles such as a greeter on the Jungle Cruise and off-stage roles like an electrician in the maintenance department.

Just like his animated feature films, Walt's Theme Park had to be "show-ready." He paid attention to every minute detail—colors, smells, and temperature were critical to producing the entire show experience.

Whether you are delivering newspapers, taking a reservation over the phone, or cleaning a hotel room, you have an important role in the show. Picture yourself as a director of a movie or a play. You would plan for and anticipate numerous aspects of the show experience. The first thing you would do is determine how the *story* should engage the audience. What do you hope people will feel upon leaving the theater: sad, happy, disturbed? Second, how will your *setting* (staging, costumes, and lighting) contribute to the overall image or mood? Third, how will the actors' performances or their *roles* contribute to the entire show? And last, how will the *backstage* processes contribute to the overall success of the show? Remember, every business really is show business!

## A Passion for Guests Sparks Innovation

In order to more clearly listen to and understand the "voice" of their Guests, Disney has invested over a billion dollars in a high-tech program known as MyMagic+. The technology is responsible for MagicBands, the flashy and fun-colored radio frequency identification (RFID) enabled wristbands that have become somewhat of a status symbol for Disney devotees. Upon entering any of the Walt Disney World Parks, Guests tap their wristbands against a sleek and shiny Mickey Mouse–shaped terminal that validates their entry as the Mickey head lights up in green.

The lion's share of the credit for initiating this system goes to the man who is widely believed to be Bob Iger's heir apparent, the 25-year Disney veteran Tom Staggs. In his position as Chief Operating Officer, Tom is keenly engaged in guiding the corporate culture in the footsteps of Walt Disney, and that includes a belief in innovation that enhances the Guest experience. MyMagic+ allows Guests to manage the many facets of their Walt Disney World visits with great ease in a uniquely creative fashion. By using the My Disney Experience planning page or a mobile app, you can book and link your FastPass+, meals, and hotel reservations together—all with your credit card and even a PhotoPass. The result is truly one of a kind and convenient for both Disney and the Guest.

As time goes by, Tom and his team will be "all ears" to discover how this innovation can help make Guests' experiences even more magical than ever before. The launch of MyMagic+ at Walt Disney World has been so positive that the next step is rolling the service out to all of the other Parks. Tom has said that he is "very confident in . . . the return on that investment in terms of Guest experience and in terms of the financials of the business."

## Turn Your Employees into Guests

One of the most innovative ways to create a magical, memorable guest experience is to turn your *employees* into guests. To complete their orientation, new employees of the luxury hotel chain Four Seasons Hotels and Resorts are required to spend a weekend at one of their properties to experience five-star service firsthand. John Young, retired Executive Vice President of Human Resources described it to us:

> Orientation is probably the biggest single training program that contains the necessary messages about our culture. It is spread over the first three months of employment.
>
> There are seven stages of orientation and the culminating event is the trial stay. Each new employee has the opportunity to stay at one of our hotels as though he or she were a guest—everyone from the dishwasher on up through the organization. We believe that this is very important because many of our people have not had the opportunity to stay in a five-star hotel because they can't afford to stay at our properties. So, after orientation, they have complimentary group privileges, and they get the opportunity to stay at any of our properties around the world. In the trial stay, they complete a rather extensive guest service questionnaire that cites our standards. Then they rate how their experience compared to those standards.

And you can be certain that Four Seasons would do anything in its power to solve a problem that an employee encountered just as they would for a non-company guest.

## Customer Engagement Equals Company Engagement

Long-term brand loyalty results from consistently producing magical and memorable guest experiences and certainly, Disney is evidence of this truth. And yet, if guests do not perceive that their problems are being solved to their satisfaction, they are "three times less likely to be fully engaged with the property or brand." Gallup uses an instrument to assess three levels of customer engagement:

- **Fully engaged.** Evidence of a long-term "loving" relationship with a company
- **Indifferent.** Displays no emotional connection with a company's product or service
- **Actively disengaged.** Evidence of an adversarial relationship demonstrated by complaints about a company's product or service

According to behavioral economists, over two-thirds of customer buying decisions are based on one's "heart" rather than one's "head." That means that if you fully engage your customers through experiences that delight them as only you can do, and if you instill problem-resolution processes that maintain that engagement, you will realize positive financial results.

Gallup also found that the degree to which employees were "engaged" in their work was a huge variable in their success. They found that 71 percent of all U.S. employees were "somewhat disengaged" in their work and that 17 percent were "totally disengaged." The Gallup study was an enormous undertaking that encompassed 4.5 million employees in 332 companies. The results also revealed that the top quartile of companies in which employees were engaged had 2.6 times greater earnings per share than disengaged companies. At first, we thought that perhaps the Gallup study was flawed. But in our follow-up research, we discovered that Gallup was right on with their results. Tower Perrin, a large consulting firm, studied a mere 664,000 employees and discovered that "highly engaged" companies were 78 percent more productive and 40 percent more profitable. A Corporate Leadership Council study indicated that "engaged" organizations grew three times faster than "non-engaged" organizations. And in a study of mini-mills, engaged workers had 34 percent fewer labor hours and 63 percent better scrap rates. Even in a hot, dirty steel mill, employee engagement works! The results of all of these studies are so dramatic, and engagement is seemingly easy to develop, that we wonder why so few companies practice consistent employee and customer engagement!

## Do Whatever It Takes to Solve Customer Problems

Some years ago, while introducing Bill's keynote address to a group of over 250 customer service representatives, the company President stated, "We must rededicate ourselves to solving customer problems. That means we must do what our customers ask of us unless it is illegal, immoral, or unethical. Just do it. Execution is the key." We agree. Leaders must make solving customer problems and addressing their complaints a top priority.

A story we heard while facilitating a Dream Retreat speaks to one company's passion for addressing customer complaints. From a father of a Limited store manager in Arizona, we learned that the company will dismiss a store manager who receives three unresolved customer complaints.

At first, we were somewhat taken aback by the severity of this practice, but after a little research into the effects of customer complaints on the bottom line, we realized that the policy makes very good sense. Years ago, the Technical Assistance Research Programs Corporation of Washington, D.C., publisher of statistics on customer complaints, revealed that for every customer complaint that an organization receives, there are 26 other dissatisfied customers who will remain silent. Each of the 27 dissatisfied customers will tell 8 to 16 others about the experience, and 10 percent will tell more than 20 other potential customers. If you do the math, you will find that three complaints translate into almost 1,000 potential customers hearing about the poor service a company provided.

And this study was conducted before social media became what it is today.

Consider this example. In 2008, songwriter and country singer Dave Carroll was on a United Airlines flight connecting through Chicago's O'Hare International Airport. Prior to leaving the gate, Dave was looking out the window and noticed baggage handlers throwing guitars. Upon reaching his destination, he was not surprised to find that his Taylor guitar had been damaged. After seven months of negotiations with United, he was unable to be compensated for the $1,200 damage to his guitar. He told United that if he were a lawyer, he would sue for damages, but he was a songwriter, and he informed them that he was going to write a song, "United Breaks Guitars," post it on YouTube, and hope that it would eventually get 1 million views.

Dave did exactly that, and the video immediately went viral, getting over a million hits in the first few days. News organizations and late night television hosts picked up the story, and within two weeks, over 100 million people had heard the song "United Breaks Guitars." To date, Dave's original YouTube video has received over 15 million hits.

Twenty years ago, it would take *months* for 1,000 people to learn about a poor service incident, and if that level of service continued over time, it would affect the bottom line or even force the business to close. But in today's environment, customers can use their smartphones to document and post incidents in real time, resulting in millions of people hearing about your poor service. The effect on your business could be immediate!

Four Seasons Hotels and Resorts goes to great lengths to make life easier for their guests. Their unusual sensitivity to their guests' needs is amply illustrated in the following example from their hotel in New York.

Just as a guest was being whisked away in a cab, the doorman noticed that the man's briefcase was lying by the curb. Looking inside, he located the phone number of the man's firm and called his assistant to explain what had happened.

"He's on his way to a very urgent meeting in Boston," she said, "and I'm sure he needs the papers in his briefcase."

Without hesitation, and without any approval from management, the doorman asked for the guest's flight number and volunteered to take the briefcase to him at the airport before he departed. With a substitute on duty to cover his responsibilities, the doorman jumped into a cab and raced to the airport, but he was delayed in traffic and arrived too late.

The doorman again called the assistant, who thanked him for his efforts while expressing regret over the whole situation. But the doorman told her not to worry because he had just purchased a ticket on the next shuttle to Boston and would personally deliver the briefcase to the man at his meeting. Without asking anyone's approval, the doorman flew to Boston and saved the day!

In most companies, one of two scenarios would happen next. Either the doorman would be a hero for solving the guest's problem, or he would be fired for flying off to Boston. At Four Seasons, he was neither a hero nor a scapegoat because extraordinary service is all in a day's work. Every Four

Seasons employee is expected to do whatever it takes to ensure that each guest has a positive and memorable experience. The environment demands it.

Problem solving is so ingrained that Four Seasons employees have been known to jump into action long before an individual has even become a guest, as Bill discovered when working with the CEO of a large firm in Chicago.

In preparation for a major retreat where key managers from around the world would be in attendance, Bill suggested using a hotel at the airport to conserve expenses. But the CEO insisted on using Four Seasons, and he explained his preference by telling an extraordinary tale about the hotel's downtown location.

The CEO was a board member at a Chicago museum that enlisted former First Lady Nancy Reagan as the featured speaker at its annual fundraising event. The CEO was asked to provide Mrs. Reagan's introduction and was expected to join other board members in the receiving line to greet her. Arriving at the Four Seasons hotel in his best business suit and with his well-rehearsed speech in hand, he noticed that people entering the grand ballroom were in formal attire. Not having checked his invitation for several weeks, he had forgotten that this was a black-tie event.

There he was in his business suit with no time to go home and change. As he stood in the lobby contemplating what he should do, the concierge, seeing the look of consternation on his face, approached him and asked, "Is there anything I can do for you, sir?" After the CEO explained his dilemma, the concierge volunteered, "One of the waiters is off today, and I know he wouldn't mind if you wore his tuxedo."

The two men went to the locker room and found a clean shirt, but the tuxedo had been taken to the cleaners. The CEO thanked the concierge for his trouble, but the concierge refused to give up. "You can wear my tuxedo!" he offered as he began to disrobe.

Not deterred by the fact that he was two sizes larger than the CEO, the concierge attempted to staple the arms and legs to make them look presentable. And when that didn't work, the concierge called the hotel tailor who came immediately and fixed the tuxedo on the spot.

The CEO took his place in the receiving line and no one was the wiser!

To top off the whole thing, when he returned to the locker room after the event, he found that his business suit had been pressed and hung neatly on a hanger. Wishing to express his gratitude to the concierge, the CEO pulled out all the cash in his pocket and his checkbook. But the concierge refused to accept any payment, instead insisting that he had only been doing his job, which was to serve the guests and solve their problems.

"But I'm not even a guest," the CEO said. "I just walked in off the street." To which the concierge replied, "Well, maybe someday you will be."

From that point on, the CEO was sold on Four Seasons and decided that the honored guest at the first dinner of their retreat would be that concierge. The CEO presented him with a brass clock, which he graciously accepted while reiterating, "I was only doing my job." Only doing his job resulted in a six-figure revenue stream for Four Seasons!

● ● ●

Innovative problem solving has given rise to centuries' worth of inventions and products, most of which we take for granted and many of which we would be hard-pressed to do without. Consider the ubiquitous Post-it notes, those sticky little squares of paper that decorate every imaginable surface in homes and offices everywhere. Can you even picture your office without them?

Well, these handy creations weren't thought up by some wild-eyed inventor in a research and development department. Instead, their creator was a member of his church choir, and he was annoyed that he often lost his place in the hymnal. While working one day at 3M, a solution dawned on him. He experimented with some glue that had never been used because of its inferior bonding qualities. While it wasn't strong enough to serve its intended purpose, it turned out to be just right for holding little yellow squares in place on a hymnal page. What began as the solution to an individual problem turned into a wildly successful and profitable product line.

Customer problems are sometimes difficult to discern because they surface only under certain conditions or situations. Nevertheless, believing in the power of listening is the first step in unearthing problems, creating innovative solutions, and providing the kind of customer experience that will set your organization apart from the crowd.

## Superior Process Equals Superior Service

How many companies have an adequate—not extraordinary, mind you, just adequate—process in place for providing customer service? Sadly, the answer is very few, if we are to judge by the inordinate amounts of time that most of us waste on the phone waiting for a human voice to respond to our call and to rescue us from the annoying music we are forced to listen to.

In an effort to help Mead Johnson Nutrition improve its customer service, we facilitated a complaint analysis team. The team was given responsibility for reengineering the customer service process, specifically for figuring out how to cut the time that callers were kept on hold. At Mead Johnson, mothers might call in because their children are sick and they have questions about the baby formula they are using. No mother with a sick child has the time or the patience to hang on the phone. She needs and often demands immediate assistance.

A surprising statistic that surfaced from the team's work was that a majority of the calls came during the team's lunch hour. It was obvious that employee lunch hours needed to be staggered, with some taking an earlier lunch, and others going later. This simple solution considerably cut the time callers had to spend on hold.

Clearly, innovation in processes is alive and well in some organizations. As Dr. William Cross, retired Vice President at Mead Johnson, said:

> We have tried very hard to find out how we are meeting our customers' needs and where we need to improve. Putting all the emphasis on the customers' needs and continually improving how we meet those needs—that's how we have been able to eliminate waste from our systems.

In our experience, large manufacturing companies often rank customer problem solving far down on their list of priorities. Senior management, in many instances, believes that middle managers should devote all their energies to strategy, systems, and training issues. Most plant managers seem to be trapped in a world of direct supervision and paperwork.

Besides allotting scant time for customer interaction, plant managers also have little time for determining misalignments between short-term objectives and their long-term vision and mission. The Vision Align tool described in Chapter 3 provides a method of incorporating the "voice" of the customer into the manufacturing process. We urge plant managers to spend at least 30 percent of their time on customer needs and problem solving.

However, before a company can hope to excel with an innovative product, service, or process, it must know its market. What we find most disturbing is that the majority of organizations know neither what customers want nor what their customers' problems are. To demonstrate this point, we have asked workshop participants to list the most important features or services needed at a retreat or seminar. Top answers consistently include unlimited coffee and easy access to restrooms. When we ask hotel managers what things most attract business customers to their hotels, they usually say, "Our great food, ample parking, and atmosphere." What's more, this phenomenon is not unique to the hotel industry. From computers to automobiles to restaurants, we have found the same story. Many companies simply do not know or understand their customers.

Even Disney has made mistakes when entering new markets. Euro-Disney, the 4,800-acre Theme Park built outside Paris, got a lot of negative press when it failed to understand its audience before opening in 1992. The Company opened a Park that was suitable for an American audience in a country whose culture differed from ours in many respects. For example, when the Park first opened, there was no wine being served in the Park. No wine? In France? The French have never accepted American culture with wholehearted enthusiasm to begin with, so they sourly regarded EuroDisney as just another example of Yankee imperialism.

The Company quickly made changes, and today the renamed Disneyland Paris is the number one tourist destination in all of Europe. Mistakes can indeed be a valuable learning tool if a company has a solid problem-resolution process that fosters the discovery of workable solutions.

## Getting Your Company on Track

From the beginning, Walt Disney instilled his organization with the idea that every Guest deserves magical moments. Since nothing is more important at The Walt Disney Company, Cast Members buy into that belief, one that is solidified during formal training programs at Disney University. New recruits come to understand how they can play a significant role in creating that "magic" and be a part of something with a higher purpose.

In most organizations, however, the people who have the primary contact with the customer are usually the least educated, least trained, and least respected, and they have the least input regarding the direction of the company. And unfortunately, too many customer service training programs deal only with how to smile and greet the customer, leaving service providers without a clue about how to solve a problem. Treating customers with respect and communicating in a pleasant manner are indeed important, but smiles alone will not improve customer service.

If your organization is among the ranks of the clueless, try doing the following two things well, and listen for favorable customer responses:

1. **Become a customer problem solver.** We are convinced that the quality of orientation at most companies would have to increase tenfold to reach the level of "pathetic." Traditional orientation programs often consist of rules, regulations, and policies. Organizations then disguise unskilled frontline employees by hanging a sign on them that reads Trainee. What that really means is, "Don't expect me to know anything; I'm trying to figure out what goes on here too." Within the first week of employment, your frontline coworkers should be able to answer the following questions with assurance:

- What products and services do we provide? It is not a matter of being able to point to the catalog and describe the products but rather of knowing how to solve the problems and fill the needs of the customers.
- What are the organization's vision and values?
- What is the story or mission for my department?
- Who are our competitors, and what is our competitive advantage?
- To whom do I turn for assistance with a problem I cannot solve?

2. **Gain customer feedback.** Customer perceptions are very powerful and often become reality. Therefore, every system in the organization must be evaluated through customers' eyes. Two critical questions to ask yourself are these:

- What is the level of ease of doing business with our organization?
- What do customers consider to be exceptional service?

Many customer feedback tools, such as surveys and focus groups, require a considerable investment of people, time, and money to put in place. Evaluate your budget to ensure that you are not skimping on these critical activities. Also be sure to recognize that you have a wealth of customer information at your fingertips just waiting to be tapped. Consider anyone who has customer contact as a barometer for measuring both positive and negative customer perceptions.

Simple efforts such as calling customers on a weekly basis lets them know that you care about their experiences. These efforts also send a clear message to employees about the value of customer perceptions. An uncomplicated and relatively inexpensive customer relationship measurement tool is called the Net Promoter Score (NPS). Developed by Fred Reichheld, Bain & Company, and Satmetrix, the NPS measures customer loyalty by having customers answer a simple question: "How likely is it that you would recommend our company [or product or service] to a friend or colleague? (In government or healthcare environments, the question would be, "How likely are you to speak favorably about your experience with us?") Typically, the answer is scored on a 0 to 10 scale. A score of 9 or 10 is labeled Promoters, or loyal enthusiasts; a score of 7 and 8 is labeled Passives; and a score of 0 to 6 is labeled Detractors, or unhappy customers. The NPS is calculated by subtracting the percentage of customers who are Detractors from the percentage of customers who are Promoters. So, if you had 45 Promoters, 20 Passives, and 35 Detractors, your NPS would be 10 percent (45 percent minus 35 percent). A range of 10 to 15 percent is an average NPS, above 15 percent translates to good growth, and 50 percent or more represents "Disney-like" world-class service.

Visit https://www.surveymonkey.com/mp/net-promoter-score/ for an easy way to capture customer data and calculate your NPS.

Another method for gaining customer feedback is through the storyboarding technique, the subject of Chapter 10. No matter the size of your organization, we recommend that you continually learn about your customers' perceptions by listening to your frontliners, calculating your Net Promoter Score (or other comparable instruments), or conducting customer feedback storyboards. By applying any or all of these methods, you will build long-term relationships with your customers.

Jan Carlzon, former CEO and turn-around architect of Scandinavian Airlines (SAS), famously coined the term "moments of truth," which is any situation in which a customer comes in contact with any aspect of the company, however remote or brief, and thereby has an opportunity to form an impression. (The Walt Disney Company refers to these as "touch points.") Through numerous interviews with his customers, Jan made the startling discovery that his perceptions of his company did not match those of his customers. In Jan's own words, "We asked them about different things: What is your perception of our head office? What is your perception of our technical and maintenance station? What is your perception about our aircraft? What is your perception about meeting with [our] people? We found out that the only perception they really had was the *meeting with [our] people.*"

As a result of these interviews, Jan instituted an extensive customer service initiative focused on moments of truth that began with 5,000 managers and continued throughout the entire organization. In less than two years, he transformed SAS from a $29 million loss to a $71 million profit while the international airline industry was collectively losing over $2 billion. And he did this without any layoffs, mergers, or extended airline routes. The phenomenal results were realized because of Jan's commitment to turning moments of truth into exceptional experiences for SAS customers.

## The Positive and Negative Power of Perception

The Physics Department at San Jose State University prided itself on having a freshman physics class that was so difficult that 50 percent of the students routinely flunked out of or dropped the class. One semester, a professor decided to do an experiment. In the first of two identical classes, he stated during his opening lecture that 50 percent of the students would flunk or drop out. In his second class, he stated that the normal flunk-out rate was 50 percent, but in looking through the students' grades, he was astounded to see that everyone in this class had an exceptional aptitude in math and science (even though he knew that both classes had a similar mix of students).

You can probably guess the results. In the first class, 50 percent of the students dropped out or flunked. In the second class, every student passed with a grade of C or better.

The point of this story is that perceptions really do become reality.

## Perception Becomes a Grim Reality

The power of perception takes on a strangely disturbing cast in this story of a railroad worker in California.

The man was sent to check on some freight in a refrigerated boxcar. While inside the car, the doors shut accidentally, trapping him inside.

*(continued)*

When the man failed to check in at the end of the shift, a coworker found him dead in the boxcar. The following words were written on the walls: "No one is hearing my cries for help. My hands and feet are getting colder. I don't know how much longer I can last."

The eerie truth of this story is that the boxcar wasn't in use because its refrigeration unit was not functioning properly and wouldn't get cold. The temperature outside was in the eighties, and although the temperature in the boxcar was slightly lower, it was nowhere near freezing. There was also plenty of air for the man to breathe.

So what happened? The man's perception of freezing to death was so vivid that it became reality.

One example of a company with a heightened understanding of customer perceptions and a firm set of long-term beliefs is Plumbing & Industrial Supply, based in Evansville, Indiana. One day, when an elderly gentleman came to the retail counter area of this business, he received a reception that is not typical of most businesses.

The apparently lonely old fellow asked a lot of general questions and didn't seem as if he were a serious buyer. "My initial reaction," said the counter attendant, "was to return to my other duties of stocking shelves and processing orders. However, having just attended a three-day retreat in which we talked about treating the customer as if he were a guest in our own home, I continued to converse with the man for about two hours."

The following day, this seemingly unlikely customer returned to place a $500 order. What's more, he related that he had told his sons, who were taking over his construction business, about the fine hospitality he had received the day before. He assured the counter attendant that his company looked forward to a long-term business relationship with Plumbing & Industrial Supply! Since we first worked with the company in the early 1990s, they have expanded to four locations, and they continue to provide "responsive-dependable-capable" customer service.

Walt Disney would surely have appreciated the counter attendant's story, for he always focused special attention on those who dealt directly with Theme Park Guests—the ticket takers, the waiters, the security officers, and the people who operated the attractions. Walt recognized that those people were the ones who were working directly with the customer and making an invaluable, direct impression on the Disney Guest.

Prior to the opening of Disneyland in 1955, at the very first Cast Member orientation session, Walt Disney said this:

> To make the dream of Disneyland come true, took the combined skills and talents of artisans, carpenters, engineers, scientists, and planners. The dream they built now becomes your heritage. It is you who will make Disneyland truly a "magic kingdom" and a happy place for millions of Guests who will visit us now and in the future years. In creating happiness for our Guests, I hope you'll find happiness in your work and being an important part of Disneyland.

If you have ever visited one of the Disney Theme Parks, you will realize that Walt's words continue to resonate, and Cast Members are honoring the Company's heritage. Chances are that you've had a Cast Member stop to chat with you and ask which attractions you've been on, check if you need anything, make sure you're having a good time, and so forth. In other words, they treat their Guests like any good host or Walt would have.

To ensure that his frontline Cast Members would always deliver superior and pleasing service to the Guests, Walt Disney went out of his way to make sure that they were satisfied with their jobs and with the Company. No one had to tell Walt that individuals and teams who are happy take pride in their work and do it well.

## Parting Thoughts

Front line equals bottom line is still an accepted rule at The Walt Disney Company. Walt also recognized that teamwork is a necessary component of the good show. Many of our clients are utilizing enabled teams and reaping the benefits of more efficient and effective performance. In the next chapter, you will read about the importance of the team member experience.

### Our Featured Organization: Flanagin's Bulk Mail Service

#### AN EXPERIENCE THAT TRANSCENDS SERVICE

We all know them—iconic companies like Starbucks and McDonald's who have remarkably transformed commodity-based businesses into "go-to" places for millions of people throughout the world. And yet, it didn't take a household name to achieve the same result for a business in small-town America. Valparaiso, Indiana, is home to Flanagin's Bulk Mail Service—a place where locals can get a dose of Disney-style "magic" even if they aren't buyers!

First of all, the business of delivering the "stuff" that appears in your mailbox is a commodity whose service is interchangeable with those offered by other mail service companies. And in a heartbeat, most of us would jump from one to another based upon price alone . . . unless, of course, a company does something that draws us in and entices us to stay.

In 1996 when Donna Flanagin established her bulk mail business with her two daughters, Erica and Monica, they quickly became known for providing first-class service with first-rate savings. But Donna wasn't interested in being known simply for expertise, value, or usefulness to her customers. She wanted to create an *experience* for them.

As is true for so many of us, Disney is a meaningful and memorable part of Donna's life. She chose Disneyland for her honeymoon and was so impressed with the Park's cleanliness that after Erica and Monica were born, the entire family continued the tradition of visiting Disney on a regular basis.

When Donna began to contemplate a model for her new business, Disney immediately came to mind. Donna knew she wanted to create a lasting memory for her customers just as Disney has done for her and her family. One day, while brainstorming with her daughters, the idea of "Flanagin's Fairies" began to take form. They decided that Erica and Monica would soon become enchanted creatures who would make believers of a whole mass of children!

The town where they live and work is also the original home of the late Orville Redenbacher's popcorn empire. So they decided to participate in the annual popcorn festival parade, and Donna spent nearly four months designing elaborate costumes that would transform the girls into Disney-like characters.

On parade day, the crowd's enthusiasm for Flanagin's Fairies inspired Donna to think about more ways to engage her potential customers. They staged a "meet and greet" for families to interact with the Fairies, and within a few minutes, children began swarming around them like bees to honey. Donna said, "We decided we would take pictures with the children and sign autographs on the spot. It turned out to be way more awesome than we had ever thought. It was a beautiful day, and the costumes really sparkled. People were just amazed and kept coming up to us to say positive things. And, even more amazing, the kids were just standing there staring in awe. It was just gorgeous!"

In prior years, Flanagin's had been a part of the popcorn festival, but they came to realize that there was a significant difference between walking in the parade as a "business" and walking as a "beautiful Fairy." After the Flanagin's Fairies debut, they were in great demand. From that point on, most children who walked through Flanagin's doors believed they were entering a magical land where Fairies lived! Soon, just as there is at most of Disney's Magic Kingdoms, there was a Main Street where children and adults alike could experience "magic" and "wonder."

Another invaluable lesson that Donna learned from Disney was that the reception area of a business should be clearly separated from the processing or backstage area. She erected a divider to accomplish this objective, but the staff realized it prevented them from seeing the guests arriving, so they installed windows with colorful awnings. Next came a lamppost, a park bench, little footprints, the smell of cookies in the air, music, birds chirping . . . a whole experience that begins with the first glimpse of the cleverly designed parking signs. Children who visit with their parents or grandparents feel special when they are asked to draw a picture and then see it mounted on the front door for all the guests to admire. The quaint town has indeed become a "go to" place that creates happiness for those who enter into the Fairy world of Flanagin's.

Donna exclaims, "How exciting is it to have people who come to deliver say, 'Oh, I love delivering to you. It's so fun!'"

The Flanagin Fairies, including Fairy Gladmother Donna, are always thinking up new ways to "wow" both their guests and all who meet them in public places. They continue to take inspiration from Disney when they design their annual parade floats and begin their philanthropic projects. Ever cognizant of tying the business together with the Fairies, Flanagin's has discovered the secret of doing something unique and different with a commodity business and thereby has reinvented the customer experience. Even *Bloomberg Businessweek* has written about Donna's creativity and methods of building long-term relationships with those who have come to know Flanagin's as so much more than a place that offers bulk mail solutions. Donna confessed, "I built the business basically knowing nothing." But the Fairy Gladmother *believed* . . . and with the help of her Fairies, made it all happen!

## Questions to Ask

- Do you know and understand the needs of your customers or guests?

- Do you produce good show experiences that foster long-term relationships with your customers or guests?

- Do you listen to the voice of the customer or guest to help spark innovation?

- Are your employees enabled to engage your customers or guests and solve their problems?

## Actions to Take

- Ask employees to experience how customers or guests are being treated in your organization.

- Establish a mechanism for customers or guests to comment on their experiences with your organization.

- Encourage employees to regularly visit or call customers or guests to discuss their problems and dreams and to receive feedback.

- Identify moments of truth, and strive to create a magical, memorable experience—however remote or brief that experience may be.

**Chapter Chats with Bill: http://capojac.com/disneyway/4/**

# Chapter 5

# All for One and
# One for All

*Many hands, and hearts, and minds generally contribute to anyone's notable achievements.*

Walt Disney

He was renowned for his creativity and superior craftsmanship and was successful beyond compare, yet even the great Walt Disney did not presume to be able to accomplish his goals without the contributions of a well-coordinated team working alongside him. "I don't propose to be an authority on anything at all," he once explained. "I follow the opinions of ordinary people I meet, and I take pride in the close-knit teamwork of my organization."

That Walt Disney so readily acknowledged the value of collaboration is a measure of his greatness—or perhaps a cause of it. In any event, his belief in the team concept was such that he promoted it both in his films and throughout his Company. In fact, teamwork is a crucial element underpinning the Disney "Be our Guest" philosophy: To wit, exceeding Guests' expectations requires a well-rehearsed Cast, with every member playing a significant role in the show.

In the area of feature animation, The Walt Disney Company has traditionally tapped the collective power of its workforce by using a long-standing process for determining the value of various concepts for production. As a first step, the senior leaders discuss ideas from several sources to decide which to pursue.

As a project moves along, directors, art directors, and the head of background production all join in the give-and-take of planning. The dialogue eventually produces a consensus, and Company insiders insist that no one ever assert an attitude of possessiveness. The teamwork continues throughout the long process of animation, camera work, adding sound, and editing until, at last, a film is ready for release.

References to *teamwork* also are sprinkled throughout Disney films, but none better illustrates Walt's belief in the value of collaboration than *Snow White and the Seven Dwarfs*. For many of us, those seven distinctive little fellows—Happy, Sleepy, Doc, Bashful, Sneezy (originally named Jumpy), Grumpy, and Dopey—are childhood friends. Each was carefully drawn with his own distinguishing characteristics, yet we remember them first and foremost as a team, always going off to work each morning whistling a happy tune. Walt purposely made the notion of cooperative endeavor an integral part of that script, with the dwarfs illustrating how different talents and personalities can be brought together to accomplish shared goals.

For many of us, the word *team* conjures up images of a football field or memories of the Little League games we played during our school years. In sports, teams have always aroused emotions of intense loyalty and enthusiastic support. By adopting the team concept, we can transport this loyalty, enthusiasm, and commitment associated with the playing field to the business arena. It's important to lay the preliminary groundwork for successful teaming, namely, to instill a shared sense of purpose and commitment to the team.

At Disney, team commitment is fostered in many ways, including the storytelling technique. And on movie projects, where teamwork is essential, Disney deviates from the norm in that collaboration is not just a one-time thing, with the participants gathered for one particular film. Many of the teammates have worked together before, and their collective long-term relationship greatly enhances the creative process. This is especially true when it comes to animated films, which demand special, well-honed skills.

Back in the early 1990s, Pixar's original *Toy Story* gang—John Lasseter, Andrew Stanton, Pete Docter, Lee Unkrich, and the late Joe Ranft—melded together their storytelling genius to produce what critics have called "the fourth best-reviewed film of all time." Arguably one of the most successful teams in entertainment history, the four surviving members are together again to bring their beloved Woody and Buzz Lightyear back to the big screen in *Toy Story 4*, due to be released in June 2018. The team has long been one in spirit, and they are united in a common mission. John Lasseter said, "We love these characters so much; they are like family to us." Back before Pixar was part of Disney, this team endured constant bullying from Jeffery Katzenberg, the volatile former head of Walt Disney Studios who challenged them to bring more "edge" to the character of Woody. On the brink of destruction was the team's more "childlike" and lovable Woody, but John Lasseter was not about to give in without a fight. In the end, the team's cohesive bond was evident, and they were able to convince Disney management to allow Woody to emerge as a more sympathetic character. Teams can flourish when they unite to forge new frontiers and when they refuse to compromise their values—even if it means pushing back on yielding, high-ranking corporate "bullies." To learn more about how team collaboration and trust can help guard against micromanagement by these bullies, check out Chapter 7, "Stand Together Against the Bullies," in our book *Innovate the Pixar Way: Business Lessons from the World's Most Creative Corporate Playground*.

## Great Leadership Inspires

Walt Disney adopted a unique leadership definition for his culture, and it is far and away the best one we have ever discovered: "the ability to establish and manage a creative climate in which individuals and teams are self-motivated to the successful achievement of long-term goals in an environment of mutual respect and trust."

When Bob Iger became CEO of Disney in 2005, his actions were clear evidence that he believed in each aspect of Walt's leadership principles. Establishing a new organizational structure was at the top of his agenda from day one. Contrary to most companies of Disney's magnitude, Bob made a decision not to name a corporate Chief Technology Officer (CTO). He contends that CEOs need to *think* like CTOs, and in reality, he himself is acting as the "unnamed" CTO of The Walt Disney Company. However, he appointed a CTO for each of the individual business units, thereby allowing them greater autonomy and enabling them to develop an environment of mutual respect and trust. Bob said, "It gives the businesses the ability to experiment and try even if they fail on some of the things they do, without a corporate watchdog looking over their shoulder all the time."

All the CTOs of the respective business units meet several times a year to discuss their dreams, challenges, insights, and information. This CTO "council" has instituted "hackathons" and Best of Disney meetings—annual symposiums in which 50 new innovations are displayed to the entire Company.

The best ideas and suggestions can be lost in a normal hierarchical business atmosphere, but the culture that Bob has established and is managing prevents that tragedy from happening. Within the business units, there is a collaborative and trusting spirit that allows the members to try, fail, learn, and try again. It stands to reason that when innovation is the key to producing long-term goals, even a team's radical premises are to be encouraged, not squelched.

For the past decade, Bob Iger's exceptional leadership has been the benchmark for both the selection and development of team leaders throughout the vast Disney empire. Much depends on the selection of a leader who will play a pivotal role in determining team results. This individual has an enormous responsibility to set the tone for the team, both through personal attributes and through the choice of individual team members. He or she must be capable of exercising firm and fair leadership that respects each member's personal values and understand the role each individual plays. And of course, a successful leader will establish and manage a climate that encourages creativity while keeping team members on track to accomplish their long-term goals.

Four Seasons Hotels and Resorts Founder and Chairman Isadore "Issy" Sharp established his company on the Golden Rule—"Treat others as we would wish to be treated"—an uncommon, yet now proven effective management strategy. Issy tells his leaders the following:

> Our competitive edge is service delivered by frontline employees we expect you to develop. It is not one of the usual goals of management, such as increased sales, market share, profit, or growth, not even a goal of service quality. Your success depends upon the success of your employees, so your number one priority can't be what you as managers want. Your priority has to be, as far as possible, an environment and a structure that gives your employees what *they* want. Your role, then, will be a leader, not a boss. Your job will be to bring out the best in all individuals and weld them into a winning team.

One of the best examples of how Four Seasons displays the ways in which they care for their employees is when they take over an existing property that had previously been managed under another brand. Before they reopen a property, they contract painters to give all of the employee areas a fresh coat of paint, they place fresh uniforms for each employee in the locker rooms, and management even cooks a meal for the entire team of employees! Few companies seem willing or able to develop trust between employees and management or to care for employees to quite the extent we have witnessed at The Walt Disney Company and Four Seasons.

● ● ●

The Disney approach stems, we believe, from a long history of teamwork and cooperation between management and Cast Members that dates back to the way Walt managed the Company in the early days. Remember the story we recounted in the opening chapter in which Walt added fireflies to his Disney-land Pirates of the Caribbean attraction in response to the suggestion of a construction worker at the Park?

An astonishing indication of the depth of Cast Member trust and empowerment at Disney is the fact that Cast Members in Guest Relations, the people who take the tickets at the Theme Park entrances, have $500,000 in tickets and cash at their disposal. They can give this out to Guests who lose or forget their tickets, run out of money with which to get home, or encounter any other problem that merits attention. That's an extraordinary sum of money to place at the discretion of Cast Members, but the Company obviously trusts these empowered and self-motivated workers to use their sound judgment.

## Creating a Solid Foundation

Many teams manage to craft mission statements that sound wonderful, but as we have witnessed in many cases, they are often little more than an exercise with no real substance. However, as Disney Cast Members believe, creating a powerful story can rally and motivate team members to perform their roles in their own unique show. In order to produce the best show, all departments within your organization should rally around a story that engages their customers; ensure that their setting visually complements the story or mood they are trying to create for themselves and for customers; understand their respective team roles and how they complement one another; and constantly challenge their backstage processes to make sure their team functions as a cohesive unit. It all begins with a story.

At Disney's BoardWalk in Florida, Trattoria al Forno serves up some of the finest Italian cuisine in all of Disney. And, as is done for so many of Disney's attractions, there is a story that the restaurant team created that is engaging to Cast Members and Guests alike:

> Trattoria al Forno has been a BoardWalk institution for as long as anyone can remember, with the best Italian cuisine on the shore. And it doesn't get more Italian than the Oliveri family who has owned and operated the place from the very beginning. The restaurant has been handed down from one generation to the next, but the current owners use the same family recipes, using only the freshest ingredients to create the robust Italian flavors of their homeland.
>
> Domenico "Dom" Oliveri and his wife Concetta, or "Connie," immigrated to America from Italy in the early part of the twentieth century. They ran a modest tavern and boarding house that grew along the burgeoning BoardWalk. Connie's cooking quickly attracted a loyal following, and the family business expanded as a restaurant, converting rooms in the boarding house into additional dining rooms just to keep up with demand, including the living room, a formal parlor, and eventually the tavern. Dom called the new café Trattoria al Forno, inspired by the great wood-fired oven he used to make his signature pizza pies.
>
> Today, the newest Oliveri generation runs the place, mixing family recipes with newer, more innovative dishes that draw on authentic Italian flavors as well as other tasty Mediterranean influences. Their authentic and innovative menu reflects their family spirit and the rustic Italian kitchens where homemade meals were shared and savored. . . .
>
> Trattoria al Forno remains a favorite destination among the locals and tourists alike, blending the old and new, and the traditional and unique, to create something for every palate. Like the BoardWalk itself, the family restaurant is a melting pot of cultures and flavors. It represents the best of Italy and everything about

Italian-American culture that has helped make this country great. And as far as the Oliveris are concerned, their family business will go on feeding visitors to the shore as long as there is a BoardWalk.

This example of a company with a unique story wins high marks in our book for producing a great deal of emotion—love for the Guest, passion for the product and as Chef Dom says, "experiencing the beauty of Italy through my stomach!" And Bill, who is a member of an Italian family that sat down to an exquisite feast every Sunday during his childhood, looked forward to trying Chef Dom's BoardWalk Italian cuisine for the first time. Even though he knew it was a brand new restaurant, he felt it was more like an old family-owned dining experience. Knowing that Disney has a story for all of their attractions, Bill asked the waitress if she knew the history of the restaurant. Without hesitation, she recited the story of the Oliveri family. Certainly the tale would not be important to most diners, but it was important to the server. The key here is that the server believed that the family's story, though fictitious, created that special old-world Italian-American family dining experience.

A good team story will enable its members to create a desired "mood," more effectively solve problems, and make better decisions than could a handful of loners working on their own. Bringing people together in both natural and cross-functional work groups often sparks a flurry of new ideas that, in turn, produce solutions to problems. Because cross-functional work groups draw on the diverse experiences and opinions of a number of people from across the organization, they are better able to look at the company as a whole and suggest integrated product, service, and process improvements.

● ● ●

In general, an organization's top management must formally lay the groundwork and champion a team-based structure. Just such an example drew our attention at an East Coast utility.

We have done consulting work for many utility companies, usually auditing on a management level. In the process, we look at the cost of materials and how trucks are purchased. As they are sometimes used for maintenance work or emergencies, utility trucks are a familiar sight on suburban streets and country roads. These vehicles constitute a major investment for utility companies. Traditionally, whether the buying is done by a group in the corporate structure or, as sometimes happens, by a special purchasing group, the responsibility usually rests in the hands of white-collar executive personnel. The work crews that operate from the trucks and the people who drive and maintain them often have nothing to do with acquiring them.

At our East Coast client's organization, the Vice President in charge of materials was new on the job and had spent many years as a purchasing manager for an airline company. When we asked him how he went about buying needed supplies, his honesty and candor were both refreshing and instructive. He readily admitted that he didn't know anything about utility trucks, even though he was charged with buying hundreds of them. So what did he do?

"I got a group of line workers together," he said, "the people who were using the trucks, plus people from purchasing and accounting, and I said to them, 'Go into a room and don't come out until you can give me the specs for a truck.' And you know what? We saved a ton of money, and for the first time ever, the line workers were really pleased with the equipment we got for them."

Contrast that story with one we heard from a group of line workers at another utility. Here, the purchasing department bought trucks without any consultation from line workers, and those line workers were then forced to come up with their own solution: "When we get a new truck in," they told us, "we cut things off of it and weld things onto it. In two or three weeks, we have that truck the way we want it."

Innovative? Absolutely. Efficient? No way! But this is exactly the kind of thing that happens when management is wedded to the oft-heard principle, "That's the way we've always done things here." Through either hubris or inertia, outmoded and costly methods of operation remain in place year after year, leader after leader.

But this need not be so. Any manager can imitate the innovative Vice President at the first utility who organized a multifunctional team of people to work together to find the best possible solution to a problem. Rather than following an inefficient and imprudent practice, however "standard," and ordering a fleet of expensive trucks or some other high-priced item, a manager can take the initiative to change any wrongheaded procedure. But taking that initiative often means bringing the frontline people into the process, people who know what is needed, as in the case of the utility that acquired trucks that met the workers' actual needs. At the same time, this team saved the company a lot of money, planning well in advance of the purchase and coming in well under budget.

When properly structured, teams can improve everything from the bottom line to employee satisfaction with the job. In fact, much of the research we see suggests that in a tight market for the top-notch recruits in technology, production, and other fields that demand both high intelligence and high levels of skills, people are attracted to jobs with the most expansive descriptions and opportunities for advancement. Salary is important, to be sure, but it is often not the first criterion that the best people have in mind when they begin evaluating job possibilities or offers. As R. S. Dreyer stated in an article for *Supervision* magazine, people work not only for the salary but also "for the satisfaction they derive from accomplishment. They work to be part of a team . . . [and] for the feeling of pride they get out of being employed by a fine organization."

In 2014, TINYpulse—a firm that helps organizational leaders better understand their corporate cultures—conducted a survey that supports Dreyer's contention. A cross-section of employees in more than 500 organizations participated in an assessment of "The Seven Trends Impacting Today's Workplace." Choosing 1 of 10 answers, they responded to specific questions such as, "What motivates you to excel and go the extra mile at your organization?" The following are the rankings of the responses to this question regarding what motivates them most on the job:

- Camaraderie, peer motivation (20 percent)
- Intrinsic desire to do a good job (17 percent)
- Feeling encouraged and recognized (13 percent)
- Having a real impact (10 percent)
- Growing professionally (8 percent)
- Meeting client or customer needs (8 percent)
- Money and benefits (7 percent)
- Positive supervisor or senior management (4 percent)
- Belief in the company or product (4 percent)
- Other (9 percent)

A team we worked with at Bristol-Myers Squibb is one of our favorite testimonials on the subject of employee motivation. The team met for one hour, once a week, to make changes in the quality and productivity of their infant formula production line. After being enabled to improve their processes, management asked them to make a presentation of their results. After the presentation, one of the managers asked the team members, "How do you like this team concept?" A line attendant, an employee whose job it was to make sure that the line didn't jam up, told us her story about working at a plant that produced infant formula. This employee was responsible for correcting any problems that occurred on the production line, which happened infrequently. It's a bit like being a traffic cop, except that watching the line all day can be monotonous and boring. When she was put on a team, however, her whole attitude about the job changed.

Here's how she explained it: "Before I joined the team, I was always proud to say that I worked for Bristol-Myers, but when asked what my specific job was, I usually changed the subject. The truth was that I was embarrassed to say I was a line attendant. Now it's different. I tell anyone who asks that I'm a member of a team that is responsible for making the best quality product at the most affordable cost for mothers and babies throughout the world."

Talk about pride in workmanship! And the only thing that changed in her job was meeting with her fellow team members for one hour, once a week, to discuss changes. But, in essence, more than that had changed—her values had changed.

## Factors in Successful Team Building

Not every team experience is going to be a success, of course. There are those who complain that when they introduced the team concept in their companies, it didn't work. But when the team approach fails, there is usually a good reason for it.

To begin, setting up teams is not always easy. As we stated earlier, leadership is the key. The composition of the rest of the team is a major factor in its success or failure too. You must first determine all the stakeholders on a particular project, then move to find the best representative of each of the needed skill sets. Walt Disney was a master at putting people together with different, but compatible, gifts so that they could learn from one another. Back when the concept designs were being formulated for the original Haunted Mansion at Disneyland, Walt brought together Rolly Grump, a master of 3D artwork and developer of kinetic sculptures, with Yale Gracey, a master illusionist. Rolly and Yale eventually took over an entire warehouse at the Disney Studio where they produced and showcased their exciting special effects that amazed their coworkers, Disneyland tour guides, and Walt Disney himself. Today, Rolly and Yale are hailed as Disney legends.

And as basic as it sounds, we always urge our clients to consider the personalities of potential team members. Leaders must also make sure to include detail-oriented people as well as big-picture thinkers. You don't want to end up with a group in which everyone looks at the end result but no one is paying attention to all the little things that will make it happen. Diversity is important, but in the end, it's all about synergy, balance, and raising the bar for one another.

At the core of every healthy team is mutual respect and trust. *Merriam-Webster's Collegiate Dictionary* defines *respect* as "to consider worthy of high regard" and *trust* as "to place confidence in or rely on someone or something." Over the years, we have facilitated many teams, some that have been newly formed and others that have been together for years. In both cases, the team members' knowledge, acceptance, and appreciation of one another's special instincts and "gifts" in the workplace have been significant factors in their development and success. Many of our teams utilize instruments such as the Myers-Briggs Type Indicator, Gallup StrengthsFinder, Kolbe Indexes, and DiSC, all of which can be instrumental in creating long-term trust bonds within teams and aid in conflict resolution.

In many team facilitation situations, we utilize the Myers-Briggs Type Indicator for their development and to overcome dysfunctional team dynamics. Expert facilitation can help turn an entire team around if it's heading off in a wrong direction, especially if its leader loses touch with the members and their issues. Such is the case of a person we'll call John, one of 24 team leaders we counseled at a large international manufacturing company. On the results of a quarterly team self-evaluation instrument, John's team always came in last, and its members could never hit performance targets quite as well as their counterparts. At one no-holds-barred session we attended, a team member broke down in tears when she addressed John: "You are forcing us to be a team, and we don't want to be."

We had seen enough of these kinds of sessions to know that seldom do the members of a group collectively decide that they don't want to be a team, even if they are aware that it takes a long time and effort to develop that synergy. Instead, there were other issues here that needed to be surfaced.

As the team leader, John demonstrated tremendous courage in his willingness to listen to complaints and suggestions in such a public forum as this session presented. Encouraged to speak their minds, team members expressed their anger about John's lack of support and direction and his absence in spirit when the team hit a wall and needed a boost to overcome a problem. John sat quietly, taking notes and listening intently.

In the ensuing months, we worked with the team in their discovery of the members' unique personality styles and began to repair some team damage. One of the key issues was that the woman whose emotional outburst earlier had set the tone for the meeting with management felt that she was a bit of a lone ranger. In fact, upon sharing her Myers-Briggs results with her team, she quickly discovered that her style was nearly the opposite of most of her fellow coworkers. Gradually, the team began to build upon their shared strengths, and the members gained more empathy for their differences. Knowledge often breeds acceptance, and in the case of John and his team, the Myers-Briggs became a catalyst for a more productive and trusting environment.

The newly energized team, with John on board, decided to meet twice a week to discuss issues and to solve problems that were plaguing their internal customers. Open communication and positive results became visible, which was in part due to the fact that John had become a respected leader in the eyes of his fellow team members.

Over the next two years, this team grew both emotionally and professionally. Completing their subsequent rounds of team self-assessments, they found that they had indeed become a team rather than a collection of individuals wearing the same logos on their shirts. From top management to shop floor employees, everyone saw the difference both in attitude and in performance. As for John, his new leadership style received kudos from people inside and outside the plant, and within one year he was promoted to the corporate office—not bad for a guy who just a year or so earlier had produced fear within his team. Now those members were singing a different song, praising not only John's success but also their own for the progress they had made as a team.

As we state in *The Disney Way Fieldbook: How to Implement Walt Disney's Vision of "Dream, Believe, Dare, Do" in Your Own Company*, human beings need a civilized way to work out issues so that they can achieve success. As the founding members of The Walt Disney Company, Walt and Roy Disney often assumed conflicting positions when faced with key business decisions. And yet, they managed to avoid any irreparable damage to their solid bond of mutual respect and trust. Walt believed it was his job to dream up new ideas and Roy's job to figure out a way to pay for them. If you are the leader of a team, your job is to facilitate healthy relationships between team members and help them avoid building destructive ones that could cause them to fail.

## The Advantages of Colocating

When we help bring together members of a new team, we stress the importance of the individuals' functioning as a cohesive unit from the outset. They must not think of themselves as a committee, with one person representing marketing, another there to protect the interests of the purchasing department, and so on. Instead of someone saying, "Well, I've done my design piece," or "I've given my financial statement," and then sitting back to wait for someone else to produce the deliverable, the entire team must ask, "How can we all do this together?"

To foster the necessary cooperative attitude and to increase productivity, we emphasize the necessity of bringing teams together to work in a central location, a process known as colocating. Walt Disney often referred to these locations as planning centers, and his Company has found that its people are much more efficient and willing to take the initiative when they can discuss a problem or ask questions of someone sitting nearby. Brainstorming sessions have a way of happening spontaneously under colocated conditions.

Back in the 1970s, MIT Sloan Professor Thomas J. Allen, Jr., taught managerial psychology for nearly four decades and conducted research on the relationship between distance and frequency of communication in the workplace. For six months, Allen examined the communication patterns among 512 employees in seven organizations. He found that at a distance of 30 feet or less, the quality of communication is five times better than it is at a distance of 100 feet. Allen's research also showed that beyond 100 feet, distance is immaterial because communication is simply ineffective—period. In other words, ease of communication is largely dependent on physical location.

Even before we saw this scientific study, we had reached a similar conclusion based on our own experience. When questions need to be asked or issues discussed, proximity enables interaction. It was with the idea of bringing people together to facilitate communication and improve production that triggered Chrysler to construct a five-year plan to redesign its engineering facilities at a cost of $1 billion in 1990. Bringing together all major engineering functions into one facility, this physical reorganization contributed substantially to the revival of the company.

For some colocated teams, interruptions are somewhat of a stumbling block to creativity and meeting deadlines. When there are too many people stopping by your office or if you perceive that there is always someone demanding your time and attention, a "time-out" period can be a welcome relief. Every so often, any team needs to recharge its batteries.

Mindvalley, the award-winning Malaysian company founded by Vishen Lakhiani, has a team of approximately 200 employees from over 35 different countries determined "to spread enlightened ideas to 1 billion people by 2050." One of their most innovative ideas was the creation of Learn Day—a day that occurs *every* month and during which the entire company is focused on "studying," not "working." When employees need to take a break, they can unleash their "spirit" through song, dance, laughter, or even tears. (After learning this fact, to us, the typical "break" that involves grabbing a cup of coffee or making a trip to the necessary room sounds really boring!) For a company that prides itself on "disruptive systems that Push Humanity Forward," we would expect nothing less than a deviation from the norm.

Give your team members a chance to renew themselves; then bring them together and share successes, failures, experiences, and ideas. They can be catalysts that propel your next big innovation. Designate space, perhaps a wall, in your team room to post creative ideas. Encourage everyone to stop by on a regular basis to add pieces—comments, photos, props—to the team's Idea Storyboard. (In Chapter 10, we describe the storyboarding process in more detail.) Collaboration is critical to the process of generating ideas and problems in any team, but it seems to happen more naturally in a colocated environment.

With the goal of increasing employee engagement and loyalty, companies such as General Mills and Aetna are now offering flexibility in workspace arrangements. A 2010 survey conducted by the Society for Human Resource Management (SHRM) revealed that 58 percent of human resource professionals claim "flexibility" as the number one factor in attracting fresh talent. As a follow-up to their NextGen global generational study, PricewaterhouseCoopers (PwC) wrote an article, "Engaging and Empowering Millennials," that supports SHRM's findings. The survey results of 44,000

PwC employees revealed a significant difference between what motivates and satisfies millennial or Generation Y and Generation X (those born between 1965 and 1970) workers. Generation X values control over their work, development opportunities, and pay satisfaction whereas millennials passionately seek flexibility, appreciation, and team collaboration.

The late Steve Jobs designed Pixar's football-sized atrium to promote both personal workspace freedom and collaboration. You might think it's a waste of space, but Steve realized that when people and teams can gather together to colocate at will, good things happen and constructive ideas are exchanged.

## Rewards That Promote Teamwork

It almost goes without saying that some type of reward system should be in place to recognize superior performance. However, most managers we encounter feel that a little bit of healthy individual competition is as important, if not more important, than teamwork. They really believe competition is good for the organization and will even boost productivity. Most of us have been encouraged since we were very young to compete with one another in school as well as sports. People rationalize that a competitive spirit is a simple fact of human nature.

Alfie Kohn, author of *No Contest: The Case Against Competition*, has spent decades reviewing the effects of competition and cooperation in hundreds of organizations. His conclusion is quite clear: "Superior performance not only does not require competition; it seems to require its absence." David and Roger Johnson of the University of Minnesota report the following results from an educational environment study: 173 studies found that cooperation promotes higher achievement than competition or independent efforts, whereas 13 studies found that competition promotes higher achievement. Another 78 studies found no significant statistical difference.

Red Auerbach, the indefatigable coach of the Boston Celtics, won 16 NBA championships under his direction and never kept individual statistics on his players. Hubie Brown, the basketball commentator and former coach, remembers the Celtics' style that Auerbach helped create: "Red knew how to push the right button on each guy to get him to be subservient to the team. . . . The Celtics understood the maxim 'There is no I in Team.'"

The benefits of a team reward system as opposed to a competitive one are so compelling that even in a competitive society we must take notice. Everyone benefits from feeling appreciated, and team rewards are an excellent way to encourage the hoped-for sense of community and cohesiveness among team members.

During our work with a global team at Whirlpool, we challenged the organization to weight the reward system more heavily toward team performance instead of individual performance. We believe that when teams achieve exceptional results, appropriate bonuses and pay raises should go to the entire team, not just to certain people that the organization judges to be key contributors. Anything else undermines the entire structure of effective teamwork. If everyone is truly working together toward a common goal, then everyone should be rewarded equally.

In the case of Whirlpool, the global team leader was forced to go to bat for the team to ensure equal recognition. He argued that the combined efforts of each and every team member made his group one of the top-rated performers in the entire company. Furthermore, he insisted on equality, and he offered to give up his own personal bonus to get it.

This leader exhibited exceptional integrity and commitment in his battle to secure the proper recognition for his team, but it's not always necessary to go to such great lengths to reward team members. In fact, rewards don't have to be in the form of money and prizes. A reward can be something as simple as a pizza party over the lunch hour. In some cases, we've worked with top leaders who chose to host a barbecue, actually cooking the burgers and hot dogs and serving the team themselves. A personal effort is a particularly effective way of showing appreciation.

Through his benevolent belief system, our friend Tony Castillo demonstrates appreciation and unites his employees through a unique "reward" system that is not dependent upon their past work experience or skills. Tony is the owner of several McDonald's restaurants in West Michigan, and he was one of only four McDonald's owners to be invited to the White House in 2008 in celebration of Hispanic Heritage Month. As a recent recipient of the McDonald's Golden Arch Award—a lifetime achievement recognition earned by fewer than 1 percent of the company's more than 10,000 owners and operators—he is highly respected for his standards of excellence in both developing and preserving his employee base.

Tony creates job opportunities that spark his employees to reach for their dreams and explore their true potential. Although most of the new recruits begin by earning a minimum wage, those who become loyal team members soon earn above the median wage of fast-food workers. And, unlike most factory workers, Tony's employees enjoy flexible schedules, they are protected from layoffs during economic downturns, and they also receive a week of paid vacation, a benefit that is atypical of the fast-food business and at other McDonald's restaurants. When considering candidates to hire, Tony says, "I look at people who might have a hard time getting a job and might not have transportation. It gives them a great opportunity to acquire some important skills by getting a job. If that job helps them buy a home or a car, that's important stuff." Those McDonald's employees are aware that they are some of the most rewarded in the industry, and rightfully so, they credit Tony as the catalyst for launching their careers.

## Self-Management Gains Ground

A few years ago, a Brazilian university leader asked Bill to document the best practices of their nation's "Pixar-like" innovative organizations. One of the most fascinating companies in *any* country is Semco, a trendsetter in "self-management"—a system that expects employees to think for themselves, continually question "everything," and solve problems in a collaborative fashion. Unlike thousands of Brazil's companies that have been shut down due to the country's struggling economy, this industrial pump manufacturer is thriving. Since 1980, Semco has been led by Ricardo Semler who has achieved international fame as one of the most prominent creators of a "corporate democracy" organizational structure.

As we stated in Chapter 3, leaders who expect their employees to be "actively engaged" need to encourage them to think and act like "owners." This is precisely what Ricardo set out to accomplish when he took over his father's company at the age of 21. Ricardo believes that centralization and a hierarchical structure of management in organizations is a formula for disaster. He said, "Managers have been consulting employees for centuries. It's only when bosses give up decision making and let their employees govern themselves that the possibility exists for a business jointly managed by workers and executives."

As Semco's CEO, Ricardo has allowed employees to design their own jobs, select their own supervisors, and determine their own levels of compensation. As the company grew, he instituted additional innovative cultural initiatives including abolishing dress codes, offering flex time, and encouraging employees to take ownership of their roles and responsibilities. At Semco, there is no such thing as a "dead end job," and there is no human resources department or job descriptions that can limit employee freedom.

With a growth rate of a staggering 900 percent in the first decade of Ricardo's leadership, the company's results have inspired many other leaders to consider changing their cultures accordingly.

One such organization is United States–based Zappos, whose leader Tony Hsieh has adopted an alternative to the traditional workplace—a *Holacracy*. The term is derived from "holon," a term Arthur Koestler coined in his 1967 book, *The Ghost in the Machine*. A holon is an autonomous unit that is nevertheless a dependent and interdependent part of a larger whole. In the 2015 book *Holacracy: The New Management System for a Rapidly Changing World*, author and Ternary Software Founder Brian Robertson explains the concept that he trademarked as a best practice for organizations.

In 1999, Tony Hsieh launched Zappos as an online shoe store that has evolved into a trendy place to buy the latest and coolest goods, from diamond watches to diaper bags. Although Amazon.com purchased the company in 2009 for $1.2 billion, Zappos maintains both its autonomy and founding principles that have contributed to its success.

Like Brazil's Semco, Zappos is not a worker cooperative, so there is no shared ownership. In simple terms, a Holacracy has clusters of semiautonomous groups that may function in a democratic fashion to achieve results. As an introduction to the new Holacracy structure at Zappos, Tony wrote a 4,700-word letter to his employees that described how the change would enable them "to act more like entrepreneurs."

For those employees who expressed discomfort with the world of self-management, Tony granted them an "exit offer" that included three months of severance pay. In mid-2015, 14 percent of the company's 1,500 employees opted out of the culture in which the values of Holacracy, according to Tony, will be fully implemented within three to five years. Since Zappos is on the cutting edge of cultural transformation with respect to work design, employees are required to embrace a new system that does not support the habits that have been engrained in many of them over the years. In over

20 years of consulting, we have met many employees who came to realize that changing their deeply held personal values and beliefs to mesh with those required in the workplace is too stressful and too difficult to accomplish. On the other hand, when employees choose to stay with an organization and commit to a long-term endeavor, they can become part a culture that is no longer ridden with stifling bureaucracy. More importantly, they can help solidify an organizational structure that promotes autonomy and creativity. This is Tony's "dream" for Zappos.

Similar to Amazon.com's leadership posture with Zappos, Disney's leadership has allowed Pixar to maintain its unique identity and organizational structure. Although Pixar is not totally "self-managed," Ed Catmull, Co-founder of Pixar Animation Studios and President of Walt Disney and Pixar Animation Studios, and John Lasseter, Chief Creative Officer of Pixar, Walt Disney Animation Studios and DisneyToon Studios have promoted a "playground" spirit where "art is a team sport." The original team that brilliantly created Pixar's blockbuster film *Toy Story* sparked the idea of a process known as a Braintrust, a group that comes together to help one another with new ideas and to identify and solve problems. At Pixar, a Braintrust group is fluid, so the reasons why members join and then leave depend on their roles in the various stages of a film's development. Ed said, "One of the things we realized is that the Braintrust should have no authority. Our group could not tell the director what to do, and as a consequence, the person responsible for the production would never have to come into the room in a defensive posture knowing the group could undermine him."

Pixar's Braintrust culture also helps make their "postmortem" process more of a true learning experience in which there is no room for personal attacks. At the end of each project, they identify things they will do differently and things they will repeat in the next film. When Disney leaders asked Ed and John to run Disney's animation unit, the pair brought Pixar's collaborative spirit into the parent Company and began to change their culture. Ed said, "For us, it was like, how often do you get to take your principles and apply them to an entirely different group of people?" Right from the start, Ed and John told the film directors, "You don't have to listen to anyone's notes, not even ours, and that was rather shocking to them. We brought them up to watch Pixar idea sessions, and then we took our Braintrust over there and gave them notes."

Organizations that prove to be totally self-managed are a rarity today, even though many have explored the possibility of adopting the innovative concept. LRN, a consulting firm whose mission is "to inspire principled performance" recently conducted a survey of over 36,000 employees in 18 countries and discovered that only 3 percent are "self-governing"; that's fewer than 1 in 30 companies.

"Self-governing" companies are also synonymous with "self-managed" organizations, in which traditional power and authority are replaced with collaboration and values-based decision making without management directives. Those who fall in the survey category of "self-governing" claim higher levels of the following: innovation, employee engagement, customer satisfaction, and financial performance.

Over a half century ago, Peter Drucker wrote in his iconic book *The Practice of Management*: "To make management by self-control a reality requires more than acceptance of the concept as right and desirable. It requires new tools and far-reaching changes in traditional thinking and practices." After so many years, it's sad to think that the old paradigm of a top-down, management-driven corporate culture still rules! In 2015 during his segment as a guest on the BBC's radio program *Companies Without Managers*, American management expert Dr. Gary Hamel explained his position regarding the scarcity of self-managed organizations: "The only hypothesis I have is that we still have this residual set of beliefs that invisibly sabotage so many of these things: we believe that change must be imposed."

The greatest inhibitor to a change in organizational structure, beliefs, and behaviors may be management's fear of losing control and ultimately, power. Furthermore, self-management flies in the face of elitist management privileges and bonuses that are still common in workplaces today. At Morning Star—the world's largest tomato ingredient processor, based in Woodland, California—you won't find "fat cats" receiving jaw-dropping sums of money while others in the employee base struggle to pay their monthly bills. The company has been called "one of the best-managed companies in the world" and boasts an unusually low pay gap between the highest and lowest wage earners. In fact, Morning Star's highest-paid employee earns a mere six times what the lowest-paid earns (including seasonal hires) compared with the S&P 500's reported 380-to-1 spread between the top leader and the average employee. Paul Green, Jr., of Morning Star's Self-Management Institute stated: "Self-management is, at a very, very high level, exactly the way you live when you go home from work. We just ask you to keep that hat on when you come to work at Morning Star."

Although self-management is still viewed by many skeptics as an "experiment," we are encouraged by the leaders who believe in the "new" organizational model that has produced companywide collaboration and a marketplace advantage for some exceptional, innovative, and forward-thinking organizations.

## Concrete Results

Teams have a variety of roles and potential uses. We have set them up to examine customer complaints and determine their root causes. We have structured teams around process reengineering. We have asked outside suppliers to come and join in discussions about partnering possibilities in purchasing, engineering, and manufacturing functions. We have created steering teams whose role is to oversee the entire process.

Teams can be set up for a specific, one-time goal, of course, but we often suggest that they continue to function on an ongoing basis after they have fulfilled their primary purpose. Even though the members will probably meet for only about an hour a week, the proper harnessing of this collective energy can produce worthwhile results.

It's important to recognize that when teams work well together, they are spectacularly successful in solving problems and delivering results quickly and cost-effectively. At their best—and we have seen many that rate that superlative description—teams are about harnessing the collective talents of a diverse group of employees to produce a good show. The sum is far greater than the parts, and that adds up to an important tool for companies that want to wind up on the winning side.

## Parting Thoughts

A company that has recognized the power of collective effort is primed for the next phase of the Believe principle: go outside the corporate family to draw on the talents of suppliers and partners. In the next chapter, we'll look at what secure, long-term external alliances can mean for your organization.

## Our Featured Organization:
## Grand Lake, Colorado

### ELEVATE—A TEAM INITIATIVE

Henry David Thoreau said, "I know of no more encouraging fact than the unquestionable ability of man to elevate his life by conscious endeavor." Thoreau's quote need not only apply to a single individual. In fact, one entire community—Grand Lake, Colorado—has proven that they, as a team, have an "unquestionable ability" to "elevate" the lives of so many through a team-based "conscious endeavor." Most significantly, the results are far beyond what any of the members could have done on their own.

At the western edge of Rocky Mountain National Park, Grand Lake is a dream-like place that has been dubbed the "snowmobile capital of Colorado," and yet it is equally captivating in its summer splendor. The sheer beauty, tranquility, and therapeutic aura of the entire region would seem to dwarf the worries of everyone fortunate enough to call it home. But when its citizens were unable to save their beloved community school, the ensuing void and pain that resulted were anything but small.

For the town of Grand Lake, the school had always been a central gathering place, not only for parents and children but for the entire community as well. The flurry of activity that defined the school had produced a unified spirit of belonging. Unfortunately though, with declining enrollment, the school district's 2011 decision to relocate the children left the building without a purpose. Something had to be done. The town simply could not abandon the school and destroy their community culture of connectedness. Mayor Judy Burke recounted, "We decided that because it had not only been of educational but also of social importance to the town, we would go ahead and purchase the building."

As is typical of most counties and towns, there are so many stakeholders involved in making major decisions that getting them on the "same page" is a daunting task. But Grand Lake, Colorado, is NOT most places. No, this is a place where "unifiers," not "dividers," work together and make conscious choices that *elevate* their dreams and the dreams of others.

One of the most gifted unifiers we have ever known is DiAnn Butler, Grand County's Economic Development Coordinator. In the late 1990s after the first edition of *The Disney Way* was released, DiAnn was one of our early enthusiasts who embraced Walt's principles. At that time, she was launching a new program, Distinctive Homes, in her Destinations West company. DiAnn had always been a loyal Disney fan, and when she called to request our assistance with her business, she explained that she had read *The Disney Way* from cover to cover.

Then, in early 2015, DiAnn once again reached out to us to help facilitate the revitalization of Grand County. She reflected, "I remember that our office manager reminded me that our *Disney Way* retreat at Destinations West helped our team understand our core values and aligned our team moving forward."

After 15 years, DiAnn still believed in the Dream, Believe, Dare, Do principles, and certainly for Grand Lake, the inspiration sparked by Walt Disney came to the right place at the right time. In the spring of 2015, she invited Bill to travel to Grand Lake and speak to the community of 461 residents. The keynote and workshop event enticed 160 people to come to their local repertory theater to learn what it takes to embrace a brand new culture. Ed Moyer, Assistant County Manager and Director of Community Development, stated, "*The Disney Way* keynote was where we learned how to become customer centric, and the storyboarding workshop started the groundswell and the grassroots efforts going."

What was about to happen was totally unexpected. After *The Disney Way* event, Bill met with the team of community leaders, and they began to discuss how they could repurpose the old school building. Over dinner, Bill asked the team, "Wouldn't it be exciting to have a center for customer-centric culture right here in Colorado where we could bring people from all over the country to learn *The Disney Way* principles?" Then, a week later, DiAnn called Bill and asked him, "Are you serious about helping us create this 'center'? It could have a huge economic impact if we could bring in 100 or so workshop participants every spring and fall [Grand Lake's downtime between their peak tourist seasons]." Bill answered, "Absolutely."

Mike Tompkins, Co-owner of the Western Riviera motel in Grand Lake, reflected, "Everyone in the community had been thinking about different uses for the building—an arts center, a learning center, a workout center—and when DiAnn told us about this idea, it just clicked. It just seemed that, with the beauty and educational foundation of the building, and for a town that is so tourism and service related, it would be good for Grand County employees to go through *The Disney Way* program. But now we have the added bonus of bringing people from outside the area." Co-owner Jackie Tompkins added, "It is emotional for me that our entire team is happy to see a vision come out of something that was so controversial. It is something that can be real and positive for all of us."

Soon the reinvented school building became the Grand Lake Center where the signature business program—"If Walt Ran Your Organization! Training Series"—is now being offered. This four-course curriculum—Dream, Believe, Dare, Do—was launched in the fall of 2015, and spring and fall sessions are being planned for years to come. DiAnn effervesced, "I am excited for Grand County because this means one of the experts on the success formula of Walt Disney, a consultant to world leaders in industry and entertainment, will be in our county. Here, he will help hopefully thousands of people provide some of the most magical and amazing guest experiences in the world."

The Grand Lake Center has become the symbol of a revitalization of an entire region. But Grand Lake Town Manager, Jim White, cautions, "To provide the best experience to guests in Grand Lake and throughout the county, we need to promote being customer centric in-house, in the county first and foremost. We can't have people coming here to learn *The Disney Way*, then go down the street and have a bad experience."

We are looking ahead to the future of Grand Lake and are thrilled to have a vital role in the growth of the entire county. Truly, we are believers in their fabulous united team of community leaders who will no doubt continue to, in their words, "educate, collaborate, and elevate each other to new heights" beyond their wildest dreams!

## Questions to Ask

- Do you establish and manage a creative climate in which individuals and teams are self-motivated to the successful achievement of long-term goals in an environment of mutual respect and trust?

- Does the physical layout of offices and other work areas prohibit the easy sharing of ideas and the formation of teams?

- Do you encourage cooperation rather than competition among employees?

- Do your teams receive the recognition and rewards they deserve?

## Actions to Take

- Enable employees to find meaning in their work as individuals and as a team.

- Examine the physical layout of the workplace, and colocate teams in a systematic fashion to make the best use of the space.

- Celebrate and reward team accomplishments.

- Periodically refocus and rebuild teams in a retreat setting.

**Chapter Chats with Bill: http://capojac.com/disneyway/5/**

# Chapter 6

# Share the Spotlight

*We believe in our idea: a family park where parents and children could have fun together.*

Partners Plaque in the Magic Kingdom,
Walt Disney World

Long before *collaboration* became a buzzword in business culture, Walt Disney was "sharing the spotlight" with those who shared his dreams. His words "We believe in *our* idea" were evidence enough that Walt valued mutually beneficial partnerships. Walt certainly had had his share of individual success, becoming a cultural icon around the world because of his many achievements. But even though he had been blessed with creative genius, amazing entertainment instincts, and an astute commercial sense, Walt recognized early on that he could not achieve his dreams alone.

Were it not for his first partnership with his brother, Roy, Walt Disney might have remained an obscure animator and cartoonist. When the Disney Brothers Studio opened in 1923, Roy invested his entire savings of $200 in the venture, and it was Roy who took over the finances—such as they were—in those early days. This family partnership had its rocky moments, to be sure, but in the final analysis, the two brothers accomplished much more in partnership than either could have done alone. Without Roy's assistance, Mickey, Donald, Pluto, and the host of other beloved Disney characters might well have remained nothing more than figments of Walt's imagination.

Walt knew too that not only must an alliance work for both partners but he also knew that each partner must work at forming and maintaining a successful affiliation. A partnership is, after all, an investment in the future, and just like any other investment, it must be carefully considered and skillfully managed to produce the optimum return. What's more, you must know who your partner is and be sure he or she shares your values.

The latter lesson is one that Walt learned all too painfully in one of the first deals he made outside the family orbit: a disastrous partnership with the distributor of his Oswald the Rabbit cartoons. Walt originally signed a contract with a New York distributor, Margaret Winkler. Trouble began when she married and her husband, Charles Mintz, took over her business. In a 1926 distribution deal involving Universal Pictures, Mintz persuaded the Disney brothers—whom he always referred to as "the bumpkins"—to create a new cartoon to compete with the very popular Felix the Cat. The result was the imaginative and successful Oswald series.

Mintz, however, was determined to acquire the Disney studio. When the distribution contract expired, he cut the studio's payments by nearly a third and threatened to take over the operation. After all, according to the contract, he owned Oswald. Walt was devastated, but he had no choice other than to comply with the contract.

Some three quarters of a century later, Disney CEO Bob Iger was bound and determined to bring Oswald the Lucky Rabbit back to his rightful home. Believe it or not, the deal was made to trade Disney's ABC/ESPN sportscaster Al Michaels to NBCUniversal in exchange for Oswald. Walt Disney's daughter, the late Diane Disney Miller, stated, "When Bob was named CEO, he told me he wanted to bring Oswald back to Disney, and I appreciate that he is a man of his word. Having Oswald around again is going to be a lot of fun." And the word "fun" definitely fits the quirky floppy-eared rabbit whose gestures are reminiscent of Walt's early days of hand-drawn animation!

The entire Oswald contract fiasco proved to be a serendipitous turn of events because the failed partnership led to the birth of one of the most famous cultural icons of all time—Mickey Mouse. With his newfound freedom to create new characters, Walt was convinced that from that point on, he must own his work. And he never forgot that partnering with like-minded people is critical to the success of the relationship.

Mickey may have led the parade, but Disney was not a one-mouse band by a long shot. In his teenage years, Walt met the man who would become one of his closest friends, collaborators, and eventually his chief animator at the original Disney Brothers Studio. His name was Ub Iwerks. Their bond developed during their early days of working together in Kansas City, where they began to explore their passions for art and the uncharted world of animation.

Years later, after Charles Mintz stole Oswald along with most of the Disney animators, Walt turned to Ub for support. In one of the darkest times in Walt's life, he could not foresee that his new character, Mickey Mouse, would soon become one of the brightest cinematic stars in the entire world. From the start, Walt gave the famous icon an authentically heroic personality, and he even lent his own voice to make Mickey come alive. Ub, whose technical genius was hailed by animators throughout the country, possessed the ability to make even inanimate objects appear to move on film. He took Walt's concept for Mickey Mouse, and he began to develop the physical look of a small boy as we know Mickey today. As Walt's nephew, the late Roy E. Disney, said of Ub, "He animated Mickey. Without Ub, there wouldn't have been a Mickey." Together, as futurists in the field of animation, Walt and Ub pushed the envelope in both technology and animation.

But as is true of many collaborative partnerships, things change, egos get bruised, and pride rears its ugly head. The result is derailment of a joint vision and a once-treasured relationship. Being overshadowed by Walt's newfound fame, Ub seized the opportunity to launch his own studio, and the two childhood buddies went their separate ways. Under such circumstances, few partners ever rekindle their bond. But Walt and Ub weren't just any two people. They were pioneers whose cartoons made people believe, as John Lasseter said, "they were no longer looking at drawings." Out of their unique blend of talents came the smash hit *Steamboat Willie*, the first synchronized sound cartoon, followed by years of continuing to push technological horizons in the industry.

After a decade apart, life had changed for both Walt and Ub. Walt was absorbed by his passion to combine live action and animation, a dream that would build upon some of the techniques that he and Ub had developed back in the 1920s. And Ub came to realize that his cartoons didn't have the audience appeal of Mickey Mouse, so he closed the door to his studio forever. But as we always say, "There are no accidents in the universe." At this point, it was the 1940s, and Walt needed Ub to help the Walt Disney Studios continue to bring the imaginable to reality. Walt knew it was high time to put the past behind him, and he invited his cherished collaborator to return to

Disney. Fortunately, Walt's enthusiasm for a reunion was reciprocated. The two went on to accomplish what neither of them could do alone—growing the field of animation into the art form we know today. In 1966 upon Walt's death, a heartbroken Ub told his son, "That's the end of an era."

No other company in the notoriously chancy entertainment business has ever achieved the stability, phenomenal growth, and multidirectional expansion of Disney. The talents of two great partners—one a brother and one a creative collaborator—helped Walt's dream become a reality.

## The Makings of a Good Partnership

A *strategic alliance* is a type of partnership that encompasses a wide range of collaborative opportunities between two or more organizations with shared goals, and they are often created for the short term. Sometimes, collaborations can be useful for specific projects involving common strategic goals such as bartering goods and services or cross-marketing.

True partnerships presuppose the willingness not only to "share the spotlight" but also to work out what is best for all parties in a straightforward fashion. In addition to sharing a vision and values, effective partnerships share risk, resources, and the rewards derived from win-win efforts. Partnerships take many forms, from managers and coworkers to collaborative partnerships within counties.

Here are the Four Essential Elements of a "Share the Spotlight" Strategy:

1. **Find a good partner with whom you share a common vision or dream.** Spend the time to get to know one another, and work together to gain a deep understanding of each other's priorities and perspectives.

2. **Discover what each partner does best, and allocate tasks and responsibilities accordingly.** Divide and conquer. Focus on getting things accomplished, respect one another's personal space, and make sure you show appreciation for your partner's unique talents.

3. **Continually communicate information and personal perspectives on your joint venture.** You can't overcommunicate. Talk with one another about new ideas, and have fun together. The Pixar terminology is "yes, and," rather than "no, this is better," and it is the basis of their collaborative culture, one that fosters collective creativity and keeps the vibe and energy upbeat and alive!

4. **Think with a long-term horizon, and be honest about the value of the partnership in terms of realizing your dream.** You can't expect to create an ideal partnership within a few weeks, months, or perhaps even a year. And remember that things change over time. You can switch roles, and survive. But make certain that the choices you make are right for both parties. In an environment of mutual respect and trust, take every opportunity to celebrate each partner's contributions to the fulfillment of your dream!

## Partnerships Can Secure Prosperity

Partnerships were obviously an integral part of Walt Disney's business strategy, often serving as lifelines in times of financial distress. In the 1930s alone, a string of partnerships pulled the Company back from the edge of bankruptcy. These partnerships ranged from an exclusive arrangement with Technicolor, to licensing contracts that put Mickey and Minnie's faces on toys and clothes, to deals for a syndicated newspaper comic strip and a deal for the publication of the *Mickey Mouse Book*. At this particular time in Walt's career, the cash flow from cartoons was little more than a trickle (he often had to wait months to be paid by his distributors), and the partnerships were crucial to survival.

During the building of Disneyland in the 1950s, Walt again found himself short on cash. Even though ABC had invested $500,000 and guaranteed a bank loan of $4.5 million, the price tag for finishing the Park came to some $17 million. Walt cashed in his life insurance policy and then began to search for ways to close the financing gap. The novel solution he came up with was corporate sponsorships, which, in effect, are another form of partnership. Disney signed agreements both with Coca-Cola and Frito-Lay, giving them exclusive concessions at Disneyland.

He also brought in small, unknown partners, even allowing a corset maker and a real estate agent to set up shop in the Park. Walt partnered with the late Art Linkletter and asked him to emcee the gala grand opening of Disneyland. In those days, Art was one of the best-known celebrities in Hollywood. When Walt told Art that he would love for him to emcee the event, he was sure he could not afford Art's fees. Art recalled the discussion: "Walt said, 'I'm at a great disadvantage in talking to you. Why don't you have an agent like everybody else?' I said, 'Well, Walt, I just do my own stuff. We're friends. I'll do it for practically nothing.' Walt asked, 'Will you?' I said, 'Certainly. We do things for our friends. Now, for instance, you have some things you are going to contract out. You aren't going to do everything there. Restaurants and parking and film [will be available] for everybody who comes there to buy film.'" At that time, Art owned several Kodak film franchises, and he asked Walt for the photo concession at Disneyland for the first 10 years. Art remembered: "Walt said, 'Good. It's a deal. Now you see what can get done without agents.' The Kodak people once said to me, 'Mr. Linkletter, you own the world's largest automatic film vending machine, Disneyland.'" Kodak, in the pre-digital photography days, once told Disney that 5 percent of all photos taken in North America are taken at Disneyland or Walt Disney World. One can only imagine the millions of dollars that this 10-year concession generated for Art's 90-minute appearance.

In building Walt Disney World, the Company took the same tack, entering agreements that gave the likes of Exxon, AT&T, and General Motors pavilion space at Epcot. In fact, this Park is a testimony to partnering. When Michael Eisner and Frank Wells took over the leadership of The Walt Disney Company in 1984, 18 years after Walt's death and 13 years after the opening of Walt Disney World, those original partnerships were still contributing hundreds of thousands annually to the Company's coffers.

## Partnerships Can Help Expand Your Horizons

One of Walt Disney's first remunerative partnerships was with a small New York stationery firm. He signed a contract giving the firm the rights to sell schoolchildren's writing pads with a portrait of Mickey Mouse printed on them. The firm paid a mere $300 for the rights, but it was 1929, and Disney was broke and eager for every nickel he could get. "As usual, Roy and I needed the money," he said later.

Although on its face the deal was a small one, it opened Disney's eyes to the possibilities of making money through ancillary uses of his creative product. He never overlooked an opportunity to do so from then on, and licensing arrangements became central to his management philosophy. A couple of years later, he licensed the sale of Mickey Mouse watches, which initially sold at the rate of about 1 million per year. Other similar agreements brought in 10 percent of the Company's income over a decade-long period. All the while, Walt kept a sharp eye out for any violations of his copyright, just as The Walt Disney Company does today.

But even Walt could not have dreamt of the multi-million-dollar cornucopia of Disney products that has evolved from that first Mickey Mouse school tablet. The Company licenses its cartoon characters' images to manufacturers, and then products bearing those pictures are sold by retailers around the world. There are Company-owned and operated stores, as well as a Disney website that markets movies, books, art, clothing, jewelry, collectibles, and a host of other products, all bearing the likeness of various familiar Disney figures and all produced under license from The Walt Disney Company.

Most of Walt's numerous partnerships were formed for purely business reasons, but one of his most unlikely affiliations stemmed from a creative communion that developed quite by chance. One evening, Walt was eating alone in a fashionable Hollywood restaurant when he spotted the famous conductor of the Philadelphia Orchestra, Leopold Stokowski, who was also dining alone. So Walt invited Leopold to join him. Stokowski was a giant in the world of classical music, and with his mane of white hair and sweeping gestures, he looked every inch the maestro, whether leading an orchestra or chatting with a friend over dinner.

Discussing future plans, Walt mentioned that he was about to start work on a new Mickey Mouse cartoon, *The Sorcerer's Apprentice*. Leopold expressed an interest in conducting the score and even offered to waive his fee. Over the dinner table, the two men then discussed the possibility of making an animated feature set to the music of great composers. Out of this conversation grew the 1940 movie *Fantasia*. (In Chapter 2 we mentioned the contest Disney ran to determine this movie's title.) Walt and Leopold were equally charmed by the concept.

In *Fantasia*, Stokowski conducted everything from Beethoven to the avant-garde music of Igor Stravinsky, while animated figures interpreted the compositions through dance. Visual interpretation of orchestral music was a new concept, and *Fantasia* won raves from the critics. Bosley Crowther of the *New York Times* described it as "simply terrific, as terrific as anything that has ever happened on the screen," while another critic described it as "a new artistic experience of great beauty." But, because it was so unlike any other Disney movie, the public rejected it. And today the film is highly regarded, especially among film historians.

While the film was deemed a financial failure at the time, Walt viewed few things as absolute failures. He knew that even unsuccessful ventures provide valuable lessons, and such hard-won knowledge can be put to use elsewhere. Taking its cue from Walt, The Walt Disney Company does not consign failed projects to the trash heap. Rather, it considers them to be assets of the Company that may be tried again later or perhaps utilized in a different capacity. The partnership with Stokowski served Disney well in a creative and artistic sense, and it represented a great step forward in the fusion of animation, color, and sound.

One of Disney's more recent partnerships was spawned at just the right moment in time, and it helped them escape the collapse of Disney Interactive, the division that produces games and website experiences. Until 2014, Disney Interactive had been losing more than *$1 billion* over the previous five years. Jimmy Pitaro, President of Disney Interactive said, "We were too big and trying to do too many things." Because of the division's inability to move the stock price, its Disney parent began to treat the division like a nuisance stepchild. Soon, a reorganization that included layoffs was in motion, and because of the fear that the division might go belly-up, Disney Interactive could no longer attract talent from the outside.

Finally, Disney ditched its old product lines such as console games and sank $100 million into Infinity—an interactive game that allows Disney characters such as Goofy and Donald Duck to interact and go on adventures together. Rather than go at it alone, they formed a partnership with Line, a Japanese company that created an app to provide free phone calls and messaging services throughout Japan. In an agreement with Disney, Line developed a mobile game based on Tsum Tsum—circular and stackable stuffed animals that appear to be an infantile version of classic Disney characters. These toys function as screen cleaners and were an overnight sensation in Japan. The accompanying mobile game went viral, reached the number one app spot on both iOS and Android in Japan where it was downloaded approximately 30 million times.

Riding the wave of success in the Japanese market, The Walt Disney Company quickly brought the animated characters to the United States through a puzzle app for English-speaking audiences and began selling a new line of the plush Tsum Tsum toys in Disney Parks and on the online Disney Store. The first year that Disney Interactive turned a profit since it had been operating independently in 2008 was 2014 when it earned a respectable $116 million on some $1.3 billion in sales—all because of this new partnership.

Success in terms of a partnership such as Disney and Line is possible only when the licensed products connect with the customer or Guest both functionally and emotionally. Paul Candland, President of the Japanese arm of The Walt Disney Company, said, "Disney Tsum Tsum is both a physical product and a digital game, which allows our Guests to enjoy a multidimensional experience. We are hopeful that the Disney Tsum Tsum franchise will be loved and enjoyed by Guests around the world."

A carefully chosen partnership can enable you to increase your revenue by expanding into new markets and securing new customers. And when you invest time and resources in the early stages, you may increase your chances of forming a successful, long-lasting relationship.

## Creating Good Show Experiences Through Partnerships

Finding a valuable partner to help you provide a good show experience for your employees and customers can lead to profitable financial results. This was certainly true for Mello Smello. Founded by husband and wife team, Jon and Leah Miner, the two teamed up with 3M in 1980 to create and produce Scratch 'n Sniff stickers of Disney characters. Over the past 20 years, Mello Smello has developed an innovative variety of other products, and it has grown to become a multi-million-dollar business and a valued partner to the nation's largest retailers, including Walmart, Target, and Walgreen's.

In 1986, the late Evelyn Overton who inspired her son, David, to launch The Cheesecake Factory restaurant chain, learned how accepting the guidance of a larger, better-known branded company could result in a great partnership. Evelyn had always prided herself on her strict methods of creating fabulous cheesecakes. Cleanliness and accuracy were huge factors in each and every step of the operation. When The Cheesecake Factory was about to land its first national bakery account, Darden Restaurants, the company made some critical observations of Evelyn's kitchen operations. Max Byfuglin, President of The Cheesecake Factory Bakery, Inc., described Darden's reaction this way:

> Darden looked at our company as an entrepreneurial West Coast company that had true quality with their cakes. Evelyn was proud of cracking the eggs on the rim of the bowl, but the first time Darden came to visit us in 1986, they said, "You can't do that." Evelyn was also proud of the butcher tables in the bakery, and they said, "You can't use those." After that visit, I got a three-page letter saying that they'd love to do business with us, but first, here's a list of the things we would need to do. We were just building a new bakery down the

street, so I was able to incorporate their suggestions in the areas of quality and safety. That was the beginning of becoming a national company on the bakery side. Darden has been a great partner for us.

As The Cheesecake Factory discovered, a great partnership can dramatically increase both your reputation and your profitability. Later in 2016, in partnership with The Walt Disney Company, The Cheesecake Factory will open its Asian flagship store at Shanghai Disney. Founder, Chairman, & CEO David Overton commented, "This is just the next step to having The Cheesecake Factory grow into the future."

## Selecting a Partner for the Long Term

At Disney, partnerships are viewed as long-term investments in the Company's future prosperity. The Company continues to exemplify, just as Walt did, the principle that alliances must work for both partners if they are to endure. For Tom Staggs, former head of Disney Theme Parks and current COO, partnering with the celebrated filmmaker James Cameron was irresistible. Securing the global rights to the *Avatar* franchise seemed a sure-fire bet to produce Theme Park "gold." Not only has *Avatar* set a global box-office record, but the 3D digital projection technologies developed by James Cameron are beyond compare. The result is one of the most dramatic and visually breathtaking movies of all time.

The partnership with The Walt Disney Company afforded James the opportunity to work with the Imagineers to translate the Avatar experience to Disney's Guests by producing a series of the most anticipated Theme Park attractions in years. In the words of Bob Iger, "James Cameron is a groundbreaking filmmaker who shares our passion for creativity, technological innovation, and delivering the best experience possible. With this agreement, we have the extraordinary opportunity to combine James's talent and vision with the imagination and expertise of Disney."

The fruits of Disney's partnership with James Cameron's Lightstorm Entertainment begin in the Disney's Animal Kingdom Theme Park—a natural environmental choice for the creation of Pandora, the Land of Avatar. Signed in 2011, the contract represents a long-term relationship to eventually develop more *Avatar*-themed attractions to enhance the Disney brand. As James Cameron explained, "I think one of the things that people loved about the movie is that they felt as if they had visited Pandora, and now, thanks to Disney's amazing Imagineers, people are going to truly experience Pandora firsthand. From the details in the plants to the production and design, extraordinary thought and care has gone into this entire world. The teams have really created something special, and it's not going to be like anything else." That "something special" is what continues to fuel Disney Theme Parks and Resorts growth. In fact, the Parks and Resorts division yields about twice as much in revenue as studio entertainment—the segment that produces Disney movies. In Disney's fiscal 2014, the Theme Parks led growth for the Company, and the partnership with James Cameron holds promise to be a valuable asset in its continued prosperity.

When you and your partner share a common vision, your diverse contributions can work together to achieve great success!

## A Legendary Partnership

One of the Company's most valuable partnerships in its entire history is with Pixar. In our book *Innovate the Pixar Way: Business Lessons from the World's Most Creative Corporate Playground*, we tell the story of Bob Iger's first major decision as CEO of The Walt Disney Company being the purchase of Pixar from the late Steve Jobs for $7.4 billion in stock in 2006. Since the past relationship between the two organizations had been scarred by years of dysfunctionality, mostly orchestrated by former "command and control" Disney CEO Michael Eisner, Bob's ability to make the deal was no small feat.

Rather than having the foresight to buy Pixar during its start-up days, Michael had staged a business arrangement with the young superstar company in which Pixar was in essence a commodity rather than a true partner. According to Ed Catmull, Co-founder of Pixar and current President of Pixar and Walt Disney Animation Studios, Eisner and his team were even secretly plotting to craft a sequel to Pixar's iconic film *Toy Story*. But when Bob Iger finally took the reins of the Company in 2005, he told Steve Jobs that he was "well aware of how strained the relationship had become" and that "I know you think it's going to be business as usual, but I'd like to prove to you that it's not."

Fortunately, Steve trusted Bob enough to give him a chance. Bob believed that Apple's CEO was a very valuable technology partner and that Pixar was the "pixie dust" that Disney animation needed to revive its life.

When Bob had been CEO for just over a week and the Pixar acquisition had not yet been finalized, he stood with Steve on a stage in the Bay area during the showcasing of Apple's new video iPod. Bob told the crowd that Disney's ABC shows would be available on the iTunes store. Before this point, only music was sold on the iTunes store, so this was groundbreaking news. The trust bond that was forming between Bob and Steve within those first few weeks of Bob's new role at Disney would strengthen with time. As evidence of this deep personal relationship, Steve requested that Bob replace him on the Apple board after his death, a position Bob still holds today.

Since Steve's death in 2011, the partnership between Disney and Apple has been further solidified. Disney was one of the first media companies to develop apps for iPhones and iPads. Apple Pay, the device maker's new mobile-payment system, is now used in Disney stores. Referring to the six-year relationship between Bob and Steve, Ed Catmull reflected, "In the subsequent years they thought of each other as true partners."

Clearly, the core of their special relationship was mutual respect and trust. And as our friend the late great Stephen Covey said, "Trust is the glue of life. It's the most essential ingredient in effective communication. It's the foundational principle that holds all relationships."

## Partnerships Reflect Your Values

Disney has occasionally made the mistake of ignoring its standards when working in a partnership. And every time, management has had to backtrack to figure out when the mistake was made and then re-embrace its time-tested principles. No matter how big or how successful a company becomes, partnerships, whether they are with other companies, employees, suppliers, customers, or the community, are a valuable asset that needs to be cultivated.

The late Michael Vance, former head of Disney University, recalled the story of when he and Roy Disney visited the construction site during the building of Walt Disney World. As the two men entered the site, the first thing they saw was a large sign announcing that all contractors should immediately report to construction shack 47 upon entering the premises. Reading that clear and curt order, Roy turned to Mike and asked, "What does that convey to you?" Without hesitation, Mike responded, "It says that we don't trust our suppliers to be on the property." "Right," Roy replied. "And who's responsible for communicating the Disney culture and values to all employees on the property?"

As it happens, that is one of the goals of Disney University, so Mike put together a team that designed and built a new reception center. Now contractors and suppliers at Walt Disney World are treated like the valued partners they are. The reception center offers coffee, soft drinks, and meeting rooms, all in a pleasant and welcoming atmosphere.

As Roy explained to Mike, not only were their values at stake but also the wider reputation of the Company. He said, "We need to be partners with our contractors for the Park to open on time, but even more importantly, they have to be proud to be a part of this, so they will call friends and family all over the country and tell them to come down to see what they've done."

When it comes to any team or partnership, the importance of mutual respect and trust cannot be overemphasized. Only once this has been earned and given can diversity be valued. Informational diversity, or gathering together people who bring different information, opinions, and perspectives to the table, heightens creativity, produces better problem solving and decision making, and enhances the competitive advantage of the parties involved. The same results are realized with social diversity—for example, the experiences and unique viewpoints that people of different races and genders can add to a collaborative process.

Walt Disney was an inclusive leader who was willing to communicate and collaborate with anyone with whom he worked, regardless of gender, race, culture, or creed. In fact, the following statement suggests that Walt was ahead of his time with regard to equality for women in the workplace: "If a woman can do the work as well, she is worth as much as a man, and I honestly believe they may eventually contribute something to this business that men never would or could."

The Walt Disney Company's statement regarding Supplier Diversity Outreach reflects the values of its founding father: "We actively seek diverse suppliers through participation in national, regional, and local minority- and women-owned business development organizations, advocacy groups, and trade shows."

## Parting Thoughts

With the Disney philosophy as inspiration, you should strive to cultivate relationships in which you "share the spotlight" with "costars." And, once on the path to making your shared dreams come true, don't forget to keep communicating. Ongoing dialogue helps to build and maintain trust, reduces the chances of making assumptions, and encourages the partners to stay the course together.

In the next chapter, we will look at what it means to take calculated risks and how an organization can thrive on the opportunities that arise when one is willing to accept challenge.

## Our Featured Organization: TYRA Beauty

### INSPIRED BY A LEGEND
### IN THE WORDS OF BILL

In January 2015, we received an email from a small entrepreneurial company in Los Angeles that contained two messages. One, the company's leader had studied and loved *The Disney Way* and was using it as a guide for her new company; and two, she invited us to come to LA to help reinforce *The Disney Way* principles within her company's culture. Since I was traveling with other clients at that time, I didn't really give the email much thought until I arrived back in my office a week or so later. When I spoke with Lynn, I asked, "Wasn't that a flattering email we received from that little company on the West Coast?" She looked at me in utter amazement and replied, "Are you kidding me? Don't you know who TYRA BANKS is?" At first, I felt like I had been living under a rock, but after I saw some of Tyra's photos online I told Lynn, "Of course, I know HER!"

The opportunity to work with Tyra and her **TYRA** *Beauty* company couldn't have come at a better time. Within a week of receiving the **TYRA** *Beauty* email, McGraw-Hill asked us to write the third edition of *The Disney Way*, and I was hoping that Tyra's company story would be a valuable addition to the book.

When I finally arrived in LA to work with **TYRA** *Beauty*, it didn't take me long to realize that Tyra and her company emulated the "share the spotlight" principle. Tyra shared with me her passion for Walt Disney's creative genius. She stated, "Everything I do from *America's Next Top Model* to **TYRA** *Beauty* has a lot of the principles instilled by Walt, and everything really engages the senses while creating something that people can have fun with and learn along the way too." Tyra continued, "I remember going past certain rides like Big Thunder Mountain Railroad and smelling steam. It was like every ride had something . . . smell, taste, touch . . . but it's also the magic of it. Seeing the Magic Castle and seeing

Tinker Bell go down the line awakened something in me, and not only did I enjoy experiencing that magic but I also wanted to create it."

Listening to Tyra speak, I couldn't help but wonder why one of the most famous people in the world, who could endorse any number of products with minimal effort, would choose to start her own a line of cosmetics. I had my question answered when I learned how Tyra's childhood experiences and beliefs would eventually drive her passion to create life-changing opportunities for her independent sales associates called Beautytainers. (Tyra is a master at creating new words: Beautytainment is "where beauty and entertainment collide!")

For Tyra, there is a motivator than transcends "beauty." As Tyra shared with me, "My mother, when I was very young, stayed in the marriage with my father far too long based on finances and self-esteem. She said if she had had her own money and self-worth, she would have left the situation sooner, and that has really been like an iron on my chest. I want to instill in these Beautytainers financial freedom and self-esteem. . . . Financial freedom can mean happiness and the opportunity for being a good role model for their children."

Before **TYRA** *Beauty*, there was "only" Tyra Banks—the mega-famous television personality, talk-show host, Executive Producer, Creator of *America's Next Top Model*, and former supermodel who has nearly 50 million followers on social media! When Tyra announced on *Good Morning America* that she was going to start a "movement" of entre-preneurs, she quickly had thousands upon thousands of email subscribers who were ready to learn more. They didn't seem to care that the direct-selling facet of **TYRA** *Beauty* had not officially launched yet—they simply believed in *her*. Tyra's fans already *knew* her, and they *believed* that she was committed to helping them look good and feel good about them-selves. Tyra said, "Natural beauty is so unfair. Mine came from bottles and lotions and things; fake hair and makeup made me look a certain way. So I love what makeup can do for women."

In the worldwide marketplace, there are countless cosmetics lines from which to choose. **TYRA** *Beauty* General Manager Anita Krpata acknowledges, "People love Tyra, but that does not mean they are going to love our products." The **TYRA** *Beauty* team is determined to offer products that are very innovative and transformative. In the early stages of product development, they bring in hundreds of competitor samples and evaluate them to determine what is missing. Kim Giannini, Director of Beautytainer Experience, explained the process: "We put so much love in creating our products. Tyra might say, 'I love this, but I wanted it to be a little softer or have a little more sheen.' So, we go to our manufacturer in Italy and restructure it. The product has to be something that is really going to be useful. It can't be something that people will buy just because it's *her*. The product is full of love, and it's coming through. That's where innovative and useful products like OOPS Liner and the In A Stick products that feature TY-Glide technology came about."

The dream of providing a way for women to take control of their lives is Tyra's core passion for **TYRA** *Beauty*, and this message came through loud and clear to those who desired to be crowned as Beautytainers. Anita told me, "When we opened our business on day one, we had a crush of people sign up, and seven months later that number had doubled, and it continues to grow. When we opened our doors in the fall of 2015, we had over 10,000 people wanting to become Beautytainers, where most businesses would hope to have this after a few years in business."

It would be tempting for any business with this type of popularity to merely sign up as many direct sales representatives as possible and hope for the best, or as one of our clients says, "spray and pray." That method would never work for **TYRA** *Beauty*. As Kim assured me, "We handpicked 346 [sales representatives] because we wanted a goal of 200. We wanted people who had experience but also people who had a certain spirit." The prelaunch period was imperative to **TYRA** *Beauty*, who knew that real-time testing by this handpicked group of Beautytainers is what would ultimately lead to the success of the product.

Tyra has indeed shaken up the world of direct selling. Unlike so many pyramid-structured companies in which the bottom tiers "feed" those at the top, Beautytainer leaders must sell the product, and they are also responsible for coaching their team members. Secondarily, Kim remarked, "Their commissions don't come out of the pockets of the people below them. They are compensated for leading their teams and generating team sales volume."

The **TYRA** *Beauty* headquarters team believes that their primary role is to support their illustrious army of salespeople in every way possible. Once a quarter, every employee is required to "walk in the shoes of the Beautytainer." They do this by selling a set amount of product, enrolling a certain number of Beautytainers, or spending up to one full day answering calls in their Customer Care call center.

A great headquarters staff and a passionate direct sales force, however, will not guarantee success. When I asked Anita to describe her biggest challenge, she replied, "Planning for growth. Our philosophy has always been to be start-up scrappy with billion-dollar goals, and navigating that can be really tricky." Tyra added, "If you are successful in the direct sales business, it's like a hockey stick [or a rapid exponential growth in sales]. So we are implementing different systems as we scale up, so we don't have an implosion."

Will **TYRA** *Beauty* succeed? The odds are stacked against it: 75 percent of all start-ups fail, and 90 percent of new products fail. In my experience, successful businesses are characterized by a customer-centric culture, a relentless spirit of innovation, and great leadership.

The following is my assessment of how Tyra and **TYRA** *Beauty* are demonstrating results in those elements.

## CUSTOMER-CENTRIC CULTURE

Over the long-term, if Tyra continues to instill the passion required for her team to stay focused on serving the Beautytainers, there should be no problem. As she continuously promotes and promises, "We see the world through the eyes of the Beautytainer."

## INNOVATION

Tyra's cosmetics experience as a result of her modeling and her film and television roles has led her to develop practical and innovative products and techniques. However, Tyra confesses, "It is difficult to ask the manufacturer to produce a small lot size of 10,000 SKUs (stock keeping units) during start-up and have any degree of priority when they are producing millions for other customers. From a financial perspective, we are not a priority." As with any start-up operation that relies on a manufacturing partner, until volumes are large enough to schedule regular production runs, they are at the mercy of their partner's availability. By the time you are reading this story, I hope **TYRA** *Beauty* will have become large enough to warrant priority scheduling!

## LEADERSHIP DEFINED

Dissecting Walt Disney's definition of *leadership* is a practical method for evaluating the responsibilities of any leader: "the ability to **establish and manage** a **creative climate** in which **individuals and teams are self-motivated** to the successful achievement of **long-term goals** in an environment of **mutual respect and trust**."

After spending three days with an organization, one gets a sense of its leadership style. Considering Walt's definition of *leadership*, here is my critique of Tyra and her team with respect to the key components:

### ESTABLISH AND MANAGE

Walt Disney believed in developing people through their work and encouraged them to have fun. Anita has masterfully created a three-day onboarding orientation to begin the staff development process. Like The Walt Disney Company, new hires are immersed in the culture of the organization and the expected customer service behaviors. Kim told me, "You have to know what's going on out there to do your job. So we do an onboarding, and then everyone has to do customer service. There is nothing without that connection!"

As for fun, Anita affirmed, "Fun revolves around the fact that people like to be social. We made it a point to pick a location that is in and of itself fun. It's near entertainment studios [and] a very cool and happening part of LA with arts, music, and food right outside our door. Our office décor is inspiring, whimsical, and different." An atmosphere of "fun" also envelopes the **TYRA** *Beauty* home office. The "POW der" room, as Anita says, "puts a smile on your face even though you see it every day." The "Tyra's Gonna Think I'm Crazy But . . ." room serves as a brainstorming space that tempts team members to think as far out of the box as possible. And, rather than sign a guest book in their lobby, you can sign and kiss the "schmooch" book!

### CREATIVE CLIMATE

Tyra has redefined the cosmetic shopping experience through her legendary creativity. **TYRA** *Beauty* doesn't just sell mascara, blush, and lipstick. The company provides an over-the-top experience and solves customer problems using TyTy Tips and Tricks, Four Fast Fierce Finger Techniques, and other cool Tyra-termed methods.

### INDIVIDUALS AND TEAMS ARE SELF-MOTIVATED

Tyra's "scrappy" start-up team is definitely self-motivated. One of the best examples came from the behaviors they exhibited during *The Disney Way* three-day retreat. Each day, the **TYRA** *Beauty* team members arrived at the retreat ready to get down to business. Even before each session began, they were on their laptops answering emails and working on projects, and they did the same during breaks and lunchtime. I am still amazed that even though they all were apparently swamped with work and projects (and taking two workdays in addition to half of their weekend for the retreat didn't help), whenever it was time to start, everyone was ready and focused. I credit Tyra with setting the example.

I routinely begin *The Disney Way* retreat with the topic of "commitment." The participants—both employees and leaders alike—commit to a set of ground rules that includes no ringing cell phones, no texting, and no side talking. Customarily, employees tend to look for behavioral clues from their leaders that, in turn, shape their own behaviors. In the 1970s, corporate culture pioneer Larry Senn coined the term "shadow of the leader" to describe this phenomenon. Star power aside, Tyra clearly casts a "long shadow" with her team. She was always on time and never broke any of the ground rules. I believe many CEOs could take a lesson from Tyra on focus and commitment.

### LONG-TERM GOALS

In preparation for launching **TYRA** *Beauty*, Tyra and Anita attended Harvard Business School's (HBS) executive education program that was conducted as an intensive five-day sales and strategy session. Tyra also attended college-level finance classes to prepare for Harvard's maximizing financial resources curriculum.

At the time, the media, rather than reporting on Tyra's long-term commitment to properly prepare to become the CEO of **TYRA** *Beauty*, was all abuzz with the accusations that Tyra falsely claimed she had received a Harvard MBA. Why would anyone spend nine weeks over three years and a considerable amount of money (even for a supermodel) simply to make this claim? I guess they saw her picture with the Harvard Business School Owner/President Manager (OPM) Program "diploma," but they failed to see her on the Jimmy Kimmel show during which she told him, "It's not the same as being a Harvard Business School student, and I won't be getting an MBA." She also toured *CBS Sunday Morning News* around campus describing her HBS OPM experience.

## MUTUAL RESPECT AND TRUST

These critical values are evidenced in the behavioral patterns of the **TYRA** *Beauty* team. Anita shared, "One of our philosophies is that we don't talk *about* each other. We talk *to* each other. We are all committed to the same goal and share the same love."

More than any other element of Walt's definition of *leadership*, mutual respect and trust or lack thereof can make or break both organizations and teams. In young organizations, there's often a special team camaraderie that develops and solidifies fairly quickly. They share a common goal, and they realize the importance of mutual respect and trust at the outset. We've witnessed many a start-up team working long into the night, sharing successes and setbacks, and eating cold pizza. These teams are committed to doing whatever it takes to navigate through the unknown and stay the course together. But with corporate growth come new hires and personnel changes that can dramatically alter the dynamic of an existing team. Kim related, "The most important thing I learned [at **TYRA** *Beauty*] is that you have to be open to growing and keep an open mind about bringing people in who might not click with everybody. You never know, they might bring new stuff. You can't think that since everything is great now, you have to keep it exactly how it is. In the end, you will stop your growth and the growth of your company by thinking that way."

In our book *Leading at the Speed of Change*, we wrote, "The paradox of the new economy is the more power you give away, the more powerful you will become." Tyra Banks is living this principle. As Anita told me:

We positioned [**TYRA** *Beauty*] not as "We are going to start a direct-selling business." It was a movement that you can be your own boss, and Tyra can be your mentor in doing this. It was a different message. . . . Partner with Tyra, and she will help you become the CEO of your life, and she has these really innovative and amazing products with you in mind. . . . By sharing her experience in beauty, business, and entertainment to create a line of products that aren't ho-hum or straight up, Tyra created the opposite of the run-of-the-mill products that sit on department store shelves and blend into all the other cosmetic lines out there. She didn't just slap her name on someone else's product the way a lot of other celebrity lines do. Tyra formulated each of these to pack a punch, a pow, a wow that will transform what you've got into what you want. But it doesn't end there. Tyra will also share her influence in media that reaches five generations and multiple demographics to help you broaden your network and expand your customer base and earning potential. Global domination is on the to-do list, and if anyone can do it—it's our CEO, Tyra Banks.

With Tyra's "share the spotlight" philosophy, there's little doubt in my mind that her company is off to a great start. Her words during a moment of self-reflection are what truly convinced me that **TYRA** *Beauty*, like its leader, will emerge as a superstar:

I'm interested in creating a legacy like Walt Disney. That means more than him, the person. It's about his dreams, his beliefs, and his fantasies that have outlived him. I am willing to invest my own money—this is 100 percent self-funded—to accomplish that. I'm not interested in popularity. I am interested in legacy and influence. It's more about having a lasting impact on the present generation and the ones beyond me.

## Questions to Ask

- Do you build collaborative partnerships with internal customers?

- Do you believe that business success requires diverse individuals from across the organization to work together as a united team?

- Does your organization have true partnerships with suppliers and vendors?

- Do you routinely meet with your suppliers and vendors to involve them in strategic planning and develop compatible cultures?

- Do you believe that the best ideas often come from those outside your own organization?

## Actions to Take

- Build collaborative teams to reach shared goals.

- Gain feedback from employees on a regular basis by asking the following questions:

  — How are we doing as a company in developing partnerships with employees?

  — Do we invite your input and creativity on problems and solutions regarding organizational issues?

- How are we doing as a company in developing partnerships with our suppliers?

- Think in terms of long-term partnerships. Determine what partnerships will add value to your business and work at making them successful!

- Meet with key suppliers two days or more per quarter to discuss ways to solve customer problems and fulfill customer dreams.

**Chapter Chats with Bill: http://capojac.com/disneyway/6/**

# Dare

# Chapter 7

# Dare to Dare

*When you're curious, you find lots of things to do. One thing it takes to accomplish something is courage.*

Walt Disney

Premier players can be found in all corners of the business world, and one thing they have in common is a willingness to take bold risks. They clearly understand that grasping at a dream requires one to reach beyond the sure thing. Even more, they seem to relish the opportunity. Walt Disney was such a player.

In fact, if there was a cornerstone upon which The Walt Disney Company rested, it would have to be inscribed with one short word: Dare. Throughout the 43 years that Walt ran the Company, he dared to meet challenges, he dared to take risks, and ultimately, he dared to excel.

From the time that he decided to produce his first cartoon, Walt pushed the limits of ordinary achievement. He pioneered the use of sound in animated cartoons with *Steamboat Willie*. He signed his contract with Technicolor before the revolutionary process had even been accepted by the industry as a whole, and he astutely insisted on a two-year exclusive for his cartoons. He originated feature-length cartoons with *Snow White* and defied the odds at a time when no one thought anyone would ever sit through a 90-minute cartoon.

Even Walt's decision to build Disneyland represented a new and risky concept in entertainment. Up until that time, amusement parks had something of an unsavory connotation, an association with the tawdriness of pre-1950s carnivals. It took the vision of Walt Disney to imagine a place that would incorporate historical reconstructions, displays, and rides, and it took the daring of Walt Disney to build it into a world-famous tourist destination.

The Disney "experience" illustrates how a company that is willing to take calculated risks can advance the level of development of a product or service, and in the process reap huge rewards. Ed Catmull, Co-founder of Pixar Animation Studios and President of Walt Disney and Pixar Animation Studios, has made risk taking a key link in the Company's chain of most enduring values. He said, "We as executives have to resist our natural tendency to avoid or minimize risks, which, of course, is much easier said than done. This instinct leads executives to choose to copy successes rather than try to create something brand new. That's why you see so many movies that are so much alike. It also explains why a lot of films aren't very good. If you want to be original, you have to accept the uncertainly, even when it's uncomfortable, and have the capability to recover when your organization takes a big risk and fails." But not all corporate executives and managers fall into this enviable category. Too many opt for the safest route because they fear failure or loss. They allow themselves to get bogged down in corporate bureaucracy, which can keep the management process from flowing as it should.

But such behavior is not written in stone. Companies can change the buttoned-down, risk-avoidance atmosphere that— dictates status quo first, innovation later—if at all. We have helped numerous leaders learn to prioritize their objectives and to take a holistic view of their companies, thereby putting risk taking into the proper perspective. In this chapter, we will look at how leaders dared to take calculated risks and lifted their organizations to previously unimagined levels of achievement.

## Solid Fundamentals Support Risk Taking

Psychologists might describe Walt Disney as a born risk taker, someone whose fear of failure was outweighed by the need to tackle new challenges. His brother, Roy, was more cautious and often referred to Walt as "crazy" or "wacky." But then Roy was in charge of the family cash box, which in the early days his brother depleted with alarming frequency, leaving it to Roy to persuade bankers to agree to new loans or extend old ones.

Although politically and personally conservative by nature, Walt accepted no conventional boundaries when it came to his work. He was sure of his values and beliefs, sure of his own talent and that of his Cast Members, sure of his instincts, and sure that if given the proper chance, this outstanding combination would eventually prevail.

That is not to say that he jumped at every idea that came his way, but he certainly didn't hesitate to take a chance if a concept met his artistic and financial criteria. First and foremost, any potential project had to pass Walt's trademark "entertainment" test. Then if he felt that a project fit with his vision, he would leap, often ahead of the pack.

Another business giant who is not afraid to dare to realize his dreams is Alan Mulally who became Ford's CEO in 2006. The fresh-faced former savior of Boeing after the terrorist attacks on September 11, 2001 set out to shake up one of the most systemically dysfunctional cultures of all time. And he did it in such a way that even the most egotistical, self-protective leaders of his team were soon acquiescing to Alan's unconventional new way of defining their individual lines of business. In his secret "war room," his top managers were required to classify their initiatives using a streetlight metaphor: a "red," "yellow," or "green" light.

When the very first manager, current CEO Mark Fields, stood up in a weekly staff meeting and confessed, "I have a red light," Alan jumped to his feet and began to applaud. Unlike the old Ford where personal vulnerability could translate to being fired, no longer would admitting weakness be considered as true weakness. And there was no room for blaming someone else for one's own failures. The new paradigm was to put the issue on the table as quickly as possible—fail forward fast. By all means, Alan wanted this to be a safe environment for the best minds to come up with the best ideas. What was so foreign to his staff was the raw transparency that was both expected and celebrated week in and week out. The numbers spoke for themselves, and everyone's job was to make sure they did not play the "numbers games" of the past—this was different data for different audiences.

Setting the stage for the turnaround was Alan's Pixar-like style of collaboration in which team members made one another look good. He created "One Ford"—one company with one set of products. He dared to fuse Ford with Ford of Europe, Ford of Asia, and the plethora of divisions and subsidiaries, and in his words, "merge with ourselves." He also streamlined Ford's product lines that once featured more than 97 different models under several brands.

Alan's turnaround plan included the intricacies of mortgaging every-thing he could (yes, that meant the famous blue oval logo too!) and raising the capital critical to ensure that the company didn't collapse in an economic downturn. With the resulting load of debt of over $30 billion, the stakes were high, but the plan was a success. Ford did not let the well run dry on product development, even when times got really tough.

But without the new culture in place, Alan couldn't have succeeded. Without any experience in the automotive industry, he dared to put in place what he believed—growing a culture and a brand takes a well-oiled team to build a long-standing and thriving organization. In 2009, Ford stock sold for $1.96, and in the fourth quarter of 2015, it was just over $15.00 per share—a staggering 750 percent increase!

We are often asked, "How does culture really affect the bottom line?" Since our college days, we have witnessed both organizational leaders and academics debate the relevance of corporate culture. Lou Gerstner, Chairman and CEO of IBM from 1993 to 2002, was credited with turning around the company's fortunes. He stated, "Culture isn't just one aspect of the game—it is the game. In the end, an organization is nothing more than the collective capacity of its people to create value."

True, but those "people" *need* great corporate leaders such as Walt Disney, Lou Gerstner, and Alan Mulally. They engage their teams by pro-viding them with the tools and information needed for the best results, trusting them to do their jobs, and giving them permission to take risks.

## Avoiding the Short-Term Mentality

Admittedly, being able to determine whether taking an action or not taking it will put employees and/or customers in jeopardy is not always easy. What's more, some managers are so determined to protect their own turf that they prefer the status quo to any proposition that might threaten their position, no matter how reasonable. This is akin to the *short-term mentality* (or living for today at the expense of tomorrow), and it is the kiss of death when it comes to innovation and risk taking. Many great companies have slipped into decline because of this mindset, which combines an inability to take on challenges with a dangerous self-satisfaction with past achievements.

Walt Disney, of course, exhibited the exact opposite of that mindset. When it came to technological advances, for example, he knew that no one could cling to past achievements and survive, so he always had his antennae up in search of new technology. When the movie industry stubbornly refused to sell or lease any of its products to the television networks in the 1940s and early 1950s, Walt took a different view. He saw television's potential market value, and he embraced the opportunities the new medium offered and realized that it presented yet another outlet for his product.

Although Walt was clever enough to recognize the potential television held, he still spurned the networks' initial approach. As always, he was determined to control the environment in which his work was released, and he feared that the black-and-white screen would not do justice to his color cartoons and films.

When he did make a television deal in 1953, he made it with the fledgling American Broadcasting Company (ABC), in part because that network had agreed to help finance Disneyland. In return, ABC received access to Disney's backlog of films and cartoons. Thus, just as movie audiences were declining markedly in the 1950s, lured away by the flickering screens right in their own living rooms, Disney was cementing an alliance that would plant his product firmly in the new medium. Today, Disney not only has a string of TV successes to its credit, including its own cable channel, but it also owns ABC outright.

In more recent times, the Company could have used some of Walt's wisdom in "controlling the environment," most notably in its strategic initiatives to grow the organization on a global scale. There were valuable lessons to be learned from their failures in developing Hong Kong Disneyland, a project that generated no money for seven long years.

Right out of the gate, The Walt Disney Company underestimated the number of Guests they would have. The Park's first year to celebrate the Chinese New Year was 2006, and the Company endured unimaginable worldwide embarrassment when crowds stormed the Park's entrance in anger. Hundreds were turned away due to a faulty ticketing system. Imagine spending hours driving to a brand new Disney Theme Park only to learn that your six-month pass didn't guarantee entrance on any given day! Many of the ones lucky enough to enter the "kingdom" had envisioned the space and grandeur of Walt Disney World as they had seen on their televisions, but they were soon disappointed to discover that Disney's smallest Park could be explored in less than a day. Even more troubling was that many of the Park's signature attractions and characters were unfamiliar to the locals, and therefore they did not produce the same emotional connection that Americans have with their beloved childhood heroes such as Cinderella or Snow

White. Another baffling example of Disney's failure to fully understand the culture of their new Guests was that the songs from the *Lion King* show were in Cantonese and English. This meant that for the 42 percent of the Park's Mandarin-speaking guests from the Mainland, many of whom were children, the experience fell way short of "magical."

After a harrowing three years, the Company made a deal with the Hong Kong government to expand the Park to include several new lands, attractions, and hotels by 2020. The transformation began with the addition of Disney characters to the It's a Small World attraction followed by Toy Story Land, the first new themed section of the Park since its opening in 2005.

Fast forward to 2016 with the hype that has surrounded Shanghai Disneyland, Disney's latest and swankiest Park. The Company has taken great care to make sure that their Guests will be "all smiles" on day one. To that end, they have added some Chinese nationals to the Imagineering development team to help create new attractions based on the Chinese culture. CEO Bob Iger's words are evidence that Disney has taken heed of past mistakes made in Hong Kong: "Main Street USA might not be that interesting to people here." And so, for the first time in Disney's Theme Park history, "Main Street USA" has been replaced with a sprawling expanse of grass on which local festivals take center stage.

Even with the impressive regional success predictors of the booming middle class, the population topping 25 million, and the 300 million people who are within a half-day's drive of the new Shanghai Park, the Company understands the dare. The Hong Kong nightmare wasn't that long ago, and in anticipating the opening of Shanghai in 2016, Bob warned, "We have to be careful about how many will come and their visitation patterns." All of Disney's Theme Parks test the Company's long-term strategic thinking, but Shanghai might be their biggest dare to date. With an annual attendance of 10 million, it will still take nearly a decade for the Company to recoup its initial investment. A safe bet? For Disney, we think so. Daring takes the courage to try, learn, and try again, an unshakable tradition for a Company that prides itself on providing the finest in family entertainment for *all* cultures.

## The Many Forms of Risk

It is usually taken for granted that risks in the business world are financial, but in our experience, risks come in various forms. A risk might even involve a change in a leader's personal behavior, management style, or willingness to place more trust in coworkers or frontline employees. Generally, a number of risks must be taken if a company is to reach its peak performance.

One of our clients was unable to risk making needed behavioral change until he was forced into it by circumstance. He was an executive and part owner of a family company. Within the company, he was perceived as an autocrat. Workers complained about his high-handed behavior and his abrupt way of giving orders. After it became clear that the executive in question had completely lost the trust of his employees, the complaints finally reached the company's CEO. The executive's department output was suffering, which was causing the company to lose money.

During discussions with this executive, we pointed out that discontent with his leadership style was undermining employee morale, and even worse, affecting efficiency. He had a tough time accepting our assessment at first, but in the end, he acquiesced. We encouraged him to take what was an enormous risk for him—empowering his staff by giving them information on business goals and performance and by asking them to participate in problem solving.

After three years of coaching, this executive was finally able to relax control and stop micromanaging everyone and everything in his department. He eventually became so comfortable with trusting his employees that he could even skip meetings, thus giving them more say. Because he was able to take a difficult personal risk, he reversed his department's decline.

Over the years, we have discovered that the risk of changing often holds a company (or an individual) back until the time comes when it is forced to make a choice. Threatened by competition or saddled with a product that has ceased to satisfy contemporary needs, many of our clients have come to us and asked for advice.

A few times we've encountered companies that talked a good line when it came to making changes only to discover that all management really wanted was to throw up a smoke screen. They planned to go through the motions of change by attending meetings with us, but they had no intention of even attempting to implement the suggested actions.

In some ways, such behavior is not all that surprising because it takes courage to accept the fact that you must change. Some companies are never able to do it, and ultimately, they slip quietly under the waves. But others dare to summon the resolve to do what must be done.

## Rethinking Human Resources

In any organization, the role of the human resources (HR) department is pivotal in terms of protecting the culture that its leaders have established. The policies they design and mandate and the way they communicate them directly affect the vibe and often even the reputation of the entire organization. Employees take their behavioral cues from those individuals who were instrumental in the hiring process, and that begins with HR.

Attracting and retaining the best candidates are two of the primary functions for which human resources departments were created. They must consistently communicate with the leaders, coaches, and team members who will be directly responsible for mentoring new hires, and they must avoid the trap of acting on their own accord at all costs. At The Walt Disney Company, Casting Centers (U.S. locations: Walt Disney World and Disneyland) engage in a carefully detailed process to discover candidates who will embody their unique culture.

In most cases, the first step in the hiring process is crafting the job description. A common problem in many organizations is an obsession with writing such documents in crisp, formal language that appears to have been inspired by a bland Internet description of a skill set. If you are looking for creative people who are engaging and interesting, begin by crafting a position description that reads like an inspirational marketing piece. Certainly the words must convey accurate expectations for the job, but the more you can infuse your company's unique spirit into the text, the more likely you are to attract candidates that will help propel your organization to success. In one of our favorite Charles Schulz Peanuts comic strips, Lucy pays a visit to Snoopy who is lounging comfortably on top of his dog house. With that "look" that only Lucy can deliver, she says to Snoopy, "I've always wondered why you decided to be a dog," to which he replies, "I was fooled by the job description."

Professionals in the field of human resources must never forget that they too have roles in the show and that they must be aligned with the overall vision and values of the organization. In an environment of mutual respect and trust, the term *resources* assumes the qualities of being approachable, trustworthy, and dedicated to treating employees as cherished members of a unified team. These are the values that will enable your newly hired "cast" to begin embracing the culture and unleashing their true potential.

When Walt Disney began his studio, he realized the importance of hiring the right people and instilling a sense of the Company culture in them from the start. Today, the Disney organization builds a global workforce by applying a key lesson from Walt: hire for attitude, not aptitude. Every potential new hire at The Walt Disney Company learns that maintaining a positive demeanor is critical to performing every role in the show.

Many other organizations seek job candidates with a certain attitude, but few "shake up" the hiring process with as much creativity as Google. In 1999, Google's first chef, Charlie Ayers, won the job in a cook-off judged by the company's 40 employees. His previous claim to fame was catering for the iconic rock group The Grateful Dead. When Charlie joined Google, he was the fifty-sixth employee. By the time he left the company in May 2005, he had attained the role of leading a kitchen staff of 135 who served 4,000 meals a day in addition to organizing parties and events for the growing Google workforce. The moral of this story is that daring to innovate your hiring process can pay big dividends!

Employees at Google live by a Code of Conduct, not by a policy manual. Any corporate policy manual that is nothing more than a deadly dull recitation of rules and regulations virtually guarantees that it will be overlooked or quickly forgotten. In sharp contrast, the Preface of Google's Code of Conduct begins: "Don't be evil. Googlers generally apply those words to how we serve our users. But 'Don't be evil' is much more than that. Yes, it's about providing our users unbiased access to information, focusing on their needs, and giving them the best products and services that we can. But it's also about doing the right thing more generally—following the law, acting honorably, and treating the other with respect."

Make your values and Codes of Conduct the primary focus of your employee handbook. The section that includes a formal set of corporate policies should always be written in a style that will not deflate the morale of new hires but rather reflect the elements of the culture you want to reinforce. The late W. Edwards Deming, considered the architect of total quality management (TQM), suggested 14 points for transforming a culture. Point Number 8 states: "Drive out fear, so that everyone may work effectively for the company." This is a good lesson to remember when creating any policy within an organization. Bombarding new hires with reams of fear producing and inexplicable policy prose will only serve to squelch their passion—a trait that is not only what made them desirable candidates from the start but that is also representative of every excellent employee.

## Make It Fun!

Recently, a 102-year-old Disney veteran named Ruthie Thompson cheerfully reminisced about her time working with Walt back in the early days: "We all worked for Walt Disney without knowing he was a 'great man' because he was a kid along with us." That persona of "fun" is perhaps one of Walt's greatest legacies. After all, he is the father of Mickey Mouse, Goofy, and cartoons called Laugh-O-Grams!

If you believe that laughter and play are nonessential ingredients in a corporate culture, consider the following: a robust laugh will burn up to 3.5 calories, and laughing releases endorphins, opioid proteins with about 10 times the pain-relieving power of morphine. Walt Disney got it right!

According to Dr. Stuart Brown, Founder of the National Institute for Play, "There is good evidence that if you allow employees to engage in something they want to do, [which] is playful, there are better outcomes in terms of productivity and motivation. . . ."

We find it utterly amazing that we need a national organization to protect and promote our right to play!

No company we know has the value of "play" more entwined in the fabric of its culture than Pixar. The world-famous creators of the groundbreaking animated feature film *Toy Story* live in the land of scooters. The story goes that one day John Lasseter brought his son's scooter into work and began riding it around. Soon other employees showed up with scooters, and before long, there was a small fleet of them. Pixar director Pete Docter remarked, "We got into these scooter races—there was a track mapped out, kind of a loop, and we'd time people and write the times on the wall. We all got into a very fierce competition over who could get the best time." In Bill's keynote presentations on the subject of Pixar's fun-infused innovative culture, he rides in on a scooter and awards it to a participant with the condition that he or she ride it in his or her workplace and let everyone know that he or she is "unleashing his or her childlike potential!"

Decades ago, the fishmongers of Pike Place Fish Market in Seattle, Washington, committed themselves to becoming "world famous." To date, the now World Famous Pike Place Fish Market has never spent a dime on advertising. Their goal is simply to interact with people and give them the experience of having been served and appreciated, whether they buy fish or not.

These fishmongers are featured in the bestselling book *FISH!*, coauthored by our friend John Christensen (who also penned the foreword for this edition of *The Disney Way*). In *FISH!*, readers learn the benefits of a fun and happy workplace. Some leaders may find the story line and principles ("Play," "Be There," "Make Their Day," and "Choose Your Attitude") elementary. They fail to realize that indeed they have the power to drive out boredom, toxic energy, and burnout in their work environments.

The *FISH!* philosophy and principles offer a common language, one that enables and energizes an entire workforce. And here's the best of all: as the culture is transformed, new attitudes develop, trust increases, performance improves, and yes, customers notice.

The idea that work should be fun is not new. In the 1985 book *Reinventing the Corporation*, John Naisbit noted, "Many businesspeople have mourned the death of the work ethic in America. But a few of us have applauded the logic of the new value taking its place: 'work should be Fun.'" The good news is that after three decades, many enlightened cultures are proving that workplace fun boosts the creativity and productivity of employees at all levels. Catherine Blake, CEO and Founder of Sales Protocol International, described her passion for helping clients find joy at work: "I feel like there is so much of our business that is boring, uninspiring, or asking people to do things. I always feel like I can make a difference, that I can bring that light or that fire to a workplace, and be the person that is fun and make people laugh. We live in a very negative world, and we need to create our own positivity. It's a decision."

## Betting on Broadway

The fact that risk taking is alive and well at The Walt Disney Company is nowhere more apparent than in its dramatic entrance onto the Broadway stage. In 1993, Disney CEO Michael Eisner was keenly interested in purchasing a theater venue for the Company's highly successful *Beauty and the Beast* stage play. That year, during a chance meeting on an airplane, he spoke with Marian Heiskell, Chairperson of New 42, the organization charged with the revival of the New York City theater district's 42nd Street. She enticed Michael to consider renovating the area's dilapidated New Amsterdam Theatre that was once home to the spectacular Ziegfeld Follies in the early 1900s. But how could Disney's "finest in family entertainment" image be secure in a region so aptly portrayed in the lyrics of the song from the hit musical *Naughty, Bawdy, Gaudy, Sporty 42nd Street*?

Clearly, Michael Eisner knew that his decision to pour millions of dollars into the theater project was a bet that The Walt Disney Company couldn't afford to lose. He also knew that at the time, the former Federal Prosecutor and then Mayor Rudy Giuliani was beefing up the New York City police force in an attempt to turn the nation's crime capital into its safest major city. But before Michael would commit to such an enormous business understanding, he decided that he would put the Mayor himself to the test. His meeting with Rudy was a turning point for the cautious Disney executive. Michael tells us about the conversation in which he shared with Mayor Giuliani his fear of the riffraff culture surrounding the iconic theater: "I said, 'Mr. Mayor, you know there is an American Civil Liberties Union, and I mean, they're just not gone.' He said, 'Look me in the eye.' And I said, 'What?' He said, 'Look me in the eye.' I said, 'Okay.' He said, 'They will be gone.' . . . So that was that, and we said yes."

The bet paid off big time! In 2015, Disney Theatrical Productions Limited had two of the top three highest-grossing shows on Broadway: *The Lion King* grossed over $2.6 million during a week in July, and *Aladdin* grossed over $1.8 million during that same week! Since 1994, there have only been a few weeks in which Disney did not have at least one of the top 10 highest-grossing Broadway productions.

The Walt Disney Company still dares to take risks, and in doing so, continues to shower its audiences with sheer magic, all the way from the big screen to the dazzling lights on Broadway's famous Great White Way.

## Parting Thoughts

Looking ahead to the next chapter, we'll see how those who dare to take risks to further their dreams implement the fourth Disney principle: Do. To make your dreams come true, you must know how to execute. It all begins with the right kind of training and orientation for every one of your employees.

## Our Featured Organization:
## University Hospitals
## Rainbow Babies & Children's Hospital

### BREAKING THROUGH: AN INNOVATIVE
### WORKFORCE THAT SAVES LIVES

Is there really anything in the world more important than protecting our children? University Hospitals (UH) Rainbow Babies & Children's Hospital in Cleveland, Ohio, helped cement the answer for us. For the children whose lives are so very fragile and who could be lost forever without constant care, the dedicated staff of 1,300 pediatric specialists is at the very center of their existence. What makes this special group of people continue to be recognized as one of most trusted in pediatric healthcare? Daring to innovate! In Bill's keynote presentations, he tells audiences, "Innovate, don't imitate. You must define a culture that is uniquely yours, one that is right for your organization. It takes time and hard work to make it happen." And with over 125 years as a true leader in its industry, Rainbow Babies & Children's Hospital has surely met this test.

The clinical teams at Rainbow have long been innovators in the delivery of care. From the seminal works of Dr. Benjamin Spock who began his research there in 1958, to the development of patient-centered care practices that are now the standard in the industry, Rainbow innovators have been at the forefront of innovation. Continuing that tradition, today's Rainbow workforce strives to continuously improve and produce breakthrough innovations. They face new and daunting challenges each and every day, from the onset of new communicable diseases (and the reoccurrence of old ones) to those associated with changing societal practices and a growing cadre of childhood conditions.

Claudia Hoyen, MD, Rainbow's Director of Innovation, describes the culture as this: "People from across the organization are very innovative and are truly interested in making the lives of kids better. Part of this desire to improve the lives of these children is natural to the organization, and the other is really just the fact that the people we attract have passion and know that we can make things better."

Recently, with thoughtful deliberation, Rainbow Babies & Children's Hospital has begun implementing *The Disney Way* philosophy within their culture of innovation. From the leader to the greeters to the parking attendants, care delivery teams and support personnel have become immersed in the Dream, Believe, Dare, Do principles.

During their 2014 Belcher-Weir Family Pediatric Innovation Day, Rainbow employees learned how to generate ideas graphically, instead of just verbally, in order to not only expand their perspectives and sharpen their focus but to also dare them to see, feel, and dream, not just think. And all of this was discovered through a *The Disney Way* storyboarding workshop experience (more on this in Chapter 10). Since this Innovation Day, the organization has experienced the successful utilization of the storyboarding technique including the following:

- The Rainbow care team are focused on enhancing the customer experience, and they have identified key touch points for modifications to the current practices.
- The senior leadership of the UH system are focused on keys to UH innovation, which started with implementing a systemwide innovation effort and naming a Chief Innovation Officer.
- As part of a strategic planning exercise, Rainbow leadership has developed a new model of care delivery to underserved children.

Over the past several years, Innovation Day has become increasingly important to both enabling the workforce and creating positive synergy within the community. Prior to the event each year, employees have the opportunity to submit ideas for improvements to preexisting treatment methods, the development of new devices or tools, or simply new ways to better care for their young patients. The ideas can be in any stage of development, so there is no pressure on the employees to submit full-blown, complex plans. The top "winner" receives a start-up grant to help make his or her innovation a reality.

Stephen Behm, Director of Technology Management at University Hospitals Case Medical Center, was instrumental in the launch of Innovation Day. He explained:

The first year we had a submission from a respiratory therapist who said, "I have to deliver these aerosol drugs to these kids who are on oxygen masks, and the only way I can is to take these two masks and tape them together." It was a big hit. She submitted the idea, we worked on it, and eventually we developed a new mask. Another company saw what we were doing, ran out and [marketed the masks], and now the product is on the market. . . . At the end of the day, we solved the problem and we were happy to do that.

Managing a creative culture that challenges the status quo and encourages risk taking involves much more than merely getting work done through people. Innovative climates need a leadership style that helps them to develop and grow, while still allowing them to have fun in the process. Dr. Claudia Hoyen believes that "being innovative is not something that is special to people who are trained in innovation. It's human nature. So, it's about allowing people to be the best that they can be. Once you get people to feel engaged, appreciated, and heard, then that builds their self-confidence and makes work easier. It's a place where you want to go because people at work have your back, and they are going to help you by going that extra mile for you and the patient."

The experiences the Rainbow staff share during their annual Innovation Day foster the culture in which individuals and teams believe they are truly making a difference. For example, learning the Dare principle, which is a necessity for being innovative, has led employees to not only challenge the status quo but also to feel free to try new things, fail, and learn from their mistakes. Steve related, "We try to fail quickly. Certainly there have been some things that haven't gone as well as we would have liked, and we have had some learning in terms of some of the projects. We are doing a lot better when it comes to applying the right resources at the right time."

Practicing the Dare principle has also inspired a renewed spirit of fun at Rainbow, evidenced by highly engaged employee competitions around the critical success factors of quality, safety, and the patient experience—through the eyes of a child. As Claudia recounted, "By employing the principles learned from *The Disney Way*, we are working to tap into our largest resource: our patients, their families, and the thousands of care-givers and support staff. Through them, we have found new ways to help children and their families that look to us for care." One of those "new ways" is the video that we hope will help you unleash your own inner child. Just writing about it makes us feel inspired and energized . . . and, most of all, appreciative for all that Rainbow Babies & Children's Hospital does for the beautiful people who don't know how truly beautiful they really are! Take a look at the video in Bill's Chapter 7 Chapter Chat.

## Questions to Ask

- Is your culture stuck in paradigms that are no longer effective for your business?
- Do you routinely give employees the opportunity to grow beyond their current responsibilities?
- Do you create an atmosphere in which failures are accepted and analyzed for learning purposes and possible future innovation?
- Do you promote cross-functional teams for the purpose of reengineering outdated processes and procedures?
- Do you promote fun in your culture?

## Actions to Take

- Grant employees the opportunity to develop and implement innovative ideas in all areas of their jobs: product, process, and service.
- Schedule off-site retreats and meetings to encourage breakthrough, risk taking ideas that may fundamentally change the way you do business.
- Allow employees to fail forward fast—try, learn, and try again.
- Make work fun!

Chapter Chats with Bill: http://capojac.com/disneyway/7/

# Do

# Chapter 8

# Practice, Practice, Practice

*The growth and development of The Walt Disney Company are directly related to the growth and development of its human resources—our Cast.*

Walt Disney

Actors, musicians, athletes, and others who perform in public must train and practice. Otherwise, they risk embarrassing themselves and incurring the displeasure of spectators. Also of great importance is the teacher or coach who tells the musician that he's hitting the wrong notes or advises the athlete about running form, and so on. Without such helpful feedback and the benefit of the more experienced mentor's knowledge, a performer's career is likely to be short-lived.

The same is true in business as well as in the public sector. To perform at their best, employees must be thoroughly trained, and they need the help of more experienced staff members. Moreover, to maintain their competencies, training can't be a one-shot thing; it must be ongoing.

Perhaps because of his background as an artist, Walt Disney fully understood the essential part that training and practice play in the development of an individual's talents. Add in his well-known penchant for perfection, and it's hardly surprising that he adamantly insisted on rigorous and continuous training for all of his Cast Members. After all, common sense dictates that everyone, from the backstage crew to the performers out front, must be thoroughly rehearsed in order to put on the really "good show." But as is true about so much else at the Company Walt built, training takes on a special quality not found in most other organizations. In planning his original studio-based school of the 1930s, Walt wrote an eight-page memo to Don Graham, the legendary art instructor at the Chouinard Art Institute in downtown Los Angeles, that outlined "a very systematic training course for young animators and also outlined a plan of approach for our older animators." With Walt's detailed plan for developing the finest artists in the industry, Don Graham carried forth the creation of a curriculum that included courses on drawing, comedy, music, dialogue, and motion, and he intertwined them in a holistic fashion.

Today, the students of Disney University (Disney U) enjoy the most exciting campus of any educational institution in the country. The required course work is brief, but it's famous for its intensity. The freshmen are all new members of the Disney family. Some are there to prepare for a summer job; others are being readied to assume a permanent position.

Disney University, which is a process, not an institution, was conceived by Walt Disney himself prior to the opening of Disneyland in the 1950s. Today, every new Cast Member, from senior executives to part-time desk clerks and tour guides, is required to undergo training prior to embarking on her or his day-to-day responsibilities. And in typical Disney fashion, the training process leaves nothing to chance, imparting knowledge not only about specific job skills and competencies but also, and perhaps more importantly, ensuring that every Cast Member has a thorough understanding of the Disney culture and traditions.

Thus, what is euphemistically called "human resources" at many organizations—which often view training as no more than an expensive but necessary evil—is given top priority in the Disney universe because Walt considered training an essential investment in the future of his Company.

Obviously, not every organization has access to the facilities and resources that make up Disney University, but every organization can adopt the attitude that underlies the Disney approach to training and developing its culture.

In this chapter, we examine that attitude and help you distinguish between training that is purely perfunctory and the kind that will enable your employees to perform at their peak.

# Training: Whose Responsibility Is It?

A few days before Disneyland was scheduled to open in 1955, a 12-year-old young man was working in the mailroom (at that time, child labor laws were not what they are today). He interrupted a meeting in Walt Disney's office to deliver a package. He told Walt, "I have a confession to make. I really do not want to work in the mailroom. I wish you would consider me for the role of Tom Sawyer on Tom Sawyer's Island, and the casting is tomorrow." Walt looked at the young man, turned to his Vice President of Casting and said, "This young man has red hair and freckles. He looks a little bit like Tom Sawyer. What do you think?" So the Vice President, taking the signal from his leader, hired the little boy as Tom Sawyer.

Two days after the Park's opening, the Vice President barged into Walt's office to explain a situation. He said, "Do you remember that Tom Sawyer *you* hired? We have to fire him!"

Walt asked, "Why, what did he do?"

The Vice President told him, "That young man has literally become Tom Sawyer."

And Walt said, "Well, what's wrong with that? Isn't that why we hired him?"

The Vice President explained, "Remember Mark Twain's novel about Tom Sawyer? He has to prove to everyone that he is the toughest kid around. The kid is beating up all your Guests. We have to fire him."

Walt was so upset over the situation that he shooed everyone but the casting executive out of his office and closed the door. Walt said to the Vice President, "You don't understand what we are trying to do here," to which the Vice President replied, "No, apparently not."

Walt clarified, "That little boy is being the best Tom Sawyer he knows how to be. It's our job to make him the best Tom Sawyer for Disney. Now, go do your job."

The incident, which had been forgotten until it was recounted by the then-retired Vice President at a celebration honoring the little red-headed boy for his 30 years of service to the Company, illustrates the underlying belief that led to the evolution of Disney University becoming a world-class training program. Because Walt Disney believed so strongly in the Company's responsibility for training its Cast Members, students at Disney U now receive a complete orientation called Traditions, in which they are immersed in the Company's values, traditions, and culture.

Once Traditions is over, Cast Members receive additional days of themed orientation for their specific locations and for their specific roles in the show. For example, during Epcot's Discovery Day, new hires learn about the importance of embracing all cultures and keeping abreast of new technology. They experience Walt Disney's original vision for the Park through a video that has long inspired the organization to continue evolving and growing.

The story of the red-headed boy suggests that Walt Disney understood the detrimental effects that the sink-or-swim mentality can have on the workplace. Under this approach, which unfortunately is prevalent at far too many companies today, people are thrown into new jobs and left to discover the riptides on their own—before they are dragged under by them. If someone is deemed worthy of being in your employ, why not take the time to pilot him or her through dangerous currents? After all, if you buy a $30,000 piece of equipment, you would likely follow the manufacturer's break-in procedure.

Consider the situation in which an orientation program is the recommended break-in procedure for new employees. Drawing on the expertise of its veterans, The Walt Disney Company designates trainers in each department to oversee and guide the work of new Cast Members. Frontline Cast Members also serve as facilitators in most training sessions, sharing their on-the-job experiences with newcomers. Believing the adage that "to teach is to learn twice," the Company thus accomplishes the dual goal of instructing new staffers while reinforcing their values and traditions among old hands. Such contact with senior staffers also makes clear to new Cast Members that opportunities for advancement are available.

But perhaps the thing that most distinguishes the Disney training approach is its initial concentration on making each new Cast Member feel as if his or her efforts will make a real difference to the Company as a whole. When employees are thoroughly grounded in what is expected of them and believe that their organizational leaders have confidence in their abilities, they can begin their jobs with an amazing degree of self-assurance. Consequently, they will perform their roles much better right from the start, increasing their value to both their employers and their customers or guests.

At a recent investor conference, Disney COO Tom Staggs proclaimed, "Maintaining this culture of excellence across all the various disciplines required in our business is extraordinarily difficult, if not impossible, for others to replicate. The Guest service orientation of our business does require a significant labor commitment, and operating labor makes up about a third of the segment's cost base. But when so many of our Guests single out inter-action with our Cast as the most important part of their visit, we know this continued investment is worth it."

## What Kind of Training?

As is reported in the Corporate Learning Factbook (Bersin Deloitte), train-ing initiatives have recently experienced a resurgence in the United States. In 2014, U.S. spending on workforce training grew by 15 percent to over $70 billion in the United States and over $130 billion worldwide, the highest growth rate in seven years. Companies are now facing new chal-lenges in talent management that require a strategic and planned approach to investing those training dollars. For some, the increase in job-hopping and the changing demographics of the workforce are disheartening, but Disney leaders continue to focus on training and developing their carefully selected Cast Members. Many organizations turn their backs on young talent because they take on the mindset that these employees will leave after only a short while. But values-driven organizations like The Walt Disney Company believe that failing to invest in their people is not an option. Most employees desire to be part of a strong culture with solid values, and at the Company, this truth produces loyalty. Creating a values-driven organization requires a significant commitment on the part of a company to achieve a coveted result—employees who are actively engaged in delivering the best possible customer experiences.

In many "customer service" companies, leaders are well protected behind their army of frontline representatives who are often powerless to do whatever it takes to solve a customer's problem. True leadership skills are in short supply, and even more disturbing is that these misguided organiza-tions are choked by the faulty premise that only a select few are worthy of becoming "leaders." Through the lens of their values-based culture, The Walt Disney Company sees *most* individuals as leaders.

Moreover, Disney's training approach is designed to retain and build a diverse talent base, including different generations, cultures, and ways of thinking. According to a PricewaterhouseCoopers (PwC) study, by the year 2020, the millennial generation will make up more than 50 percent of the workforce. These future leaders cite coaching, collaboration, flexibility, and motivation as key factors in their preferred work environments. While many organizations struggle with producing the type of atmosphere that appeals to millennials, The Walt Disney Company maintains a culture in which these factors are central to managing the development of *all* Cast Members. In the words of Al Weiss, retired President of Worldwide Operations for Walt Disney Parks and Resorts, "There are very few companies like Disney that give individuals an opportunity to grow and develop so much in their careers. Disney is truly an organization that promotes from within and allows our talented Cast Members to follow their dreams."

## Performance Learning Cycle

Unfortunately, a great many companies employ the "spray-and-pray" method of training—that is, they spray training on people, then pray that it gets absorbed. That kind of slapdash approach is at odds with what we call the Performance Learning Cycle, illustrated in Figure 8-1. The Performance Learning Cycle enforces the concept that the depth of training is just as important as the breadth. So companies that adopt this method must ask themselves, "Are we giving our employees enough of the right kind of

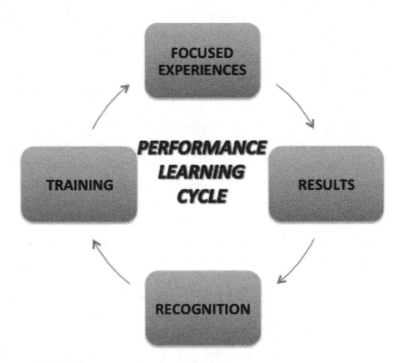

**Figure 8-1.** Performance Learning Cycle

training?" Training means providing employees with all of the tools they need in order to achieve the desired customer-focused results. Leaders should follow up by providing opportunities to apply the training in focused work experiences.

After training and practice, the next phases of the Performance Learning Cycle are the measurement of results and their timely recognition. It almost goes without saying that recognizing an employee's contribution is critical to achieving the desired behavior. Without recognition, the enthusiasm and hard work required for further improvement are likely to diminish. Recognition may take the form of either appreciative or constructive (explaining to an employee how he or she could be more effective) feedback. During this phase, a decision might be made to provide additional training and the Performance Learning Cycle would be repeated. Acknowledging the success of employees or, if needed, redirecting their training will ultimately translate into cost savings, quality improvements, reductions in cycle times, and strengthened customer relationships.

● ● ●

Appreciation means different things to different people, so how an organization chooses to recognize achievement depends on the circumstances involved and the culture of the organization. With 32 Academy Awards to his credit, more than any other individual to date, Walt Disney understood the importance of building a culture in which hard work and great results were rewarded. Inspired by the Academy Award statuette "Oscar" himself, Walt created the original "Mousecar" award which is given to individuals in honor of their special service to either the Company or the community.

In 1947, Walt gave his brother, Roy, the first of these bronze-colored Mickey Mouse statues. Since that time, The Walt Disney Company has awarded these prized keepsakes to many worthy recipients. Today, the Company uses a variety of awards to show thanks and appreciation to those Cast Members who go above and beyond what is expected of them. One of these awards is the on-the-spot recognition tool called the Great Service Fanatic card. Recipients of this particular award are eligible for monthly prize drawings. Cast Members also enjoy numerous kinds of celebrations, service pins, distinguished service citations, and internal excellence awards. But the most prestigious honor that may be bestowed upon a Cast Member is the Walt Disney Legacy Award. Recipients "are individuals who consistently

Dream, Create, and Inspire each day by supporting the business objectives and goals of Walt Disney Parks and Resorts."

You might be thinking, "Well, we can't afford to do what Disney does," but remember: a personal word of acknowledgment from a respected leader can go a long way, and small team rewards can help build morale. Even something as simple as dinner at a restaurant or an informal office party can have the positive effect you are seeking. Monetary bonuses may be appropriate as well, but when cash awards are not feasible, look for other forms of recognition.

## Habits Required in a Customer-Centric Culture

When newly learned skills are reinforced with coaching, practice, and recognition, they become habits (see Figure 8-2). The goal of learning is to develop positive habits that benefit individuals as well as organizations. When learning a foreign language, before anything else, the pupil must study enough to understand and be understood in a social situation. That is a useful but limited skill. If that person goes to live in a native-speaking

**Figure 8-2.** Habits

country, his or her limited skill will at first prove inadequate for newfound needs. The language has to become like a habit or an involuntary reaction, before the student will be fully comfortable with it, but that won't happen until he or she has practiced, and then practiced some more.

Aristotle said, "We are what we repeatedly do. . . . Excellence, then, is not an act, but a habit." If this is so, leaders who wish to pursue superior performance at all levels must work to ensure that the characteristics that define excellence are practiced, and then practiced some more, until they too become an involuntary reaction.

We believe that proper habits grow from obtaining knowledge, attitude, and skills. Knowledge is understanding what, how, and why we need to do something. Skill is applying that knowledge in a practical situation. Attitude is the desire to transform our knowledge into skills and, ultimately, into a habit. Meg Crofton, retired President of Walt Disney Parks and Resorts Operations, United States and France, advised, "Many aspects of life are beyond our control. Attitude is not one of them. It is something that we can totally control. And it is contagious."

A company that claims the corporate value of excellence must therefore establish a specific ongoing process for developing new skills based on a foundation of knowledge and the right attitude. But for such an effort to produce the desired results, a company must understand that the customer drives the process. Many times, we have encountered training programs for which an organization's human resources department has developed extensive in-depth material that neglects to mention the importance of the external customer. Employees are trained to refine their own skills and perhaps to take care of the needs of internal customers, but the all-important external customer, who provides the revenues that support the company's existence, is ignored.

Knowledge of customer needs and expectations can be taught, but attitude and motivation cannot. These elements are transmitted through the behavioral patterns of employees, and they are part of the values and sense of mission that pervade the workplace. In fact, Holocaust survivor Viktor Frankl defines *attitude* as "our response to what we have experienced." The process is summarized in Figure 8-3. That is why employee training can have a greater result when well-seasoned employees who can become role models are involved. Their behaviors provide signals to new employees as to a company's underlying culture and provide leadership during times of organizational transformation and growth.

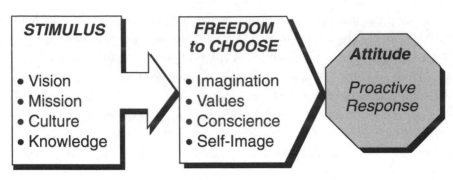

**Figure 8-3.** Attitude

To reap the optimum benefits of any training program, an entire company must be committed to it, with the main push coming from the top. When it becomes clear that top management firmly supports a cultural change effort, impressive results can follow. Over 20 years ago, when we first began to work with Evansville, Indiana–based Plumbing & Industrial Supply, the leaders had experienced minimal success in trying to implement a customer-focused culture. Prior to our involvement with the company, top management had attended various customer service and total quality management (TQM) training programs, after which they had attempted to communicate what they had learned to the lower-level employees.

In order to begin immersing the employees in the new culture and give them an opportunity to voice their concerns, we conducted a Barriers Storyboard (see Chapter 10). Their primary "barriers," or concerns, were that staff-level training was in short supply and that managers enjoyed out-of-state retreats.

The failure of the implementation was clearly taking a toll. The employees felt that *they* were the problem.

Although we relayed the findings to management, we recognized that the company's small size was at the heart of the problem. While a large company can afford to have sizable groups of people participate in a three-day retreat without substantially disrupting operations, this is not the case for a small company. We suggested another option to the president—offering our training program on weekends. But this option would still require people to be away from the workplace for one day in addition to their Saturdays and Sundays.

The President considered the idea, but he had another solution: "There is no reason why you can't have three sessions of 10 or 12 people, and [management] can take over their jobs while they are out. We can load trucks. We can drive their routes. It would probably be good for us to get back to the nitty-gritty jobs while the others are off being trained."

Besides being an excellent sign of top-level commitment to the cultural transformation, the President's suggestion helped repair the breach that had opened between management and the workers, who had felt they were being treated like second-class citizens not worthy of training. Within a short time, the customer-centric culture had permeated the organization.

## Beware the Performance Appraisal

One of most human resources departments' favorite devices is the performance appraisal. These instruments have become something of a constitutionally mandated fact of business management. In 2005, a national survey conducted by the consulting firm, People IQ revealed that 87 percent of employees and managers felt performance reviews were neither useful nor effective. In truth, we believe that these appraisals are harmful to morale and unnecessarily costly for an organization to administer.

Let us explain.

A few years ago, we asked the CEO of a major company what he considered to be his company's greatest asset. "My employees," he answered without hesitation. "I make certain that we hire the best possible people for the job." He then went on to explain his hiring policy, from the search process to the extensive interviewing of a candidate, followed by personality testing and the careful checking of references. It was an impressive list.

He concluded by saying, "My most important job is to make sure that my company is made up of winners."

When we asked him further about the company's performance appraisal system, he assured us that it too was carefully structured. Once a year, every employee was evaluated in depth by a supervisor, and the CEO was proud to report that supervisors spent a considerable amount of time and thought on the performance appraisals.

Later on, we had the opportunity to chat with the supervisors and employees of the company. When we asked about performance appraisals, everyone, without exception, agreed on the following:

1. Performance appraisals were a waste of time.
2. People dreaded the entire ritual.

3. The process did not result in positive behavioral changes.
4. The outcome was influenced by the recentness of performance.

Every year, we talk to hundreds of people, and the reaction to performance appraisals is universally negative. They are described as one of the biggest barriers to service and quality improvements.

Here's why.

Most people believe that they are above-average performers. When their appraisal evaluation rates them as average or below, they feel discouraged and misunderstood, and the quality of their work often suffers. Globoforce, a leader in the development of employee recognition programs, claims that employees who perceive performance reviews as inaccurate are two times more likely to leave their employers, and 53 percent do not consider them as motivators to work harder.

The late W. Edwards Deming once described a rationale for eliminating performance reviews:

> The effects are devastating. Such a system substitutes short-term performance for long-term planning, wrecks teamwork, and nurtures rivalry. It builds fear and leaves people bitter or despondent, unfit for work for weeks after receipt of the rating. Performance appraisals are highly subjective; they depend on the evaluator's personal attitudes. Suppose, for instance, that an employee has missed two days of work in the previous year. One supervisor might give relatively great weight to the absences, especially if the missed days have been recent, and rate the employee as "average," while another supervisor might completely ignore the missed days and assign an "excellent" rating.

Other factors also enter into the assessment of a worker, and they are often situations in which the individual has no control. For example, an employee may have the necessary education for a job and be a hard worker to boot, but further on-the-job training may be needed for the person to perform at the desired level. Some people are hired for jobs for which they do not have the appropriate education; others are evaluated on results that are heavily dependent on factors over which they have no control. Effort and commitment are really the only parts of the equation in which an employee has complete control, but it is impossible to isolate the effects of these factors.

In the final analysis, performance reviews may tempt a worker to try to please the boss at the expense either of fellow workers or, more importantly, the customers. Such efforts can undermine teamwork as well as job performance.

## Give Everyone the Opportunity to Grow

It's high time we abolish performance appraisals and establish a development planning process that will enable employees to continuously improve. If you think about it, the word *development* sends a much more positive message within a company than the term *appraisal*. If you believe that workers inherently want to do exceptional work, then you must give them the opportunity to grow through *development*, not be graded through *appraisals*.

A study conducted by the consulting firm of Blessing White revealed that when employees have been employed by their organizations for three years, their levels of engagement increase the longer they remain. However, 53 percent of employees looking for greener pastures at other companies indicated the reason for leaving was related to lack of development. Another 26 percent indicated they didn't have opportunities to grow. An additional 15 percent stated the company didn't make the most of their talents, and the final 12 percent wanted the opportunity to try something new.

At The Walt Disney Company, development planning involves collaboration between leaders and their teams of Cast Members who identify specific development goals or expected desired results, time frames, and resources needed to reach each goal. Continuous learning is a Companywide directive, and Cast Member goals are accordingly aligned. Together, a leader and a Cast Member can create an individualized learning goal that can pull from resources including more than 10,000 online and print reference materials, instructor-led courses, and keynote presentations.

Here are some of the most frequent comments and questions we hear from clients who are reluctant to replace performance reviews with development plans:

- **"People want to know how they are performing, and we do this through the performance review process."** If employees need to wait until the end of the review cycle for meaningful feedback, then your communication process, especially coaching and feedback, is sorely in need of substantial improvement. Everyone in the organization, at all levels, must be trained to give frequent and meaningful feedback. In addition, when people feel they are not getting adequate feedback from their team members, they must take the initiative to request more.

- **"If I don't have performance reviews, how do I document poor performance for discipline or termination purposes?"** All supervisors need to be educated as to what constitutes poor performance. A formal coaching, counseling, and corrective action process needs to be established. Supervisors must also be instructed in the proper ways to document unacceptable performance.

- **"How can I determine promotions and advancements without performance reviews?"** Establish clear advancement criteria for all positions. During the development planning process, discuss skills that are lacking for advancement. In accordance with company resources, offer appropriate skills training, coaching, and/or education to employees who want to grow within the organization.

- **"How do I compensate employees without performance reviews?"** Managers are often given a finite dollar amount to reward their employees during an annual compensation review. In general, employees receive approximately the same percentage increase in salary. Of course, there are a few cases of poor performers who receive little or no increase and also a few cases of truly exceptional performers who receive more than the average employee. There are numerous books and studies on the subject of compensation programs that you may find helpful when you are ready to revamp your process. We suggest designing a simple process that incorporates the following criteria:

  ○ Compensation range, by position
  ○ Automatic increases based on economic adjustments, longevity, and advancement to a new position
  ○ Lump-sum spot bonuses for those employees who truly stand out as exceptional performers
  ○ Profit-sharing process that rewards everyone when the entire organization exceeds expectations

According to the late "founder of social psychology" Kurt Lewin, effectively changing behavior requires consideration of the environment and the process as well as the person. "Behavior," he observed, "is a function of the person times the environment."

An experience of a former client illustrates the validity of Lewin's observation. The company, which made automobile engine parts, had a milling plant staffed by good but not exceptional workers. Everything went along fine most of the time, but occasionally, product quality levels would drop into the unacceptable range for no apparent reason. During one of these dips, the company's human resources department decided that the plant workers' attitudes were at fault. So HR launched a comprehensive training program in interpersonal relationships. Alas, the quality levels did not change. Why? Because this approach wrongly assumed that change comes solely from the individual. In this particular case, further investigation revealed that the quality discrepancies were the result of problems at the raw materials supplier.

Deming validates Lewin's statement. He once claimed that more than 85 percent of the U.S. quality and productivity problems are the result of the process. Therefore, it is imperative that process improvements be discussed between management and employees. Process improvements may also require changes in management policy. Leaders need to assume a proactive role by asking the following questions:

- What do you need from me (the leader) to continue to develop your skills?
- How can we both achieve great success?
- How can we remove barriers to success?

In high-performance organizations, systematic and ongoing feedback is a key element for developing a strong and skilled workforce positioned for success. One of the best methods for capturing a clear snapshot of your organization's needs is by conducting employee feedback surveys.

At The Walt Disney Company, the biannual Cast Excellence Survey is also instrumental in helping to build and protect the trusting environment for which the Company is known. The survey does not take the place of face-to-face discussions between leaders and their teams but rather, facilitates a continuous dialogue that often inspires change.

The opportunity for site-specific feedback is also critical to making Cast Members feel valued. For example, at the Magic Kingdom Park at Walt Disney World, Vice President Phil Holmes actively encourages input from all of his Cast Members. If they have a concern or an idea, all they have to do is call him or any other Cast Member in the Park. Not only does Phil publish a complete list of the phone numbers including his own, but he also generates a "You Asked, We Listened" report that includes a list of the specific feedback received, accompanied by a status report on each issue.

As should be obvious by now, an organization's leaders cannot afford to simply say to new employees, "Here's what we expect of you. Now go do it." They must be prepared to work with new employees and guide them until they become familiar with their roles, the behaviors expected of them, and the culture they will embrace. In Traditions training, stories and customs of The Walt Disney Company's unique culture foster a sense of pride and convey to Cast Members that they are a part of something greater than themselves. Former Mouseketeer Sharon Baird's poignant story exemplified this truth:

> On the opening day of Disneyland, [Mouseketeers] were in Walt Disney's private apartment above the Main Street Fire Station when the gates of the Park opened for the first time. I was standing next to [Walt] at the window, watching the Guests come pouring through the gates. When I looked up at him, he had his hands behind his back, a grin from ear to ear. I could see a lump in his throat and a tear streaming down his cheek. He had realized his dream. I was only 12 years old at the time, so it didn't mean as much to me then. But as the years go by, that image of him becomes more and more endearing.

## Parting Thoughts

When employees are inspired by their leaders and they are equipped with the tools to do their best work, they can perform at levels that may even surprise themselves. In the next chapter, we will take a look at the role proper planning plays in bringing dreams to fruition.

---

### Our Featured Organization: California State University Channel Islands (CI)

#### TRAINING FOR SUCCESS: A UNIQUE UNIVERSITY FOCUS

If you ask any university President, faculty, or staff member, "Is your school student centered?" it is hard to imagine that anyone would answer,

"No." But the truth is conventional university "wisdom" still applies for some. That is, if faculty teach their students well and provide engaging and thought-provoking lectures, students will learn. In recent years, however, there has been a global shift in higher education away from the perennial instructor-centered teaching philosophy. In a student-centered system, the instructors do not make unilateral decisions about their students' learning. Rather, they share decision-making power with their students in determining the full gamut of the learning process including what and how students learn.

Since its beginning in 2002, California State University Channel Islands (CI) has been committed to being "student centered," but it's far more than a teaching model. While most universities post signage or set up information booths to help students know where to park and where to go on the first day of the school year, CI staff are poised and ready to walk their new student "family" members through the parking lot and escort them to classes. And if any staff member is late to a meeting because a student was in need, the university President Richard R. Rush would approve!

Central to creating a "warm, welcoming, smart, and fun" student centered environment at CI is the Division of Student Affairs (DSA). The DSA happily assumes the responsibility to practice and translate those "family" values to the over 5,000 students who attend the youngest of the 23 California State University campuses.

And practice, they do! Under Dr. Wm. Gregory Sawyer's leadership, the DSA "family" of 78 staff members in five areas makes group development and training a priority. Just as they have created and designed programs and services for students that "enhance [their] university experience" and "encourage an interactive and expansive learning environment," the DSA leadership has produced this culture within their own division as well.

As Dr. Jennifer Miller, Director of Student Affairs Assessment, Research and Staff Development, (recently moved to California State University, Los Angeles as Dean of Students) explains, "We never want it to be work, work, work. There has to be some reflective piece, such as there is with *The Disney Way* seminar, as to how they are going to grow as people. [We are here] to grow and serve the students, but also how can they [the staff] be creative with everything they do."

In most universities, the administrative staff operates within firm boundaries that actually discourage creativity. For example, over two decades ago when we (Bill and Lynn) were associated with a university, we were told that sending out holiday cards to clients was against university policy! As is true of any organization, it takes leadership to produce a healthy values-driven culture that promotes creativity. Dr. Miller acknowledged, "I don't think it's normal for all institutions, but for CI, it's something our Vice President for Student Affairs (VPSA) has really prioritized."

CI is a young teaching university that enjoys a certain degree of flexibility. Even so, it would be easy to cut professional development when budgets are tight, but unlike other schools, they protect these funds. Dr. Miller is proud of their "morale funds," some of which are utilized for thank-you dinners and other situational rewards, and some of which are applied to training and development. But, she explained, "I don't have a large budget, and it takes leadership. Our top-level leadership is supportive of staff growth and development."

For the DSA, it's a conscious decision to include all areas in the division—including Assessment and Strategic Operations, Associated Students Incorporated, Housing and Residential Education, Student Life, and Wellness and Athletics—in a retreat setting. In addition to each area doing its own training, everyone benefits from cross-training and the exchange of ideas. Each DSA semiannual retreat experience is designed with the entire staff in mind. This is another huge difference between CI and many other universities we have encountered in which management receives the lion's share of the creative learning opportunities. Even in tough budgetary times, DSA's leadership and their staff members attend the full-day retreats together. In order to take care of the students, who are their first priority, the retreats occur before the school year begins in the fall, during winter break, and just after graduation in the spring.

Retreat planning begins by choosing topics of interest based on the results of regularly scheduled needs-based assessments. Gary C. Gordon II, Coordinator of Residential Education, shared, "I believe it is helpful that multiple topics related to different interests and skill levels are covered throughout the year." Michael McCormack, Coordinator of Community Programs related, "The training is forward thinking and grounded in future effective practices." In 2013, Bill facilitated the DSA staff's spring retreat—"Customer Service: The CI Way and *The Disney Way*"—to help them establish a common definition, value, and expectation of what good customer service means. Dr. Sawyer remarked, "Innovation, creativity, and visioning are fundamental to the professional growth of our staff. It was a unique pleasure to have a fellow dreamer and critical thinker visit and share another perspective of how we can continue to Dream, Believe, Dare, Do to be different for our students."

The retreats are not the only training opportunities for staff. Every other month, staff meetings are transformed into a required two-hour training session conducted by campus professionals. Also, the DSA offers optional individual training in a variety of configurations tailored to specific staff needs. Dr. Amanda Carpenter, Assistant Director of Career Development and the Henry "Hank" L. Lacayo Institute Internship Program, stated, "My career goals have expanded as a result of being exposed to various topics and experiences in the DSA training."

Dr. Miller has also made professional development planning a top priority. She said, "People don't have to ask permission to grow. They can always learn, and who knows where that will take them. Making that as clear as possible is important." Staff members are encouraged to track their own personal goals and engage in discussions as to where they want to be in a few years. Dr. Miller believes that leaders must break down barriers for staff members to be able to grow professionally. For example, for staff members who don't feel that they will have the opportunity to go to graduate school, she teaches an assessment course during the lunch hour and away from the office. Dorothy Ayer, Special Assistant to the VPSA said, "While I have worked in higher education for a number of years, never before have I had the opportunity to delve into such important topics, issues, and practices in a formalized setting."

While most university professors and administrators are entrenched in the practice of traditional roles and policies, CI's Division of Student Affairs is pioneering a different practice, and it's quickly catching on. "We get a lot of calls from those who are interested in our training methods and materials," Dr. Miller proudly proclaims, "and it is growing."

## Questions to Ask

- Do you provide a multi-day orientation process for all employees?

- Do you provide training that is tailored to the needs of your employees?

- Do your managers coach employees to reinforce important concepts after they have been formally trained?

- Do you support individual development planning rather than the demoralizing performance appraisals?

## Actions to Take

- Develop a multi-day orientation that focuses on the organization's vision, values, and culture, not its rules, regulations, and policies.

- Institute development plans in place of performance appraisals. Work in partnership with employees to create their own plans.

- Continuously provide coaching, feedback, and recognition to your leaders, employees, and coworkers.

Chapter Chats with Bill: http://capojac.com/disneyway/8/

# Chapter 9

# Make Your Elephant Fly—Plan

*When we consider a project, we really study it—not just the surface idea, but everything about it. And when we go into that new project, we believe in it all the way. We have confidence in our ability to do it right. And we work hard to do the best possible job.*

Walt Disney

Vision without a means of execution is like a plane without wings or Dumbo without his ears—it just won't fly. No matter how deep an organization's resources are, the progress of their projects greatly depends on the strength of execution, and proper execution requires thorough and detailed planning, a reality that Walt Disney understood completely.

No wand-waving or intonations of "abracadabra" preceded the building of Disney's Magic Kingdom. The cartoons, movies, Theme Parks, and all the rest of the delights that took shape in Walt's prolific imagination came into being through a precise process of planning that he employed from the very beginning of his career. Making a movie is a costly undertaking, but because animation is especially expensive and labor intensive, Walt had to plan carefully to control costs and successfully execute his ideas. Out of necessity was born a nine-step process that takes a blue-sky idea and turns it into reality.

*Dumbo*, the perennial animated favorite about the flying baby elephant, was itself a product of this rigorous Disney regimen. By putting process in creativity—in this case, using a straightforward script and story and resisting the temptation to experiment with expensive new technologies—Walt and his animators produced *Dumbo* in just one year. As one Disney executive has described it, the system says, in effect, "Within these boundaries you will create. This is the budget; these are the limitations. Make it work within this framework."

And work it has, as consistently successful and profitable flights of fancy such as *Dumbo* to *Aladdin* attest. While our clients may not be staging magic carpet rides, we have seen diverse organizations devise their own methods, both formal and informal, to ensure that a workable idea will actually come to fruition. In this chapter, we look at both the Disney blue-sky process and the variations crafted by companies in a range of industries.

## Carefully Managed Creativity: *The Disney Way*

There have always been two basic schools of thought on business creativity. The first insists that researchers and other in-house innovators be given the loosest reins possible, allowing new ideas and projects to develop on their own momentum with a maximum of independent decision making. The second approach demands that the reins be kept taut, that the generation of ideas be part of the corporate process, and like the other parts, that it be carefully managed.

Walt Disney was definitely of the second school. Although his famously forceful leadership style was largely attributable to his personality, there was also a practical consideration: the cost of making animated pictures. Makers of live-action films could shoot extra footage and then piece together their final product through artful cutting in the editing room, but animation costs were such that cartoon makers couldn't even consider this whittle-down approach.

So, to keep costs in check, Walt exercised extremely tight control of the creative process itself by instituting a rigorous, nine-step regimen for project management. Only by demanding that his people follow this standard procedure could he continue to turn dreams into tangible products, whether that be films, Theme Parks, television shows, or any of the other Disney enterprises. In the Company's system, nothing was—or is—left to chance. Figure 9-1 illustrates the planning process. The process looks like this:

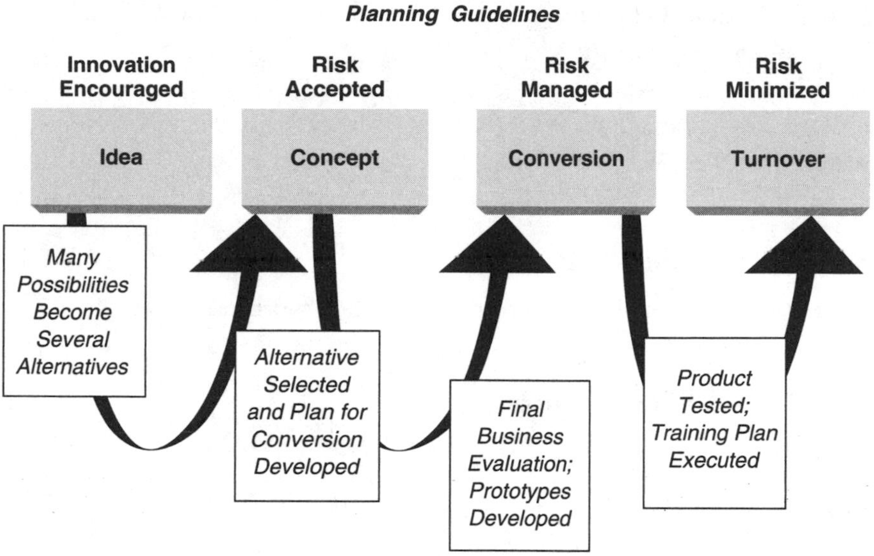

**Planning Guidelines**

**Figure 9-1.** Planning Guidelines

## Step 1. Blue Sky

- Ask "what if?" rather than "what?"
- Learn to live for a time with the discomfort of not knowing, of not being in full control.
- Take a trip through "fantasyland"; start with the story.

## Step 2. Concept Development

- Develop research.
- Evaluate alternatives.
- Recommend an idea.

## Step 3. Feasibility

- Reconcile scope.
- Prepare pro forma.

## Step 4. Schematic

- Finalize master plan.
- Outline initial business processes.

### Step 5. Design Objectives

- Finalize design details, equipment, and materials.
- Develop implementation strategy and budget.

### Step 6. Contract Documents

- Prepare contract documents.

### Step 7. Production

- Construct site infrastructure, and develop work areas.
- Produce show elements.

### Step 8. Install, Test, Adjust

- Install the show.

### Step 9. Close Out

- Assemble final project documents.
- Monitor performance.
- Get sign-off letter from operations.

And we like to add a Step 10, Celebrate a Job Well Done!

Although managers in many organizations fly by the seat of their pants, The Walt Disney Company promotes these guidelines for aligning the Company's long-term vision with short-term execution. Not only is the Company kept on track from project to project but also costs are cut and production is sped up. Such strict adherence to a set of production standards and processes enables the Company to deliver consistently successful products and services.

## Introducing the Weenie

Walt Disney seemed to have an endless supply of sources that contributed to his amazing creativity and ability to bring his dreams to fruition. Even his dog, Lady, helped him develop one of the most lasting reminders of how Walt's imagination led to well-executed plans. One day when Walt came home from work, he realized how easy it was to lead Lady anywhere he wanted her to go with a "weenie." So he thought, if a juicy piece of meat can motivate and direct a dog, what if a different kind of weenie could help Guests reach specific destinations within Disneyland?

The original Theme Park weenie was the Main Street railroad station, and to this day, it serves as an enticement to draw Guests into the Park. Since the very first time Walt described this idea to the Imagineers who helped create Disneyland, weenies have been planned as the central features of all Disney Theme Parks. Cinderella Castle at the Magic Kingdom, Spaceship Earth at Epcot, and the Tree of Life at the Animal Kingdom are all examples of Disney's famous landmarks that were not only planned as Park icons but were also designed as ways to lead Guests through their entire magical adventures.

## The Process in Practice

New technology of every kind intrigued Walt Disney, but railroading held a special fascination for him. So when he could finally afford it, he built his own miniature train on his Holmby Hills estate. He spent hours driving it around, dreaming, and planning. So when the time came to build Disneyland, it was only logical that Walt would be drawn to the idea of installing a monorail. Because The Walt Disney Company's single-track vehicle was the first ever built in the United States, there were no American engineers with the knowledge or training to construct it. So Walt turned to German engineers to help with the job.

When the monorail was completed at the end of six months, the Germans congratulated Walt on the amazing accomplishment. In six months, Walt Disney had finished what had taken Germany six or seven years to build. The Disneyland monorail represented planning and execution at its best.

## Testing Your Ideas

As described in Chapter 2, without a vision or story, there is nothing to plan. The first step, then, is the generation of new ideas that are designed to satisfy customer needs or solve customer problems. A team must be prepared to suggest, discuss, argue about, and try out any number of diverse ideas. If one or more ideas fail, no real harm is done. We remind the teams we work with that although Babe Ruth hit 714 home runs, he also struck out 1,330 times. So striking out doesn't stop someone from eventually setting a record.

Trying out ideas, or perhaps even putting parts of several ideas together to produce a prototype, helps develop an overall concept and determine whether or not it is workable. The idea for the popular Theme Park attraction Soarin' first came to life in 1996. The original idea was to have Guests fly over the California landmarks suspended from an overhead cable in front of an OMNIMAX screen, much like the Peter Pan's Flight attraction or a dry cleaner's rack. The original plan was simply too costly and required a difficult three-level Guest loading process. Just before the project was about to be canceled, Imagineer Mark Sumner developed a working prototype using an old Erector Set (toys first sold in 1913 by Mysto Manufacturing Company; metal construction sets) that substantially cut construction and labor cost while easily loading Guests on one level.

A prototype can also be evaluated and market tested, and it can serve as the centerpiece around which a process is developed. At the Disney Theme Park merchandise department, the centerpiece might just be one of the most treasured items in their Holidays for Your Home collections. In researching ideas for this festive lineup of items ranging from a mistletoe-bearing Minnie Mouse ornament to Mickey Mouse–decorated dishware, the collaborative Disney team discovered that the popularity of 1960s retro is surging. Furthermore, from that era emerged a variety of now-classic holiday traditions that all generations of families continue to enjoy. This led them to introduce, as Senior Graphic Designer Natalie Kennedy said, "a collection that was rooted in the past but wouldn't feel out of place today—something new, but also familiar." Months before the production phase was launched, the team unleashed their "childlike" imaginations during the Blue-Sky Phase from which creative direction was determined. Their cherished childhood holiday memories helps drive their passion for telling a story with each treasure they create. The entire process of bringing a new Disney product line to the market typically takes 18 months, and every idea must be carefully evaluated in terms of marketplace trends and competitor merchandise offerings.

From retail to the attractions, nothing at The Walt Disney Company is left to chance. Indeed, during the planning of the Seven Dwarfs Mine Train roller coaster at Magic Kingdom, the development of an authentic-looking mountain posed several challenges. First of all, how would the Imagineering landscape architecture team produce turf that was "believable" but not real at the same time? After all, no Cast Member could be expected to brave the summit with a lawn mower!

With the assistance of a Chinese company, the Area Development Director, Rebecca Bishop, shared the plan that included "a kind of mosaic of colored grasses . . . where heavier rains might have occurred along the mountain, the grass was a deeper green. Near the top, where not much water would be stored, it was more of a yellow grass." When the gusty winds swept across the Magic Kingdom, the faux turf needed to move the same way as real turf would, so they developed varying lengths of unruly-looking grass that, thanks to the latest technology, would not fade or change color.

Next, hundreds of larger artificial plantings such as trees, shrubs, and poppies were interspersed with live plants to complete the illusion of a totally natural mountain. Even the birds were fooled. Before long, they were nesting atop the highest trees. The bees weren't as lucky though; they would be forever frustrated trying to extract pollen from those poppies!

The latest of the Company's mega-planned Theme Park additions is Star Wars Land, the largest single land expansion in Disneyland's history. Both Star Wars Lands—one in Disneyland and the other in Disney's Hollywood Studios at Walt Disney World—will be themed as "a whole new planet" that did not exist on the big screen in the Star Wars movies. The Imagineers are creating a "gateway planet" and a "remote frontier town," which will serve as "one of the last stops before wild space," and remarkably, every Cast Member you meet will be in character as part of the mythology. Bob Chapek, Chairman of Walt Disney Parks and Resorts, revealed, "Every single thing will be in story."

Implementation of any high-stakes project demands a carefully thought out structure that establishes specific guidelines, from the initial blue-sky idea up to the final stages of completion. Certain milestones along the way must be specified as points at which management is appraised of overall progress. Those who work on a project need to know what is required at each step and how to measure their headway. Efficiency dictates that nothing be left to chance and hence, managers carefully plot every step on the chosen path.

We recognize that in today's business climate, a forceful ruler patterned after Walt Disney might generate no small amount of enmity and have a harder time maintaining control, particularly if the company involved has a somewhat freewheeling culture. In fact, a strong argument can be made for giving creative minds the maximum amount of freedom. But most organizations find that an approach that falls somewhere between absolute control and complete freedom works best for them.

We recommend that each organization design its own procedures for turning a dream into reality. Such a process works best if it grows naturally out of discussions among leaders and teams rather than being imposed from the outside. That way, it can more adequately reflect an organization's culture, history, traditions, and structure.

Many of our clients have successfully adopted rigorous processes similar to the Disney approach but tailored to manufacturing and service businesses. At one company, for example, the first phase is called the Idea. In screening the Idea, the company initially asks these questions:

- What is the compelling customer benefit?
- How is the idea going to increase shareholder value?
- Does it fit strategically into the organization?
- What resources are required to move the idea into the next phase?

Next comes the Concept phase. Here the questions are:

- What is the market assessment?
- Is the concept technically feasible?
- What is the business analysis?
- What are the preliminary design specifications?
- What plans and resources are required to move to the third phase?

The third phase is the Conversion. Here the questions are:

- What is the business case?
- What critical process and product elements can we identify?
- What is the plan of execution, and how can we make it happen?
- What costs and benefits will be associated with the final phase?

And, as the company moves into the final Execution phase, here the questions are:

- How do we release the product (if there is one)?
- When is the process going to be implemented?
- How do we get the product to the customer?
- Do we have a feedback mechanism in place to gauge the success of the product?

With carefully determined guidelines and milestones, teams or departments can proceed on their own. Micromanagement is avoided because the organization does not have to keep track of what everyone is doing at every minute of the day. There is no need to ask how the project is going. Instead, leaders can safely trust that teams are keeping tabs on progress and that appropriate appraisals will be forthcoming at specified points along the way.

Project leaders understand, of course, that if problems arise that threaten deadlines or if some assistance is needed, they are there to help. Otherwise, the message should be, "You're on your own until you've finished this phase of the project." An interesting sidelight about Disney's planning process is that many times a project may not receive the necessary funding to continue. In most companies, when this happens, a team is viewed as a failure.

At The Walt Disney Company, they look at these projects as assets that may be dusted off and continued midstream as funding or technology becomes available. The storyline for the legendary movie *The Little Mermaid*, released in 1989, really began in the late 1930s with the amazing pastel and watercolor sketches of illustrator Kay Neilsen. For some unknown reason, the original project was terminated shortly after Kay completed her sketches.

Some 50 years later, the Disney animation team discovered Kay's original storyboards and used them as a starting point for the film. *The Little Mermaid* was the Company's last animated feature to use hand-painted cells and analog technology. The animators received such inspiration from Nielsen's sketches that they gave her a "visual development" credit on the film. The movie was hailed as the phoenix of big-screen feature animation, and it was the first to spawn a TV series. The movie's music earned the Academy Award for Best Score. Additionally, "Under the Sea" won the Academy Award for Best Song, the first Disney tune to win since "Zip-A-Dee-Doo-Dah" from *Song of the South* had won in 1947.

# Planning Tools

The planning center is a practical approach for targeting the status of any one of the myriad pieces in a project. The physical size of the center and the breadth of information displayed can vary, of course, according to specific needs. All that matters is that project leaders and teams have a way of keeping abreast of individual and overall goals, specific progress toward those goals, and any problems or needs encountered at various stages of a project. In Chapter 10, we share how to use storyboarding to build the essential elements of a planning center.

Another form of the planning center is embodied in the concept of colocating, which we described in Chapter 5 in conjunction with teaming. When a Whirlpool technology team decided to colocate people from around the world to work in its Midwest facility, a subteam was charged with coordinating the colocation activities. To facilitate small-group interaction, the subteam's leader went to great lengths to create just the right environment.

This leader worked closely with two furniture suppliers to put together smaller functional areas within the total space allocated for the entire team. He also installed an active noise system that effectively tripled the perceived distance between individual team members in terms of the privacy it created. In the case of this Whirlpool global team, the illusion of greater distance was particularly important because many of the team members had a difficult time adjusting to the open-room style. In addition, the multiple languages spoken by the participants made the system imperative. Since people tend to listen when others speak a different language, it would have been virtually impossible for team members to tune out each other's conversations.

The effort involved in putting together the colocation space paid off for the Whirlpool team, which put together and executed a project that ended up surpassing everyone's expectations. The ease of communication that both planning centers and colocating promote goes a long way toward keeping a project on track and ensuring its ultimate success.

## Taking the Holistic Approach

Thinking holistically is counterintuitive for those schooled in the principles of corporate Darwinism, where only the so-called fittest survive and where the law of the jungle guides most decision making. To overcome those blocks and to help people accustom themselves to the concept of the holistic company—in which everyone works for the common good of the organization—we conduct an exercise called Broken Squares (see Scene 18 of *The Disney Way Fieldbook: How to Implement Walt Disney's Vision of "Dream, Believe, Dare, Do" in Your Own Company*) in which workshop participants sit in groups of five at separate tables. We hand each person an envelope with pieces of a puzzle. The goal is for all participants to finish their puzzles; but to succeed, they have to trade pieces without saying a word.

This is not a competition, but as the exercise progresses, invariably, some individuals begin to compete, hoard pieces, and strive to finish their own puzzles and their group's before anyone else does. After the experience, the participants who have pitted themselves against one another begin to understand that success comes from not hoarding pieces, either individually or within a group. The fastest way for all participants to finish their puzzles is for everyone to collaborate across "organizational" boundaries—in other words, to think and to act holistically, just as effective teams do.

As you set about using the tools described in this chapter to design your own planning procedures, we must add one word of caution. Don't get so involved with making plans that they become the be-all and end-all. Some teams are so proud of the fine plans they craft that they forget about implementing them. They begin to look at the plan as their deliverable. As legendary General George Patton said, "A good plan today is better than a perfect plan next week." Get in the habit of thinking "execution" immediately after you say the word "planning."

One way to help you keep the process in perspective is through your system of rewards. Set the system up so that while idea generation is rewarded, the biggest rewards and the largest celebrations are for the successful completion of the overall project. Therefore, employees will be encouraged to keep their eye on the ultimate goal.

## Parting Thoughts

That goal will be closer to your reach after you master the storyboarding technique that we will describe in the next chapter. Using it has helped our clients to conquer seemingly insoluble problems, enhance planning, and improve communication. Once you learn how to storyboard, you will find it useful in a variety of situations.

---

### Our Featured Organization:
### Joe C. Davis YMCA
### Outdoor Center/Camp Widjiwagan

**PLANNING A "KIDS AND GUESTS FIRST"
CUSTOMER-CENTRIC CULTURE**

"*Suboptimization* is when everyone is for himself. *Optimization* is when everyone is working to help the company." The late Dr. W. Edwards Deming was speaking to the importance of creating and sustaining an optimized organization. Our friend Jeff Merhige is a passionate leader who has mastered both.

In the 2007 edition of *The Disney Way*, we shared Jeff's amazing 12-year track record with Ohio's YMCA Camp Kern. There he built a sustainable workplace culture based upon the Dream, Believe, Dare, Do credo. Recently, Jeff shared with Bill, "If it weren't for you and Lynn, book or not, I wouldn't have discovered what kind of manager I wanted to be. If you guys hadn't put me on the path of looking at cultural management and empowerment, I wouldn't be half as successful as I am today."

In November 2013, Jeff assumed the role of Executive Director of the Joe C. Davis YMCA Outdoor Center/Camp Widjiwagan in Nashville, Tennessee. In this role, he charted a visionary course to become the number one camp in America in program delivery, staff training, and facility. He planned to achieve this by providing a "safe, fun, magical, and educational experience for all guests and children through the demonstration of four core values—respect, honesty, responsibility, and caring—and practicing 'kids and guests first' customer service." With the founding dream and operating philosophy in place, Joe C. Davis was destined to foster summer camp memories that kids would cherish for the rest of their lives.

To help launch the plan, Jeff invited Bill to facilitate a Dream Retreat in which staff, board members, volunteers, and major donors convened to help shape the organization's future. During the event, everyone learned how to storyboard, and the tool helped them visualize the goals they committed to achieve.

The beginning of any venture takes careful planning and execution. "I see my role as a cultural manager," Jeff told Bill, "and that is all about empowerment." He challenges his team members to consider four questions in every decision they make and exercise behaviors that demonstrate a commitment to excellence:

- Is everything you are doing safe? (This is nonnegotiable in everything we do.)
- Is everything you are doing courteous? (This includes the way we treat guests, the environment, and each other.)
- Is everything you are doing magical? (Do we constantly go beyond expectations?)
- Is everything you are doing efficient? (How can it be done better?)

Each quarter, the entire team engages in a *quarterly pulse check* (QPC) through which the staff members receive coaching and feedback. Jeff related, "It also removes fear of the 'evaluation.' . . . I am focused on instilling a belief that it's okay to fail, but it's not okay not to try. We learn from our mistakes and we move on." He has also instilled a motivating training philosophy: "Be the best version of yourself." When the staff members hear comments from parents such as "Camp changed my kid's life," that is what Jeff calls "magic" and helps bring out the very best in them. But, for some kids, that change may come much later. Jeff explained, "Down the road, if kids face a bad time in their lives, they can say, 'Wait a minute. I have met some great people, and I have had happier times.' And they will remember what that week at camp meant to them. That creates hope, and that is what we are training staff to do. They all buy into that. They want to be that memory, and they love doing it."

Jeff's first year was off to a great start with his staff marketing all new programs, contacting more than 1,200 families from the previous summer, and planning to hire seasonal staff who would be immediately immersed in the new Dream, Believe, Dare, Do culture. As a result of collaborating with IT and marketing team members, their new website produced over 1 million views by midsummer. The staff's energy and vibe was at an all-time high. As Bob Knestrick, COO of the YMCA of Middle Tennessee, shared, "Jeff keeps the message consistent and concise as he leads his team. He is someone who is easy to follow due to his energy and passion that he brings to serving our 'kids and guests first.'"

In a capital funding campaign, Jeff's enthusiastic team of volunteers and donors raised over $200,000, which allowed the YMCA to launch over nine new activity expansion projects for guests. These included four 80- to 200-foot-long tube slides, a Kangaroo jumper, and one of the only wheelchair-accessible zip lines in the United States. Within the first half of the year, the staff had completed over 25 items on their Dream list, including the creation of a 600-person amphitheater and over two dozen programs.

By the time summer arrived, the staff was fully engaged and ready to deliver "kids and guests first" customer service as well as a totally new and exciting array of day camp, resident camp, conference, and retreat programs. The Star Wars camp as well as the Percy Jackson and Harry Potter fully themed immersion camps sold out in a flash and were a huge hit.

When the evaluations were collected and tallied, those "happy" campers translated to ratings of over 90 percent "above and beyond satisfied"!

At the close of 2014, Jeff and his team were under budget, and the Outdoor Center had amassed $108,000 in revenues over the previous year end. Through a well-planned and optimized culture of employee engagement, the Joe C. Davis YMCA Outdoor Center/Camp Widjiwagan has in turn optimized the guest experience—kids making magical lifelong memories. And the seeds of the plan sprang forth from the dream of their passionate leader: "I want to give kids a better childhood. That's my pixie dust."

## Questions to Ask

- Do you have one or more planning centers in your organization where leaders and teams can work together on processes and projects?

- Does your organization have a specific process for project implementation?

- Do you encourage the development of prototypes to help develop an overall concept and determine whether or not it is workable?

- Do you celebrate specific milestones and the completion of projects?

## Actions to Take

- Develop a process for project implementation that is used throughout the organization. Provide training on the process, and champion its use.

- Create planning and communication centers for project and process activities.

- Allow individuals and teams the flexibility to work on projects without management interference.

- Set up cross-functional project teams on a routine basis.

- Develop quick and inexpensive prototypes to test products, processes, or service ideas.

**Chapter Chats with Bill: http://capojac.com/disneyway/9/**

# Chapter 10

# Capture the Magic with Storyboards

*What we do is we edit the movie before we start production. And we use storyboard drawings to do that. We quickly get away from the written page and the script, and we really develop the movie in storyboards. A comic book version of the story. And we do it the way Walt Disney did it.*

John Lasseter

Walt Disney originally conceived the idea that eventually became known as storyboarding as a way to keep track of the thousands of drawings necessary to achieve the full animation of cartoons. By having his artists pin their drawings in sequential order on a board that was hanging on the studio wall, Walt could quickly see which parts of a project were or were not completed.

From its genesis in animation, the technique has spread to many other areas. Advertising agencies use storyboarding to sketch out commercials before they shoot them. Scenes from feature movies are often storyboarded for the next day's camera work. Editors and art directors utilize storyboards as tools in producing picture books. It allows them to visualize what the final page will look like and to make sure that one page leads logically to the next.

But storyboarding is not limited to artistic endeavors. Like many ingenious concepts, storyboarding takes a simple technique—visual display—and uses it in a unique way to capture the thoughts and ideas from a group of participants. Their thoughts and ideas are recorded on cards, and then the cards are displayed on a board or a wall. The result, an "idea landscape," is more organized than the output from brainstorming, yet it retains the flexibility that teams need as they work their way through the various stages of idea generation.

Storyboarding is also a flexible, creative, and efficient method for generating solutions to complex problems that can sometimes feel overwhelming. It breaks problems into smaller, more manageable parts and focuses attention on specific components. When ideas and suggestions are displayed on a wall, they can be read by all and moved about as the participants see fit. And the confusion that can stymie breakthrough solutions is dissipated.

Leaders can also use storyboarding to conceptualize their mission statements, develop best practices for manufacturing control systems, and produce technical plans for improvements. Posted ideas or suggestions become the first step in the analysis of barriers—the investigation of their root causes and the creation of team solutions. Any process can be mapped out in this way.

In this chapter, we explain exactly how storyboarding works, and we look at a number of variations of the technique in action. As you read how companies in various settings are successfully using it to solve a range of problems, think about how you can put the technique into action in your own organization.

## The Birth of a Technique

When Walt Disney came up with the storyboarding technique in 1928, cartoon animation bore faint resemblance to the complex web of movement and color we know today. Full animation of cartoon features was still just a dream, but it was one he was striving to realize. To that end, Walt's team produced thousands more drawings than state-of-the-art animation required at that time.

The finished drawings were arranged in piles according to a predetermined narrative sequence. Then the cameraperson would photograph them, and the staff could watch them in a screening room. But with the prodigious output of drawings, it didn't take long before piles were stacked up in the studio. To bring some sense of order and to make it easier to follow a film's developing storyline, Walt instructed his artists to display their drawings on a large piece of fiberboard that measured about four feet by eight feet.

Not just finished drawings but early rough sketches were also pinned on the board. If there were problems with the storyline or if a character wasn't taking shape as Walt wanted, changes could be made before the expensive work of animation had begun. The storyboard made it possible for Walt to experiment, move drawings around, change direction, insert something he thought was missing, or discard a sequence that wasn't working. And he could do all this before the animator had spent countless hours painstakingly putting in the final details.

Decades later, in the 1960s, the display technique was picked up by Disney's employee development program when the staff recognized its value for generating solutions to problems and enhancing communications in other areas. The refined storyboarding concept has since been adapted to a variety of situations in which the introduction of the visual element makes interconnections more readily apparent. As the participants' cards are pinned to the wall, a team's thoughts and ideas begin to unfold.

Why doesn't a flip chart on an easel, a method often used in brainstorming sessions, work as well as a storyboard? On a flip chart, participants can see only one step at a time and therefore fail to get an overall picture. Moreover, flip charts can quickly become virtually unreadable as new ideas are inserted, old ideas are scratched out or moved around, and large arrows are left pointing nowhere. When using the storyboarding technique, all participants contribute their unique ideas without having to vocalize them. The lack of anonymity in brainstorming contributes a certain unease that discourages contributions. Our experience with both storyboarding and brainstorming allows us to make concrete comparisons in this regard: where a 60-minute brainstorming session with 14 participants produces, on average, 42 utterances (questions, ideas, or comments), a storyboarding session of the same size and duration typically produces anywhere from 150 to 300 utterances! Our studies have shown that in a typical 14-person brainstorming session, 5 participants produce 80 percent of the utterances, 5 participants produce 20 percent of the utterances, and the remaining 4 participants are mere observers of the meeting. In a storyboarding session, we have found that all members of the group are active participants.

Anyone who has participated in a traditional, inefficient problem-solving meeting knows the drudgery of endless discussion, time-wasting repetitions, and lengthy explanations. Since only one person can talk at a time, most peoples' minds wander from the topic being discussed to the job waiting for them back at their desks. And invariably, a few participants tend to dominate the discussion. When the meeting finally drones to a close, it is virtually impossible to remember much of what was said.

The storyboarding process works differently, as will be described in this chapter. It is a fully participatory activity that places the entire sequence of a project, a potential solution to a problem, or plan of action clearly in everyone's line of sight.

## Storyboarding: The Overview

From a procedural standpoint, storyboarding evolves in a logical progression. First, a team identifies the topic to be defined or the problem to be solved, and this is written on a card and posted at the top of a storyboard. Then, the group establishes a "purpose," which is the reason for pursuing the topic. The facilitator gives participants the time to sit and answer the question or problem, jotting down their thoughts, one idea per card. The facilitator then collects the cards as participants continue to write more thoughts.

When the group has completed the writing exercise, the facilitator reads each card aloud, invites discussion, and asks the participants to suggest how the cards might be clustered or positioned on the wall or storyboard. Once all the cards are read and discussed, the group prioritizes their most significant ideas.

## Storyboarding: The Process

### Supplies

1. A meeting room with plenty of blank wall space
2. An unbiased facilitator
3. Pin boards and pins; OR choice of drafting OR blue or green painter's tape and masking tape
4. At least 10 four- by six-inch index cards for every participant for each topic storyboarded
5. Felt-tip (preferably water-soluble) markers, blue or black (choose same color for each participant) and one red marker
6. Several different colored self-adhesive ¾-inch dots (referred to below as Priority Voting Dots, or Dots)

## Preparation

1. Place 12 three-foot vertical strips of drafting tape on a wall, sticky side out, and anchor them with four-inch horizontal strips of masking tape.

   **Tip:** If using boards rather than a wall, you can use pushpins to anchor the drafting tape strips, OR you can eliminate the tape and pin all the cards to the boards.
2. Select a facilitator.

## Procedure

1. The facilitator asks leading questions to assist the group to determine a topic, then records the topic on a card that becomes the Topic Card (see Figure 10-1). The facilitator posts the Topic Card at the top of the storyboard.

   **Tip:** Sometimes the Topic Card has been selected by someone outside of the group, but the facilitator should make sure that the group understands its meaning.
2. Responding to the Topic Card, participants silently record their thoughts or ideas on Detail Cards (see Figure 10-1), which should contain one idea per index card. Participants should place their completed cards face down in front of them for the facilitator to collect. This is *quiet time*, so there should be no idle chatter or discussion. The facilitator gathers the completed Detail Cards as participants continue to record their thoughts.

   **Tip:** The facilitator may place six Detail Cards with differing ideas at the top of the stack. When the facilitator begins reading the stack of cards, the group will hear six *different* ideas first, which may help participants to really think about the "big picture" rather than becoming stuck on one single idea or theme.
3. The facilitator reads each card aloud, one by one, and seeks the group's assistance to post them on the storyboard. Similar Detail Cards should be placed together by theme or category in columns on the storyboard.

   **Tip:** Sometimes it makes sense to duplicate a Detail Card and place the cards in two different columns. This often eliminates a lengthy debate about the placement of a card.

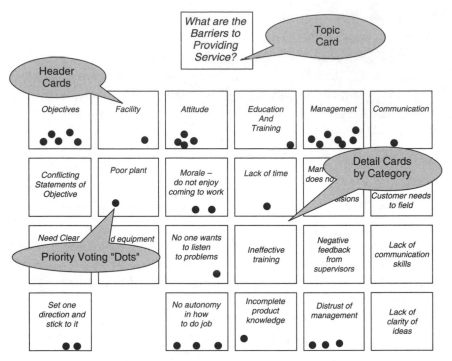

**Figure 10-1.** Storyboard example

4. Once three Detail Cards have been placed in a column, the group determines the Header Card (see Figure 10-1) that describes the column. The Header Card is then printed in red and the facilitator posts the Header Card at the top of the column.

5. Once all the Detail Cards have been discussed and posted along with their respective Header Cards, and all columns have been assigned a Header Card (even if the column has only one or two Detail Cards), the facilitator should summarize the storyboard by reading the headers. Next, with the group's input, the facilitator should review each column and point out any general big-picture idea or ideas. The group should decide if there are any changes, cards to be moved or duplicated, or additional ideas that need to be posted. If the facilitator sees that any column has many diverse ideas, he or she may challenge the group to make a new Header Card. For example, if there is a Header Card called "Communications" that addresses both internal employee communications and external customer communications, the group may create two headers, one for each.

6. The facilitator determines the number of Priority Voting Dots (see Figure 10-1) to be given to each participant.

   **Tip:** For up to 12 storyboard columns, group members should place two red Dots on their choices of "most important" Header Cards, and three blue Dots on their choices of "most important" Detail Cards. If participants feel strongly about an item, they are permitted to put any or all of their allotted Dots on the appropriate Header or Detail Cards.

   **Tip:** Increase the number of red Dots proportionately to the number of columns increased. Allow at least one more blue Dot than the number of red Dots.

7. Debrief. Here are suggested questions to ask the participants to help them process what they have experienced:

   - Does the storyboard provide a clear "snapshot" of the question or topic?
   - What are the most significant storyboard cards to be examined?
   - What storyboard cards need clarification?
   - What has been achieved so far?
   - What are our next steps?

   When a team reviews a storyboard, they may see some storyboard cards that suggest immediate action, and they may choose to create a follow-up storyboard to solve a specific problem. A storyboard card that receives many Priority Voting Dots may become the subject of a new Topic Card for a new storyboard. For example, if "facilities" is one of the Detail Cards on a Barriers Storyboard that received the most Priority Voting Dots, the group may create a new Topic Card for a new Idea Storyboard that reads, "How can we improve our facilities?" Or after reviewing the storyboard, the team may recommend an immediate procedural change to remove a barrier that was revealed on the storyboard.

8. The completed storyboard should remain on the wall for group reference or photographed, typed, and distributed to the group members and other appropriate parties.

## Additional Reminders

1. The facilitator may prepare leading questions beforehand to assist the group with determining a Topic Card.
2. Group members must record only one idea per card.

3. All participants must use the same color (blue or black) markers to write Detail Cards.
4. Once the third Detail Card has been posted in a column, stop the process of reading additional Detail Cards and ask the group to assign a Header Card.
5. As a facilitator, even when placement of a Detail Card or the naming of a Header Card is obvious to you, ask the group for input or a suggestion. (Remember, facilitators are NOT the decision makers in the storyboarding process. The storyboard belongs to the group.)

## Facilitator's Role: To Protect the People and the Process

1. Greet participants and create a pleasant, informal atmosphere.
2. Explain a brief history of Walt Disney's storyboard creation.
3. Lead the discussion to mobilize the group's creative energy and/or resolve conflicts.
4. Challenge conclusions or answers in a noncompetitive, nonhierarchical way, and provide positive feedback. If a card is vague, ask the group for clarification regarding the potential meaning of the idea or comment. Never ask, "Who wrote this card?" It is quite acceptable for the author of the card to volunteer clarification, but you must never ask for the author to make himself or herself known.
5. Keep the group focused and the pace moving.

## Overcoming Skepticism

We generally acquaint clients with the concept of storyboarding early in our association. Even though we emphasize its enormous value, acceptance is not a foregone conclusion. The idea of congregating around a space decorated with rows of cards on the wall may seem totally outlandish to people who have never witnessed a storyboarding session.

For example, an Indianapolis utility company with whom we worked had spent almost two years trying to devise a plan for changing their culture. After untold hours of management meetings, brainstorming, and arguing, the executive team still couldn't agree on a plan. When we arrived with a stack of cards and dozens of markers, the group listened politely as we explained storyboarding, but they were clearly dubious about the whole approach. Nevertheless, they agreed to give it a try.

The group appeared far from convinced at the outset of our session that tacking cards on a wall would do anything to help solve those problems that had baffled them for two years. We began by asking them for their ideas for potential solutions, which they wrote out and we posted on the board. As the cards were moved around and new ideas added, a structure for their implementation plans gradually developed.

The storyboarding process is a lot like building a house; it entails a logical progression. Just as a house begins with the architect's conceptual rendering and then moves through the various stages (foundation, subflooring, walls, and roof), so too does the storyboarding process. What starts as a "concept," or the problem to be solved, moves along in a creative interplay of ideas and suggestions until the desired solution has taken shape.

And that is exactly what happened in the session with the utility company after only two hours of storyboarding. The once-skeptical executives were astounded. One of them admitted to us afterward that the group initially thought storyboarding was, in his words, "a real Mickey Mouse technique." They couldn't imagine that it could be of benefit in their situation. But more progress was made in two hours of storyboarding than the group had made in the previous two years of endless meetings and unproductive wrangling. Everyone agreed that the storyboarding technique had crystallized the overall concept of what management wanted to achieve, clarified the necessary action steps, and defined the progression of tasks.

Many people wonder how something so simple can possibly work to unravel complex questions. After all, a five-year-old can be taught to put cards up on the wall. Yet to paraphrase a line of poetry, "simplicity is elegance," and it usually takes just one session to convince people of the richness of the storyboarding technique. The power it has to engage and stimulate people while also unleashing their productivity is remarkable.

We believe that the high level of participation demanded by storyboarding is one reason that it works so well. Instead of the typical meeting situation in which the troops are forced to endure endless and often garbled rhetoric, in a storyboarding situation the facilitator engages all people in a focused discussion.

This approach also heightens the concentration of individual group members as they become immersed in the problem at hand. Participants begin to embellish and expand on one another's ideas, unlike what often happens in brainstorming when rather than adding to the proposed idea, half the people in the group are busy marshaling their thoughts to rebut it. "That's not going to work," they think, or "My department will never buy that."

In addition, the initial anonymity allowed by not asking people to sign their names on their idea cards encourages free expression and critical thinking. The value of anonymity was brought home to us in a focus group we conducted for Illinois Power. That group, composed of folks from the community, was set up to help the Illinois Power economic development team become more effective.

Originally scheduled to run from 8:00 a.m. until noon, the session was conducted just like a conventional focus group, with people brainstorming and putting things on flip charts around the room. When we realized after two hours that no new ideas were emerging, we assumed that everyone had said everything they wanted to say. To our surprise, however, several of the team members pressed us to try the storyboarding technique that we had previously described to them. So instead of ending the meeting early, we spent the remaining two hours doing a storyboarding process. The result: At least three significant new ideas emerged concerning ways in which the development team could better serve the community.

As it turned out, some of the focus group participants had been reluctant to verbalize their ideas in front of the group. In our experience, that is often the case. Many people are simply frightened by the thought of speaking their minds in public. But stimulated by the discussion and given the chance to express themselves anonymously, they too can provide valuable input.

Storyboarding is a valuable tool for getting to the heart of customer problems, and innovative responses to customer problems is the stuff of business legends.

## Solving the Communications Dilemma

Intracompany communication is a hot topic these days. People fret about it in management meetings, employees complain about their massive amounts of emails, and everyone agrees on the need for more effective dialogue. But several questions remain: Is anyone really communicating? How many organizations have a formal plan to facilitate better communication?

A formal plan is important because not everyone responds to the various forms of communication in the same way. Some people like it written, some want information delivered face-to-face, and some don't care about the method, but they do care about the quality and the frequency. Obviously, meeting the needs of a diverse work group requires experimentation with various options. You might try quarterly town halls or skip-level meetings that allow top management to hear from people once or twice removed from the usual information chain. You might even try implementation of a 360-degree feedback approach. The point is that leaders can't depend on a hap-hazard communication system. They must consider the various styles and needs of their teams and then devise a formal plan for delivering information.

Storyboarding is an ideal way to share ideas and concepts by throwing them into the public arena for discussion and tapping a team's collective cre-ativity to figure out where and how an idea might work in any given function or department within a company. The technique helps break through inter-departmental barriers because it promotes face-to-face communication and a lively give-and-take among diverse personalities focused on a common goal.

Working with various clients, we have repeatedly noticed that story-boarding enhances a team's cohesiveness. The interplay of meaningful communication has a way of binding people together. Members of a cross-functional team are often nearly strangers to one another. That's because they work in different departments and receive different training; even their outlook is different. But once team members participate in a storyboarding session together, the employees from manufacturing or accounting or purchasing or any other department often find that they are not as far apart as they once thought. To solidify a team, we suggest they employ the storyboarding technique. That way, any ideas that surface belong to the entire team, not to individual members.

The bonding element inherent in storyboarding worked to particularly good effect with a Whirlpool global team. The members of the team spoke several different languages and came from wildly different backgrounds—not just different job descriptions but different countries, continents, and political situations. For example, among them was an engineer who had never been outside Communist China before finding himself set down in the Midwestern United States. How could such diversity be melded into one high-functioning team of men and women who were born and raised within the United States? Storyboards helped us overcome the hurdles.

We storyboarded character traits and asked team members to decide which traits they liked and which they disliked. As it turned out, there was a high level of agreement on what people liked as well as what they didn't like, regardless of nationality. The best learning of all, they said, was the discovery that they all disliked "arrogance" in others! The storyboarding experiment helped the team members appreciate one another and helped them realize that their commonalities were more significant than many of their cultural differences.

Storyboarding, then, can help any organization improve communication and planning at all levels. During a Dream Retreat that Bill facilitated for the Fred Astaire Dance Studios' leadership team, President and CEO Jack Rothweiler became completely enamored with the storyboarding process. The results of the storyboard that his team developed together enabled him to gain a clearer vision of his company's direction. Now, he utilizes the process in many others ways, including flushing out and crystallizing his ideas when developing company presentations.

## Getting Results: From Manufacturing to Chambers of Commerce

A Planning Storyboard is a flexible approach to developing a timeline or outline of the steps required to reach a desired result. One example is a retreat we conducted for a manufacturing team that was responsible for an 18-month project. We posted 18 predefined Header Cards labeled for each month—January, February, and so forth. First, we asked the team members to identify all the activities that needed to take place in January. They recorded one activity per storyboard card. We read each Detail Card, and the discussion ensued. Next, the team continued to identify activities to take place in February, one by one, and they repeated this process for each subsequent month. As a result of the discussion of the cards, some activities were added or moved to another month. Once the entire 18-month plan was completed, the team recorded their names on yellow Priority Voting Dots, as many as needed. Then they posted the Dots on cards on which they agreed to participate or in which they had interest or could add value.

As a result, something exciting and gratifying began to happen. The barriers between the various functional areas started to crumble. Technicians accepted responsibility for engineering tasks; engineers became interested in marketing concerns; and marketers assumed the critical business role of evaluating suppliers. Even their usually standoffish finance team members willingly jumped into the trenches with purchasing and marketing folks. The flow of ideas became a flood. By the end of the retreat, everyone was working together for the common good of the team.

Personal financial management is a world apart from manufacturing, but this method can work for all types of businesses, as you can see from the results of Bill's three-day retreat with ClearPoint Credit Counseling Solutions. At the retreat, ClearPoint's President and CEO Christopher Honenberger and his management team discovered how storyboarding could deepen their range of thought while developing a long-term corporate strategy. Chris remarked, "Challenge and change are inevitable in today's business environment. How a company empowers its team to meet those evolutionary realities defines its future."

The retreat was attended by 15 percent of the ClearPoint employee base and included all management and senior support staff. Together, they utilized the storyboarding tool to begin the process of systematically unearthing their business challenges and ideas for expansion. According to COO Jim Craig, "The 'so what' was that we eliminated silos and restructured the organization. It really turned around our company morale and communications."

As a result of their eye-opening storyboarding experience, ClearPoint's empowered team continues to use the tool to solve business problems and identify business opportunities on a regular basis, and using storyboards has broadened the scope of both their product and service offerings.

Another devotee of storyboarding is the Monroe County, Michigan, Chamber of Commerce Board of Directors who utilized the process during their 2015 annual planning retreat. The directors were pleasantly surprised how effective this method was compared to the typical practice of a facilitator recording all the ideas and allowing extroverts to dominate the conversation. Storyboarding engaged all the participants equally and was very efficient. After the retreat, Chamber of Commerce staff transferred the ideas from the storyboard cards to a spreadsheet for all to review. The document became their 2016 business plan. Monroe County Chamber of Commerce Executive Director Michelle Dugan exclaimed, "This was the best retreat ever!"

# A Tool to Help Transform Your Community

Our good friend Roberto ("Bert") Jara is the former leader of the nonprofit organization Latin Americans United for Progress (LAUP), whose focus is addressing the educational issues of Hispanics and Latinos in the Holland, Michigan, community.

In 2007, the four-year high school graduation rate for Hispanics at Holland High School was 49 percent. The revelation of this fact roused many in the community to action, and LAUP entrusted Bert to pull together some of the best local minds to design a program focused on raising the educational achievement of minority youth.

With the help of AT&T and the League of United Latin American Citizens (LULAC), Adelante was created to help Latino students and others explore careers, engage in community service, develop cultural identity, gain confidence, and navigate a path to post-secondary education. The Adelante students gained so much from this experience that they created a special program to further develop student leadership and prepare them for college: Más Adelante. The main goals of the program were to help the students develop critical thinking and problem-solving as well as oral and written communication skill sets.

As Bert recalled, "I reached out to Bill and Lynn and was delighted when they agreed to come teach storyboarding to my small group of students. They really clicked with the students, and the group generated an unusually large number of ideas around the idea of 'creating the ideal high school.' The storyboarding process helped to empower the students to participate in designing solutions to barriers to their success. Today, the four-year graduation rate among Hispanic students has grown from 49 to 74 percent at Holland High School."

The Más Adelante students became the "pioneers" of storyboarding in the Holland community. They used storyboarding to design their Internet blog, generate ideas for a museum exhibit and service projects, and redesign their annual youth conference with the involvement of their peers in the Adelante program. From that point forward, every LAUP project tackled by Bert's youth groups utilized the storyboarding process.

Within a couple of years, other youth workers from the community heard about how the LAUP students were using storyboarding, and they decided to utilize the tool to organize the annual Lakeshore Youth Leaders fall retreat. Bert said, "Now it's used everywhere by Holland's young people and in settings that seek to raise educational outcomes for youth. Students took the tool back to their classrooms and student councils. A high school teacher now uses the tool with a group of the lowest-achieving students to gather their input to design an educational environment that will help them thrive." And recently, the annual Holland Mayor's Roundtable event used storyboarding to gain input from youth on critical community issues such as how the town can work with the Holland Board of Public Works to become more responsible and efficient in its use of energy. Bert remarked, "That initial night of training at Más Adelante was the birth of a movement in the community that utilizes storyboarding to address a variety of issues affecting not only our students but other citizens as well."

# The Six Types of Storyboards

1. Idea Storyboard
2. Barriers Storyboard
3. Planning Storyboard
4. Customer Feedback Storyboard
5. Leadership Storyboard
6. Communications Storyboard

## Idea Storyboard

The Idea Storyboard is one of the most useful tools for developing a concept and unleashing the creative thinking of any group of people. Walt Disney once said, "We don't allow geniuses here." He did not feel that creativity was just for right-brainers. He felt that everyone was creative. All we have to do is create an environment where everyone's creative energy is captured and focused on solving a problem, and the Idea Storyboard does just that.

To facilitate an Idea Storyboard, refer to the section entitled "Storyboarding: The Process." Example topics are these: "How might we adopt a Dream, Believe, Dare, Do culture in our organization?" "How can we achieve a legendary customer service reputation?" "How can we improve quality and productivity on the XYZ production line?" As you can see, storyboard topics can be very general and deal with "soft" issues, such as culture, or very specific "hard" issues, such as process improvement production issues.

## Barriers Storyboard

The Barriers Storyboard is critical to the success of accomplishing a dream. It is used to identify existing and potential roadblocks to success.

To facilitate a Barriers Storyboard, refer to the section entitled "Storyboarding: The Process." The Topic Card should read: "What are the barriers to accomplishing XYZ? (Just fill in your dream or goal.)

## *Planning Storyboard*

As we mentioned in Chapter 9, one of the most effective tools we've found for managing a project and bringing an idea to its successful fruition is a *planning center*—that is, a room where all the various elements of an entire project and its progress can be displayed.

When The Walt Disney Company was still relatively small, with some 1,200 employees, the project teams pinned rough drafts of drawings and story ideas to the walls of their planning centers so that the exact status of their projects could be quickly ascertained. Walt Disney didn't care much for meetings or written reports. He preferred to wander into the planning centers alone, usually late at night, and scan the walls for samples of work in progress. Comparing the visuals to the vision he held in his mind told him instantly whether a cartoon or feature film project was on the right track.

Unexpectedly, planning centers can help build morale by bringing employees together and giving them a sense of involvement in all aspects of a company's processes. When cross-functional teams participate in creating a Planning Storyboard (discussed earlier in this chapter), they feel that they have a voice in developments outside their own departments, and compartmentalization gradually disappears.

Occasionally, people complain that all plans can be tracked online, and therefore, they do not see a need for a visual display. However, the whole point of a planning center is to allow people to see a holistic picture of the projects and activities throughout the organization. What's more, when two or three people congregate in an area where the significant work of the organization is visually displayed, often an impromptu meeting takes place. People communicate better face-to-face, and as discussed in Chapter 5, MIT research supports this conclusion. The quality of communication improves markedly with proximity. Close contact encourages questions and discussion, which is the kind of interaction needed to move projects along.

## *Customer Feedback Storyboard*

The Customer Feedback Storyboard is used to identify customer desires and "dreams" (see Figure 10-2). Many of our clients are unable or unwilling to spend thousands of dollars on professional marketing studies to find out just what customers are thinking and what they really want. In our Dream

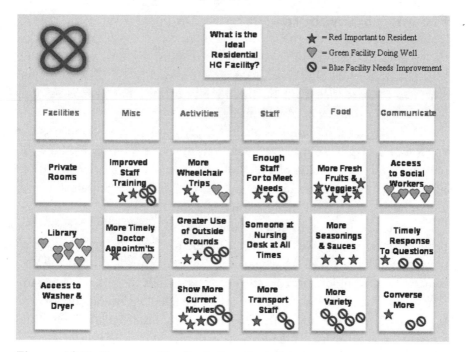

**Figure 10-2.** Customer Feedback Storyboard

Retreats and workshops, we teach the following relatively simple variation of storyboarding to accomplish this goal.

Invite a group of 15 to 20 customers who you believe have a firm interest in helping you improve one or more of your products or services. Plan to provide refreshments, a light meal, or a gift certificate to compensate them for their time. We have found that most people, especially loyal customers, welcome an opportunity to provide feedback in areas that directly affect them.

The Topic Card for this storyboard should read: "What elements create your ideal customer experience in the area of _____ [fill in your product or service]?" For example, if you are in the hotel business, you might ask your customers, "What elements create your ideal hotel experience?" Explain to them that this step is to identify what the ultimate experience should look like.

Once you have collected, read aloud, and posted all the Detail Cards and Header Cards (see Figure 10-1), distribute three red Priority Voting Dots to all of the participants, and ask them to place their Dots on the three cards that they consider to be most important. Distribute three green Priority Voting Dots to all of the participants, and ask them to place their Dots on the three cards that they believe are your strengths, or things you are doing well. Distribute three blue Priority Voting Dots to all of the participants, and ask them to place their Dots on the three cards that they believe are your weaknesses, or things you could improve.

In a 60- to 90-minute session, the storyboard will be complete, and you'll have a snapshot of what really matters to your customers and how you measure up to their criteria of an "ideal" experience with your organization. Figure 10-2 is an actual example of a Customer Feedback Storyboard from one of our clients, a residential healthcare facility.

It is not uncommon to discover that some of the things that customers believe you are doing well are unimportant to them. If you discover an obvious conflict between what you think is important and what the customers think is important, consider this as a serious red flag. If you don't change direction, your organization might be spiraling toward disaster. In Figure 10-2, you will notice that the residents considered the library and access to social workers as the two best attributes of their healthcare facility. However, not one of the residents felt these two items were important.

We recommend storyboarding with three or four different customer groups and then comparing the results. If you want to take this process a step further, ask the same question to a random group of frontline service providers and to the top management group. It may surprise you which group really has a better understanding of the customers' needs, desires, and dreams.

## Leadership Storyboard

The Leadership Storyboard is an ideal way for leaders to gain anonymous feedback that can enable them to increase their overall effectiveness (see Figure 10-3). Initially, many leaders express a bit of apprehension in championing this exercise, but nearly all with whom we have worked have found great value in the results. Due to the sensitivity of this type of feedback storyboard, the following are the steps that should be carefully followed:

1. The leader assembles his or her staff in a conference room in which they will have no distractions. If need be, present a brief overview of the mechanics of storyboarding.

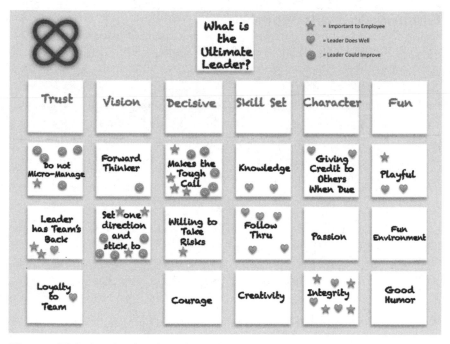

**Figure 10-3.** Leadership Storyboard

2. The leader explains that the group will have total freedom to answer the question, "What is the ultimate leader?" This is the Topic Card.

3. The leader leaves the room and will return to the group when they have completed the entire storyboarding process.

4. A facilitator or member of the group collects, reads aloud, and posts the Detail Cards and Header cards.

5. A facilitator or member of the group distributes red, green, and blue Priority Voting Dots in the same fashion and for the same general purpose as is required to conduct the Customer Feedback Storyboard. In this case, participants will place their red Dots on the three cards that they consider to be the most important leader behaviors; the green Dots on the three cards that they believe represent the leader's strengths, or things he or she is doing well; and blue Dots on the three cards that they believe represent the leader's weaknesses or opportunities for improvement.

6. The leader is then invited back into the room to review the storyboard and ask for any clarification and examples of his or her behaviors. The rule of anonymity is crucial here. The leader should not ask, "Who wrote this card?"

## Communications Storyboard

The Communications Storyboard is used to organize and communicate daily activities to those who need to know, and it should be visible as the process or project is carried out.

Thus, the Communications Storyboard becomes a team's or an individual's personal planning tool. When Walt Disney assembled a team for a project, he would require them to colocate into one room or planning center. He did not believe in lengthy meetings or reports, but he did require project teams to keep their storyboards current.

The Communications Storyboard has five areas:

1. **Activities to do.** The team or individual would post a short-term to-do list on storyboard cards, one activity per card.

2. **Activities in process.** Storyboard cards are moved from the "Activities to do" area to the "Activities in process" area as work on that task or activity begins.

3. **Activities completed.** Once an activity is completed, it is moved to this area of the storyboard.

4. **Messages.** This area of the storyboard is reserved for messages to the team or individuals (for example, from telephone calls or visitors when no one was available for communication).

5. **Hang-ups.** This space on the storyboard is reserved for problems that have not yet been resolved. Walt Disney was known to wander through the planning centers, many times after normal business hours. In addition to reviewing the Planning Storyboards, he would check the Communications Storyboards for hang-ups. For example, he might have seen a note that someone was waiting for accounting to approve a budget before the next activity could be completed. So, on the message area of the Communications Storyboard, he would write something like, "Let me know if you do not hear from accounting by noon tomorrow. Walt."

## Storyboarding Recap

Regardless of what storyboarding is being used for, one thing remains constant: its role in nurturing creative and critical thinking. People often ask the practical question, "How much space do we need to adequately storyboard?" There is no cut-and-dried answer because it depends on how many people will be present at a meeting. Two people can storyboard very satisfactorily in a small office for the purpose of visualizing their ideas or mapping out potential solutions to a problem. Try to limit the upper level of your storyboard group to 25. In our experience, groups of more than 25 often suffer from the old mindset of the typical classroom where the teacher speaks and the students are silent. This type of rigor mortis kills the intended participation that is necessary for storyboarding.

## Parting Thoughts

An American architect once mused that there are very few inferior people in the world but lots of inferior environments. "Try to enrich your environment," he advised. Storyboarding is a tool that can enrich the environment of any organization, no matter the specific needs.

In the next chapter, we focus on a truth that Walt knew so well: grand ideas are nothing without proper emphasis on the details.

---

### *Our Featured Organization: McLean County, Illinois, Unit (School) District No. 5*

#### A SUPERINTENDENT BRINGS *THE DISNEY WAY* TO PUBLIC SCHOOLS

Clearly, our nation's educational process is failing our students who are our future. Of every 10 students entering high school this year, only 7 will graduate in four years. Of those 7, 4 will go on to college, but 2 of them will need to take a remedial reading, writing, or mathematics class. We don't know of any business that can survive with an 80 percent defect rate!

One school district Superintendent—Dr. Mark Daniel—has been "attacking" the process with respect to accomplishing his dream: a way of teaching that is student centered and has the values of Disney. In 2011, he was the Superintendent of the Dowagiac Union Schools in Dowagiac, Michigan. Bill worked with Mark and other leaders from four local entities—public school system, hospital, city government, and the Dowagiac community—to help them understand what it takes to embrace a customer-centric culture. We began a week-long *The Disney Way* engagement with Bill's "If Walt Ran Your Organization" keynote that was attended by 10 percent of the Dowagiac population, a diverse audience that also included college students. Dr. Fred L. Mathews, Chairman of Southwestern Michigan College, said, "Bill's message is one that every student going into the business world should hear."

Bill also facilitated Customer Feedback Storyboard sessions with middle school and high school students. The students identified the "ideal" classroom as having the following attributes: (1) exploration and discovery; (2) interaction with the teacher and fellow students; and (3) fun. They were so excited to begin building a great future together! It reminded him of the Millennium Celebration at Walt Disney World whose theme was "Celebrate the Future Hand in Hand." Being with those students reinforced Bill's passion for student-centered experiential learning and gave him cause to celebrate!

In 2014, Mark left Dowagiac and became the Superintendent of McLean County, Illinois, Unit District No. 5 whose mission is "Educating each student to achieve personal excellence." In striving to continuously improve and achieve "excellence," Mark instituted the storyboarding technique that he had learned during *The Disney Way* week in Dowagiac. Over 450 students, principals, and community residents congregated in 21 different buildings and storyboarded two questions: (1) "What makes our school an outstanding school?" (2) "What can we do to make our school even better?" Mark explained, "They started with those two themes, and they discovered very quickly what the patterns and themes were, what strengths are in our buildings, and what areas we can concentrate on to improve. We are using the data to assist us with our strategic planning. I call it my 'Listening Tour' data."

Collectively, the storyboards revealed six themes—curriculum, instruction, transportation, facilities, community partnerships, and special education—whose data was analyzed and recorded on spreadsheets to aid in communicating the information as well as facilitating the goals of the district's strategic planning teams. Mark continues to utilize the storyboarding process to provide better input for decision making with respect to improving the school district. When communicating the results of the storyboards and preparing the numerous community stakeholders for the future, he never fails to remind them that customer service is a key to helping students "achieve personal excellence." Mark stated, "Any time I can include what is truly customer service and what that means to an educational system or educational organization, I think it benefits not only the school district but also the community as a whole."

## Questions to Ask

- Do teams of all sizes use storyboarding as a way to visualize their barriers, goals, problems, solutions, and project plans?

- Do you promote the use of storyboarding in meetings Involving sensitive topics?

- Do you offer assistance in storyboarding facilitation to teams in need?

- Do you invite your customers and suppliers to participate in storyboarding sessions to gain their feedback and assistance in planning and problem solving?

## Actions to Take

- Train all employees in the technique of storyboarding.

- Provide teams with areas to storyboard and the flexibility to leave the storyboards visible for as long as needed.

- Use storyboarding in planning sessions to develop timelines and project assignments. Use the storyboard as a dynamic tool that can be changed, revised, and updated as needed.

- Use storyboarding to gain feedback from customer groups.

- Develop a formal communications plan that defines who, what, when, and how communications are made to all employees. Schedule storyboarding sessions with all employees to gather ideas for improvement.

**Chapter Chats with Bill: http://capojac.com/disneyway/10/**

# Chapter 11

# Give Details Top Billing

*It's the details that make the Disney Parks work . . . And you have to make it a complete story, which means striving to be accurate about whatever story you're telling, down to the smallest details.*

Marty Sklar, Disney Legend

**M**any leaders place a great deal of importance on seeing the big picture or coming up with the next grand idea. But it's the details that give the big picture depth, bring the grand idea clearly into focus, and produce pride in workmanship. Paying attention to the little things is what turns the vision into a top-quality product or an outstanding service. As the great architect Mies van der Rohe once put it, "God is in the details."

In his constant pursuit of excellence, Walt Disney never failed to remember that attention to detail was the key to complete realization of his dreams. As a result, the Company he founded has no equal when it comes to creating the thousands of intricate drawings needed to produce nonpareil animation, bring together the mind-boggling number of parts required to build a Disneyland or a Walt Disney World, or carefully attend to the numerous small details that make every Guest's experience a magical one.

Often overlooked in Disney's awe-inspiring success is how the Company has managed to give extravagant attention to detail without bankrupting itself. It has achieved a careful balance between the competing demands of the bottom line and the quest for perfection. The key to this balancing act is contained in the Disney philosophy that everyone from the groundskeepers at the Parks and the animators in the studios to the number crunchers in the accounting department are responsible for doing whatever it takes to deliver the "good show." When all parties are convinced of the importance of their individual roles, nothing will be left to chance.

Most of the organizations with whom we work are far removed from the Disney environment of entertainment, yet they too have recognized that obsessive attention to detail can pay huge dividends. Thus, they are calling on "casts" of employees to present their own version of the good show to an audience composed of suppliers and customers, and in doing so, these organizations are consistently delivering quality products and services to their target markets.

## A Relentless Search for Perfection

There is a photograph in the Disney archives of Walt and 10 of his animators standing around a studio table. In the middle of the table are five live penguins. The birds are all turned toward Walt Disney as if they know where their next meal is coming from. This arresting and charming image perfectly captures so much of the Disney ethos and magic—the element of surprise, the embrace of the animal kingdom, and always, the relentless search for perfection.

Walt, who was determined to exceed Guests' expectations, was dissatisfied with the movements of his animated movie animals. They were good, but they weren't perfect. Up until that time, his animators had relied on photographic stills or movie clips to give them the models for their figures. It was clear to Walt that the animators could do better if they were able to copy the real thing—ergo, the penguins. Walt made it clear that carelessness toward details would not be tolerated because such an attitude might cause Guests to start doubting Walt's trustworthiness, the heart and soul of his management philosophy, and personal credo.

"How can we do better?" is the question Walt Disney asked at every turn. But then complacency is unnatural to the perfectionist. He strove continually to improve the quality of his products. Walt originally coined the term "plus-ing" as a way of making an idea, film, or attraction better. He told his Cast Members to keep looking for ways to improve even when they thought their work was really good.

Walt once said, "Whenever I ride an attraction, I'm thinking of what's wrong with the thing and asking myself how it can be improved." If Walt had been alive during the development of the Magic Kingdom's Seven Dwarfs Mine Train, he likely would have been evaluating every detail to make sure it would meet his lofty standards. Honoring the tradition established by their Company's founder, the Imagineers painstakingly managed every minute detail in the design of the attraction's themed cars and characters. In preparation for creating the dwarfs, they watched the original 1937 movie to learn how the dwarfs behaved and studied their facial features when they were speaking and singing. Walt Disney Imagineer Ben Van Beusekom said, "Authenticity . . . is absolutely crucial in the storytelling. In order to immerse the Guests into the story and actually have them believe that they are in the mine train, it has to be right, down to the smallest detail."

As is true of all of Disney's animated film classics, *Snow White and the Seven Dwarfs* was also a shining example of meticulous attention to detail. For example, viewers don't see drops of water just dripping from a bar of soap. Instead, they see glistening bubbles that actually twinkle in the candlelight.

Of course, creating such film magic required a staff of skilled animators, and Walt refused to leave anything to chance. To make sure that he would always have a sufficient number of talented artists to meet his demanding standards, Walt began in-house training courses and eventually made a deal that brought teachers from an art school to work with his animators.

In fact, no corner of the organization escaped Walt's obsession with perfection. Thoroughly convinced that no detail was too small to be ignored in order to provide his Guests with an exceptional experience, the leader made his touch apparent everywhere. He determined that garbage cans should be spaced exactly 25 feet apart all around Disneyland. He ordered that the highest-quality paint be used on attractions and buildings, going so far as to specify that real gold or silver be used for any gilding or silvering. He even sent John Hench, legendary Disney artist and Imagineer, to patrol Disneyland twice a month to make certain that all the colors in the Park were in harmony!

The master entertainer instinctively knew that the whole package—colors, sounds, smells—had an impact on how Guests received the show.

If this holistic, integrated approach to entertainment seems excessive, one need only think of a promising restaurant experience that went awry because of one disagreeable factor. Perhaps the food was first class, the service pleasant, and the decor attractive, but the background music assailed a diner's ears and made it impossible to enjoy the meal. One jarring element can undermine a host of favorable impressions in a restaurant or anywhere else, and Walt Disney wasn't about to risk such a misstep.

That's why street cleaners at Walt Disney World are given extra training at Disney University to ensure that they respond in a positive and helpful fashion to questions from departing Guests. It might seem strange to train street cleaners in customer service, but the Company learned a few years back that these Cast Members receive the greatest number of unstructured questions from Park Guests. For instance, an exhausted couple with three hungry children in tow might ask where they can get a quick, inexpensive dinner. To make sure that a Guest's last impression after a wonderful day in the Park isn't ruined by a don't-ask-me-it's-not-my-job attitude, The Walt Disney Company decrees extra interpersonal skills training for the cleanup crew. They take a proactive approach to head off potentially damaging situations. The Walt Disney Company realizes that the entire show is critical. The way the street cleaner treats a Guest is just as important or even more important than the way a Guest is treated on the Tower of Terror.

## Maintaining a Delicate Balance

When it came to pursuing the often elusive ideal of perfection, Walt Disney spared no expense. The previously mentioned reworking of the Jiminy Cricket character in *Pinocchio*, after the costly animation process was already well under way, is but one example. When it was discovered that the merry-go-round at Walt Disney World was installed two inches off center, the Company insisted that it be moved. "Who would notice?" you might wonder. Walt's big brother, Roy, not only noticed but he reasoned that if the carousel were not set right, thousands of Guests would take home vacation pictures that provided an imperfect memory of their visits to the Park.

In fact, Disney's PhotoPass photographers take between 100,000 and 200,000 photos per day at Walt Disney World, and many of those are taken from an angle that captures the carousel in the background. For example, Guests often are photographed as they stand in Cinderella's Castle with Fantasyland as the backdrop. Looking through the doors of the castle, the carousel is perfectly framed at the center of the opening. Maintaining the quality of the Guest experience cemented the decision to move the carousel to its correct and present location. Remember what Roy said: "When values are clear, decisions are easy."

● ● ●

In the spring of each year, Epcot hosts its spectacular International Flower and Garden Festival—one of the most photographed events in all of Disney. Those fortunate to visit the attraction in 2015 were treated to smiling nine-foot topiaries of Mickey and Minnie exquisitely decked out in farmer attire for the current year's theme, "Epcot Fresh." If you were facing them from the front, you would have seen Spaceship Earth perfectly positioned in the distant sky—again, a Disney photo opportunity for millions of Guests who expect a level of perfection. But there was amazing attention to detail in creating their backs too; even Minnie's apron was beautifully "tied"!

It's a huge expense to bring this event to life each year. For starters, 3.5 million annuals need to be planted, 500 live butterflies need to be released in the butterfly pavilion, and countless hours need to be spent creating the "face" characters such as Elsa and Anna from the movie *Frozen* that are difficult to both craft and preserve. But we must make clear that "sparing no expense" has never meant profligate spending. Walt Disney was always well aware of the bottom line, and he expected that the money spent would be returned in Guest satisfaction and Cast Member loyalty. The way Walt saw it, meticulous attention to detail provided a level of quality that Cast Members could take pride in, and he knew that when workers are proud of their product, it is reflected in the kind of service they give to Guests.

When it came to spending on items unrelated to providing the good show, however, Walt was actually known as something of a penny pincher. He never built a splendidly pompous, ego-enhancing headquarters building, nor did he ever spend a nickel on advertising his Theme Park. Walt reasoned that his television shows provided advertising aplenty, so why waste money paying for it? In today's environment, The Walt Disney Company has a large advertising budget, but it still does not waste money on backstage areas.

Walt also kept a sharp eye on financial arrangements and partnerships, not hesitating to protect his own interests. Although a licensing deal in the early 1930s brought in $300,000 the first year, with Walt's share providing half of the Company's annual profits that year, he quickly discovered a major drawback. The deal called for his percentage of the profits to increase as more items were sold, but since novelty items sold fast and then faded from the market, the licensee would make a lot more money than the Company would. Walt canceled the arrangement and set up an in-house marketing division.

Today, Disney executives ask Cast Members to balance what they call "quality Cast experience," "quality Guest experience," and "quality business practice." The product should deliver value and balance in all three areas: pleasing Cast Members, Guests, and corporate bean counters. The Company firmly believes, as Walt did, that obsessive attention to detail in all respects is the key to delivering a sterling experience that will keep Guests coming back while holding costs to a level that still maintains profit margins.

In our experience, successful organizations like Disney balance business and creative needs by insisting on strict adherence to a set of core values, emphasizing the importance of details in exceeding customer or guest expectations, and encouraging innovation and risk taking within a specified set of boundaries. Disney makes no bones about its belief that creativity works best within a specified framework.

## Measuring for Success

Paying attention to detail also means measuring results. This concept seems almost too rudimentary to mention, but experience has taught us that many organizations make little or no effort to assess results, either in terms of operating objectives or in terms of performance standards and customer satisfaction.

In our Dream Retreats, we frequently ask participants, "How many of you feel that you would be more successful if you made fewer mistakes and produced your product more quickly?" Most everyone raises a hand, but seldom does even one hand stay in the air when we follow up with, "How many of you are making quality and time measurements for your key business processes?"

We can't emphasize strongly enough how important it is to implement some system for gauging quality level, process time, customer satisfaction, and product cost, as well as negative elements such as errors of judgment and process mistakes. All too often, companies give little thought to measuring processes in their entirety, even though doing so should not be a complicated task. But without measurements, an organization cannot possibly know which processes are working efficiently and effectively, what products and services are meeting quality standards, and whether or not customer requirements are being satisfied.

Identifying processes and mapping the functions involved are keys to increasing efficiency. In many organizations, however, processes seem to be hit-or-miss affairs because they are the result of haphazard growth. When a team takes the time to map the details of a process, the results are usually an eye-opener. "Why would anyone design a process like that?" baffled leaders ask. Of course, no one actually did design it, and that's just the problem. The process simply mushroomed in all directions as well-meaning managers added a step here and required a memo there. Before long, what once was a relatively smooth-functioning process has turned into a multi-headed monster.

Dr. William Cross, the retired Vice President whom we worked with at Mead Johnson and was first mentioned in Chapter 4, suspected that his department's key business processes were flawed, and he asked his teams to evaluate them closely. They uncovered many redundant and non-value-added elements that had been built into the system over the course of several years. Dr. Cross was astounded to discover that mapping a single work process related to releasing a new product produced a "flowchart that when it was all put together end to end, was about seven feet high and about two and a half feet wide, and was in very small print. So it was extremely complex."

However, by mapping out the details of the complex process, the team was able to determine which steps could safely be discontinued. The new streamlined process reduced the usual cycle time for a product release by about two weeks.

Something similar occurred when Bill was working with the South African utilities company. After every step in the procurement process had been documented, more than 100 square feet of a wall in the project planning center were covered with index cards. Needless to say, the process was hopelessly complex and very often redundant so that capital materials procurement was taking as much as a year and a half, with seven or eight months of that eaten up by the internal bureaucracy.

Astonished company executives could only wonder how it had happened that pieces of paper were going back and forth for months on end, and for absolutely no reason at all. Once the process was streamlined, the savings in time and money were considerable.

When we work with a team on a strategic initiative, a willingness to become immersed in details is a must. Let's take another look at Mead Johnson. They examined an exhaustive process that began with the creation of a complaint analysis team to determine the path traveled by product complaints, either from an individual or from another company. It took three to four months to complete the flowchart documenting each step involved. The team interviewed every department along the route, and when the flowchart was done, each department was asked to check it for accuracy.

Simultaneously, the team followed one sample complaint through the entire handling process and clocked the amount of time each step took. Multiplying the time factor by the department's charge-out rate allowed the team to assess costs. The team discovered that a single complaint traveling through the analysis system took an average of 30 days, cost the company up to $910 from beginning to end, and wasn't even solving the problems quickly. Having established its data, the team was then able to draw up a new flowchart for an ideal system.

One change drastically reduced the number of complaints that were still being stored after the process was completed. Before the analysis, all complaints were being held for four months, even though most of them were never looked at again. The team logically determined that only those complaints that posed a potential legal threat, dealt with packaging that had allegedly been tampered with, or those that involved a federal, state, or local government agency needed to be retained. This one simple change of process saved the company considerable time.

Not all of the team's proposals and recommendations could be instituted immediately, but initial forecasts pointed to eventual savings of $123 per complaint. Dr. Cross said, "The teams have saved in dollars thus far tens of thousands, which have already [produced] a payback."

The message for management, then, is to look at your business in a holistic manner the way Disney looks at its show. Carefully examine all the details that affect the way your product or service is provided to customers. In other words, go the extra mile, or as the folks at Disney might say, "Bump the lamp."

This cryptic phrase originated when the movie *Roger Rabbit* was being made, and it relates to a scene in which someone bumps into a lamp, causing the shadow it casts to wobble. Initially, there were no shadows in the scene, which the animators immediately spotted as being unrealistic, so they went back and did the hundreds of drawings needed to bring perfection to these few seconds of the film.

## Parting Thoughts

"Bump the lamp," originally coined by retired Disney CEO Michael Eisner, has become shorthand at Disney for management's commitment to doing things the right way, down to the tiniest detail. The Walt Disney Company has raised the bar of performance—to bump the lamp and strive for excellence in all they do. We encourage you to make it the philosophy in your organization too.

In the next chapter, we reveal the "real" pixie dust . . . if you hadn't looked at the Contents page, you'd never guess what it is!

---

### *Our Featured Organization: Science Center of Iowa*

**BRINGING THE VISITOR EXPERIENCE TO LIFE**

*All sciences are vain and full of errors that are not born of experience, the mother of all knowledge.*
              Leonardo da Vinci, *Leonardo's Notebooks*

The Science Center of Iowa (SCI) was created in 1970 (originally called the Des Moines Center of Science and Industry), and it has evolved into an "innovative, dynamic, and changing environment that adapts its experience platforms, theaters, and programming to serve future generations." As da Vinci stated, "Experience" is "the mother of all knowledge," and SCI's Visitor Experience Team (VET) is entrusted to protect the visitor "experience."

Hence, the VET seeks to understand and honor the continuously evolving needs and expectations of both their visitors and their community. When it comes to truly knowing what will engage a guest today and in the future, effective systems are necessary and every detail matters. Any organization needs to look no further than Disney to understand this truth.

Along with fellow SCI leaders, the VET members became immersed in *The Disney Way* culture through a three-day workshop that Bill facilitated in the summer of 2015. The goal of this experience was to engage the participants in rethinking their organizational strategy, methods, and tools in light of Walt Disney's success principles. In the years preceding the workshop, SCI had endured multiple changes in leadership, and therefore, they lacked focus and stability in both the financial and programmatic aspects of the organization. Curt Simmons, SCI President and CEO related, "When the new creative learning center opened 10 years ago, we experienced a kickoff of success in our first two years. After this success, we experienced a significant period in which we did not invest enough in listening and responding to our community. As a result, we lost connection, and our community noticed."

*The Disney Way* workshop inspired significant cultural change, and the newly drafted "Science Center Story" helped move the organization forward with a single shared vision. As a next step in their *Disney Way* journey, the VET was inspired to help the entire workforce create the best visitor experience possible. Allison Schwanebeck, Director of Exhibits remarked, "To better serve our visitors, we have been educating ourselves on the contemporary research in our field to better understand needs and motivations."

From its inception, the VET members began gathering data through observations and surveys to analyze the SCI experience from a visitor's vantage point—from the pre-visit communications to the planning and arrival to the facility. They were also keenly focused on making sure that every department was "overprepared" to interact with the visitors on a daily basis.

Renee Harmon, Vice President of Science Learning, remarked, "It's a retooling effort. . . . We retooled our message, and we now prepare our staff to better engage the visitor and make every experience valuable." For example, the VET members have prepared a list of ideas for creating rewarding and memorable staff-visitor interactions. This document delineates suggested questions to ask visitors, how to respond to visitor questions, and how staff members should introduce themselves to visitors. Questions such as "Why is the planetarium closed?" are addressed with an explanation and the assurance that soon there will be a new and amazing experience for the visitor to enjoy.

If you've been to any of Disney's Theme Parks, you know that "closed" attractions are a common occurrence, and the Company makes every effort to assure their Guests that the end result will be worth the inconvenience and the wait. Similarly, within the new visitor-centric culture of SCI, the goal is to learn how to assist visitors in every way possible, whether that be responding to a complaint about a broken or closed exhibit or simply answering a question in a timely fashion in the spirit of true personal engagement.

SCI's Gravity Ramp Exhibit is a prime example of behavioral changes in the way SCI staff members take care of their visitors. The experience allows visitors to "race" tennis balls down three ramps with various configurations to see if any of the balls will reach the bottom of the ramp before the others. In the "old" culture, each morning the staff would place three tennis balls at the exhibit, but it wasn't long before the balls went "missing." Rather than focus on how the lack of balls ruined the exhibit quality and the visitor experience, the staff became angry and made the decision to leave the exhibit "as is." In essence, they were punishing their visitors for alleged "bad behavior." In the "new" culture, to ensure that the exhibit is "complete" for every guest, the staff provides extra balls and monitors the activity on a regular basis. The change has resulted in the expected improvement, and as a secondary benefit, visitors who are waiting to experience the exhibit may collect the extra balls so they are ready to launch them as soon as the previous visitor has moved on to another attraction. Carefully managing the details has also effectively doubled the "throughput" of the exhibit.

Gradually, the organization has shifted its focus to developing a "holistic" experience for each visitor to the facility. Staff members routinely engage visitors on the elevator rather than talking only with coworkers. Even the volunteers have realized a change in the culture. One regular volunteer commented that staff members were now directly and purposefully interacting with him on every one of his visits.

Jennifer Koska, Visitor Experience Manager, is delighted that the VET team has the "eyes" and "ears" of other SCI teams with whom they work in tandem to produce great visitor experiences. Jennifer stated, "We have been working with the Science Learning Team. Each day, they put on a lab coat and go out on the floor and talk to visitors. They are also looking for any exhibits that are broken, and they receive really good information about what we are doing. We will be looking at their feedback over time to see if there is a shift, even a small component, that we could address."

Happily, the SCI experience for many visitors has become a valuable part of their lives. Curt has received numerous letters and comments about how his staff is doing things "out of the ordinary" and putting smiles on the faces of children and parents alike. One such letter was from a mother whose son was having behavioral difficulties at school. After a week without causing any disruptions or receiving any demerits, she permitted her son to choose a place in town to visit. The boy chose the Science Center. As Curt recalled, "Not only did he enjoy it but the mother felt it really changed her son's behavior in school." Clearly, SCI's Visitor Experience Team has a lot that is worth protecting—not only the potentially life-changing experiences of each and every visitor but also all of the details that make those experiences possible.

## Questions to Ask

- Do your cross-functional teams map all the critical details of processes in order to determine which steps can be safely eliminated?
- Do your employees and teams make quality and time measurements of their critical processes?
- Are your employees constantly examining details and asking, "How can we do this better?"

## Actions to Take

- Appoint a "details squad" to get fanatical about the details that make a difference to your customers.
- Continuously evaluate the effectiveness of your processes.
- Evaluate how "little things" can make a difference in the way you serve customers or turn out products.

Chapter Chats with Bill: http://capojac.com/disneyway/11/

# Chapter 12

# Love: The Real Pixie Dust

*Love is a song that never ends.*

Bambi

Really, "love" in business? Love is just not a topic that is typically discussed in the boardroom. And yet, love is present in nearly every aspect of our lives. We listen to love songs, read poetry, and enjoy our favorite love stories. We openly express love for so many things—from our cars to our favorite sports teams. But somehow, when it comes to talking about our careers, you will seldom hear people say, "I love my job!"

Few business scholars publicly address the "soft" topic of love. They are more comfortable with less "threatening" terms such as customer engagement, employee attitude, and behavioral styles. In 2010, Peter Boatwright and Jonathan Cagan wrote *Built to Love*, an account of how to translate product strategy into emotions that invoke positive feelings for customers. However, there is so much more involved in building a great organization, and Walt Disney knew it. He exemplified not only love for his product but also for his Cast and his Guests.

## Love for Employees

*I am in no sense of the word a great artist, not even a great animator. I have always had men working for me whose skills were greater than my own.*

Walt Disney

Every human being has both physical and emotional needs. We spend most of our time meeting our physical needs, even though they are the simplest to satisfy. For our survival, all that is required is food, water, and shelter. Yet, we have learned to live in a world of "must haves." We tend to eat too much and purchase homes with more room than we truly need. Luxury isn't necessarily a bad thing, but it's certainly not a necessity for a happy and fulfilled life.

Our emotional needs are also few and every bit as important as our physical requirements, but they are not as simple to satisfy. Emotional needs, if not met, can be as debilitating as hunger, thirst, exposure to severe weather conditions, and a host of psychological disorders. Behavioral scientists tell us that an infant who is left alone and neglected will cease to develop and may choose madness and even death. You might think it's a stretch to suggest that the same is true for employees. Consider, however, that the development of employees who are "alone and neglected" may be stunted, and the results to the organization can be poor service, unacceptable quality, low productivity, and yes, sometimes even death of the organization!

But who really is responsible for taking care of employees? The answer is their leaders. For employees to become successful, they must have leaders who guide them to experience an emotional connection to both their work and fellow team members. The very best leaders bring out the best in their teams, and they are the ones who are truly "loved" by those whom they nurture. We never love our leaders because of their titles. We love them because of the way they make us feel!

In many ways, the employer-employee relationship is analogous to the traditional mating ritual. Typically, it begins with the hiring process (the courtship); then an employee experiences orientation (the engagement); and finally, the employee commits to a long-term arrangement with the organization (the marriage). And, just like a successful marriage, a successful employer-employee relationship must be based on open communication, mutual respect, and trust.

Love for employees works! Need more proof? Gallup's extensive research regarding the State of the American Workplace has revealed that disengaged workers cost American businesses $450 to $550 billion a year in lost productivity. According to the Boston Consulting Group, since 2001 companies that embrace "whole person" employee engagement have outpaced the S&P average cumulative share price by margins of up to 99 percent. Gallup also reports the following additional benefits:

- 37 percent lower absenteeism
- 48 percent fewer safety incidents
- 28 percent less inventory shrinkage
- 10 percent higher customer satisfaction
- 22 percent higher profitability

It's easy to think of love as a bunch of touchy–feely nonsense that has little use in the real world of work. But love and respect are even taught at our military academies. The cadets at the U.S. Military Academy at West Point, Officer Candidate School at Fort Benning, and the U.S. Air Force Academy are required to memorize an excerpt from Civil War General John Schofield's graduation address to the class of 1879 at West Point:

> The one mode or other of dealing with subordinates springs from a corresponding spirit in the breast of the commander. He who feels the respect which is due to others cannot fail to inspire in them respect for himself. While he who feels, and hence manifests, dis-respect toward others, especially his subordinates, cannot fail to inspire hatred against himself.

Take some time to contemplate the organizations that you most admire, and the ones we have featured in this book. Examine their corporate cultures, their values, and the way they proactively take care of their people—we guarantee you will find love!

## Love for Customers

*Whatever you do, do it well. Do it so well that when people see you do it, they will want to come back and see you do it again and they will want to bring others and show them how well you do what you do.*

Walt Disney

The Golden Rule is part and parcel of the messages in virtually every religion in the world, and it can serve as the inspiration for our love for employees and customers alike:

- **Christianity.** Do unto others as you would have them do onto you.
- **Taoism.** Regard your neighbor's gain as your own gain and your neighbor's loss as your own loss.

- **Confucianism.** One term that sums up the basis of all good conduct: loving kindness.
- **Hinduism.** The sum of duty: Do not do to others what would cause pain if done to you.
- **Islam.** Not one of you truly believes until what you wish for others, you wish for yourself.
- **Judaism.** What is hateful to you, do not do to your neighbor.
- **Native spirituality.** We are as much alive as we keep the earth alive.

The Dalai Lama stated, "Every religion emphasizes human improvement, love, respect for others, and sharing other people's suffering. On these lines, every religion has more or less the same viewpoint and the same goal." The Golden Rule is intended to apply to all whom we encounter. It isn't meant for us to selectively apply to only fellow believers, members of our race or political persuasion, or only at our places of worship.

● ● ●

Companies can demonstrate love for their customers in two ways:

1. **An emotionally charged ad campaign.** There are many fine examples, but a few come to mind. Recently, Jeep ran an ad in support of our troops in combat: "There will be a seat left open, a light left on, a favorite dinner waiting, a warm bed made . . . because in your home, in our hearts, you've been missed. You've been needed, you've been cried for, prayed for. You are the reason we push on." And, over the years, we have become captivated by the majesty of the Budweiser Clydesdales that have forever touched our hearts. Who can forget the 2014 Super Bowl ad that featured the puppy that ran away to the Clydesdale barn? Earlier in this book, we wrote about the importance of engaging customers and guests with an emotional story. Remember, a series of facts and figures gets muddled in our brains, but when our emotions are triggered, we are 22 times more likely to remember the story than a fact-based ad.

2. **One-on-one engagement.** Since 1994, Gallup has been measuring customer engagement and defines it as "the emotional connection between your customers and your company." Here are the three elements that make up the Gallup Customer Engagement Score (CES):

- The company always delivers what it promises.
- I feel proud to be a company customer.
- The company is the perfect company for people like me.

Engagement or loving your customers is not about sales. It's about service—delivering on promises, taking pride in your company, and solving unique customer problems.

Loving your customers isn't to be taken lightly. Consider the following two examples. The first is a story about Southwest Airlines. One day, Peggy Uhale boarded a flight from Chicago to Columbus, Ohio. The plane was on the tarmac waiting in line to take off when it unexpectedly turned back to the gate. A flight attendant asked Peggy to get off the plane. Peggy recalled, "I figured I was on the wrong plane. The gate agent told me to check in at the desk, and when I did, she told me to call my husband."

Peggy's husband informed her that their son who was living in Denver had injured his head and was in a coma. As soon as Southwest Airlines learned of the accident, they immediately rebooked Peggy on the next flight to Denver with no additional fees or service charges. Peggy said, "They offered a private waiting area, rerouted my luggage, allowed me to board first, and packed a lunch for when I got off the plane in Denver. My luggage was delivered to where I was staying, and I even received a call from Southwest asking how my son was doing."

Compare Southwest Airlines' "loving" customer service example to that of American Airlines' failure to exhibit any customer care whatsoever in a similar situation. Theresa Purcell was scheduled to take a commuter flight to San Diego, California. She was unable to walk and was confined to a wheelchair. As she began boarding the plane, the flight attendant told her that it was too late to provide a wheelchair ramp. Rather than miss her flight, Theresa said, "There was no other way for me to get on the plane so I crawled up to the plane." What is even more disturbing is that there was a ramp near the plane, but the agent simply refused to retrieve it. Eventually, American Airlines issued an apology, but the damage was already done. Sadly, they refused to compensate Theresa for her humiliation and harrowing experience, and they now have a lawsuit on their hands!

It is no surprise that from 2012 through 2014, American Airlines has incurred a loss of $828 million, while Southwest Airlines has reaped a profit of $2.3 billion. On a side note, Southwest Airlines has recently completed its forty-first consecutive year of profitability. This is a remarkable record. In fact, the company weathered the storms of the horrific September 11, 2001, terrorist attacks and the financial meltdown of 2008 without losing a dime or laying off one employee, while most major airlines were losing hundreds of thousands of dollars and laying off tens of thousands of employees.

Everyone from the boardroom to the storeroom must engage and demonstrate love for their customers. Offering a kind word, an honest compliment, or simply listening with true concern are heartfelt behaviors that breed customer loyalty. The late Leo Buscaglia (a.k.a. Dr. Love), author of *LOVE: What Life Is All About*, once proclaimed, "What love we've given, we'll have forever. What love we failed to give will be lost for all eternity."

## Love for Product

*When we opened Disneyland, a lot of people got the impression that it was a get-rich-quick thing, but they didn't realize that behind Disneyland was this great organization, . . . and we got into it and were doing it because we loved to do it.*

Walt Disney

In merely a dozen years, from 1930 to 1942, Walt Disney managed to transform animation from a marginal segment of the entertainment industry to a new art form. His strength as an imaginative and principled creative force grew from his willingness to take risks, to experiment, and to invest his resources and time in new ventures. Walt's stellar accomplishments might suggest that he had no difficulty in taking whatever action was needed to bring his dreams to fulfillment. It was not always easy though, particularly when a lot of skeptics stood in the way. But Walt knew that dreams are sterile things unless the dreamer can do what it takes to make them come true.

When Disneyland was being built in the early 1950s, Walt himself was passionate about every detail. He spent countless hours putting his personal stamp on everything from landscape design to attractions to music. He was not driven by financial success. Whether it was an animated feature film, an attraction at Disneyland, or a popcorn kiosk on Main Street, he loved making it the best it could be. Walt once said, "I don't make movies to make money. I make money so I can make movies." And those movies continue to captivate audiences of every generation.

In their book *Built to Love*, coauthors Boatwright and Cagan describe a three-step process for creating products that captivate customers: determine what emotions should be evoked, build that capability into the product, and then let it perform. And this certainly works.

For as long as IBM personal computers have been around, Bill has been a loyal customer. However, several years ago, he purchased an iPad, and now he's totally hooked, head over heels, in love with the brand. Since then, he has purchased an iPhone, Mac desktop, and Apple laptop.

It's one thing for the creators to love what they have created, but it's even more important that they translate that passion into winning over prospects and turning them into loyal customers. Perhaps you have had times when you witnessed the love of product or love of job that a salesperson demonstrated. Most of our finest experiences have been at Walt Disney World, whether it was at Guest Services, the attractions, or the kiosks.

We are still in awe that over 20 years ago, a Disney team reinvented the closing process for buying their timeshares. When we decided to buy time-share points at Disney's Old Key West, we felt compelled to share our fears of a cumbersome long-distance closing. The Cast Member Byron quickly assured us that Disney had indeed taken the pain out of the process. What an understatement! Within a few days, we received an accordion file with color-coded and tabbed sections, all clearly marked and explained in understandable, plain English rather than legalese. The Disney Vacation Club website claims, "Disney Vacation Club's commitment to quality is part of a heritage that began with Walt himself." Five decades after his death, we, along with millions of others, still feel the love he had for his products.

● ● ●

A great example of Walt's love for his products is his masterful art of plus-ing. As we stated earlier, he originally coined the term "plus-ing" as way of making a film, an attraction, or an idea better. He told his Cast Members to keep looking for ways to improve, even when they thought their work was really good.

One of our favorite examples of Walt's plus-ing happened late one year at Disneyland. Walt had decided to hold a Christmas parade at his new Park. Knowing that the parade would cost several hundred thousand dollars, Walt's brother, Roy, and the accountants tried to convince him not to spend the money on such an extravagant event. Their rationale was that

Guests were already coming for the Christmas holiday, and no one expected a Christmas parade.

Walt answered, "That's just the point—we should do the parade precisely because no one's expecting it. Our goal at Disneyland is to always give the people more than they expect. As long as we keep surprising them, they'll keep coming back. But if they ever stop coming, it'll cost us ten times that much to get them to come back."

## Love for Yourself

*The more you like yourself, the less you are like anyone else, which makes you unique.*

Walt Disney

Reflecting on their 41 years of marriage, Lillian Disney said, "We shared a wonderful, exciting life, and we loved every minute. He was a wonderful husband to me, and a wonderful and joyful father and grandfather." But Walt's love for his product may have outshined the other loves in his life. He announced, "I love Mickey Mouse more than any woman I've ever known." It is not hard to believe that Walt would say that he loved Mickey "more than any woman" because Mickey was his alter ego.

Walt was so comfortable with himself that he didn't need to prove how important he was. A man who worked with Walt once told us that Walt would stand in line in the studio cafeteria waiting his turn and then would reach into his pocket to pay for his meal. He wanted people to know him as "Walt," not "sir" and certainly not "Mr. Disney." Walt proclaimed, "Being a celebrity doesn't even seem to keep the fleas off our dogs, . . . and if being a celebrity won't give me an advantage over a couple of fleas, then I guess there can't be much in being a celebrity after all."

Some might think that loving one's self would be one of the easiest things to accomplish. However, it is surprising how many people find self-worth to be a lifelong struggle. How people cope with their "undesirable" personality traits varies. Some tend to blame themselves, and others pretend they don't exist by compensating for the traits in some fashion. In the first case, fear and aggression may be the result, and in the second case, a false persona may be observed. We've all encountered individuals who appear to be "too nice," "too helpful," or "too sweet." In short, there are people who live in an "unreal" world—thinking that life is either unrealistically terrible or unrealistically wonderful.

The late Martin Luther King, Jr. said, "There is some good in the worst of us and some evil in the best of us. When we discover this, we are less prone to hate our enemies." Our "good" is characterized by generosity, loving kindness, and wisdom; our "evil" is characterized by greed, hate, and delusion.

When we accept that these traits are the underlying roots of our behavior, we can start looking at our own behaviors more realistically, not blaming ourselves for unwholesome behaviors and not praising ourselves for wholesome behaviors. We can learn to cultivate wholesome behaviors and suppress unwholesome behaviors.

The training necessary to cultivate these behaviors requires a great deal of maturity. Unfortunately, the wisdom gained by maturity is not connected with age.

The Buddhists teach that love for oneself requires a three-step process. The first step is recognition. For many, this may be the hardest, for it is not easy to see what goes on inside of oneself. Leading a "contemplative" life is the key. A contemplative life does not mean sitting in the corner all day humming a mantra and meditating. It means living life with what Buddha called the "exuberance of youth." If you have ever observed preschoolers at play, they tend to approach everything that is happening around them as a learning experience. They are a great reminder that we can approach each day with that same exuberance! They also can inspire us to view our shortcomings and everyone else's in a light-hearted manner. When we take ourselves too seriously, life ceases to be fun!

The second step is learning how to cultivate wholesome behaviors and suppress unwholesome behaviors, and learning not to condemn but to understand. After we recognize what is going on in ourselves, we can then accept and understand the behaviors of others.

The third step is change. There is nothing left but to look inside ourselves and to embrace change. Once we do, we can begin loving ourselves; then, loving others becomes possible, and we can enable them to love themselves too. The French writer, poet, and pioneering aviator, Antoine de Saint-Exupéry, wrote, "Perhaps love is the process of my leading you gently back to yourself. Not whom I want you to be, but to who you are."

Only when we love ourselves can we truly experience joy. The Egyptians believed that upon death, to enter heaven or continue their journey in the afterlife, they would be asked only two questions: "Did you *bring* joy?" and "Did you *find* joy?" Walt Disney said, "In bad times and in good, I have never lost my sense of zest for life." The result of Walt Disney's genius continues to bring joy to millions, and our guess is that he found joy in every minute here on earth.

## Parting Thoughts

In the next chapter, we introduce the Ottawa Way—a county government initiative that would have made Walt Disney proud!

---

### Our Featured Organization: A Personal Story from Bill

#### WHAT I LEARNED ABOUT LOVE FROM "MA," OWNER OF THE VILLAGE TOY CENTER, BENSENVILLE, ILLINOIS

Throughout this book, we have cited many business examples of love— from Walt Disney's "mutual respect and trust" to Four Seasons Hotels and Resorts and Ottawa County, Michigan's Golden Rule, followed by **TYRA** *Beauty*'s dedication to making a better life for her army of Beauty-tainers, and finally ACTS Retirement-Life Communities credo of "loving-kindness." But before I learned of any of these role models, I was immersed in the power of love at my mother's business—The Village Toy Center in Bensenville, Illinois.

My mother was the owner and operator of The Village Toy Center for 32 years. It seemed like I was always hearing from people how "lucky" I was to have a toy store as our family business. The store was on the Chicago commuter line, across the street from the train station and was open seven days a week. We opened at 5:30 a.m. and stayed open until 6:00 p.m. to fulfill our customers' desires for their daily newspapers, candy, magazines, and tobacco products.

From grade school all the way through college, I helped my mother (whom I called "Ma") in the store alongside my father, whose main job was as a machinist at a local factory. Every morning through grade school, I would help open the store, walk to school, and then return to help out after school until closing. In high school and college, it was my job to close the store on Saturday nights and open it on Sunday mornings.

Ma, however, tirelessly worked more than 12-hour days, but she was rarely too tired to prepare an evening meal for my father, my older brothers, and me. On Friday nights, we either had pizza at the store, or my father would take us out for a late dinner after the store closed. Sunday was a very special day when Ma prepared a feast fit for a king that would begin shortly after noon when the store closed and often not end until 2:00 p.m. With all of her responsibilities in life, I never once heard her complain.

Here are five things I learned from Ma regarding love:

1. **Reject no one.** Ma not only treated everyone with loving kindness, but her heart was always open to anyone in need. One day back in the mid-1960s, a young engineer from India named Bharat visited her store during his lunch hour. Sensing that he was a bit homesick for his native country and family, Ma invited him to come back the next day and join her for lunch. What began as a chance encounter resulted in a 40-year relationship in which my parents acted as Bharat's American mother and father, and when he later married, they also "adopted" his wife, Sheela; his son, Ketan; and his daughter, Niki. You may have heard the expression "We are brothers from different mothers." Bharat and I are "brothers from the same mother's heart."

2. **Have fun and make work a game.** Whenever there was a large task to be completed such as checking in and stocking hundreds of toys for the Christmas season, Ma would say something like "Let's see if we can complete 40 items this hour." Work was never a chore.

3. **Do your best, and be true to yourself.** Ma was not concerned about "winning." She was happy to put her heart into everything she did, and it was always her best effort. Her philosophy reminded me of the phenomenal De La Salle high school football team's 151-game winning streak under the coaching of Bob Ladouceur, played by Jim Caviezel in the 2014 movie, *When the Game Stands Tall*. Each week, Coach Ladouceur required all players to make one weight lifting goal, one practice goal, and one game goal. Each player gave his goals to a fellow teammate who was responsible for determining whether the goals were fulfilled. The sharing of these goals and caring about one another's achievements were keys to the

team's performance. When asked the secret to his success, Coach Ladouceur stated that it revolved around the most basic of human emotions—love.

4. **Help others.** Despite Ma's long workdays, she was always ready to give back to her community. Whether she was organizing fundraisers for leukemia research or spending countless hours at the International Lioness organization, she was always helping others.

5. **Strive for perfection.** It was a challenge growing up in a small community where everybody knew my mother and hailed her as a model of "perfection" in so many ways. I couldn't get away with even the slightest misbehavior because Ma would always find out the truth. My mother taught me that perfection is something you may never achieve, but you should never give up trying. She encouraged me to speak with confidence but never be condescending. And when choosing between "right" or "kind," she would say, "pick kind because it is the right thing to do."

It took me a long time to realize how valuable those early lessons in life really were. For quite a few years, I often lamented that our family business wasn't as financially successful as it could have been. But I've come to realize that true success transcends profitability, titles, or the number of possessions one has accumulated over a lifetime.

Twenty years before her death, Ma sold The Village Toy Center. After she passed way, there was a constant stream of family, friends, and former customers (some of whom had not seen her in 20 years) who came to pay their respects during her visitation. On the cold and damp January day of the funeral, there was standing room only in the church, and the outpouring of love was overwhelming.

Shortly after Ma's death, I rediscovered a poem by Ralph Waldo Emerson entitled "What Is Success?" It reads as follows:

*To laugh often and much.*
*To win the respect of intelligent people and the affection of children.*
*To earn the appreciation of honest critics and endure the betrayal of false friends.*
*To find the best in others.*

*To leave the world a bit better, whether by a healthy child, a
garden patch, or redeemed social condition.*
*To know that even one life breathed easier because you lived;
this is to have succeeded.*

By Emerson's definition, Ma was a phenomenal success. In one of
Leo Buscaglia's final interviews before his death in 1998, he stated, "The
essence of love is getting out of oneself and into others. When we care less
about our feelings . . . and begin to concern ourselves with the feelings,
rights, happiness, and security of others, we will have found the true
power of love." Leo's passionate words are reminiscent of Niki Shah's
2015 Christmas tribute to my mother: "I woke up this morning thinking
about Grandma Capodagli. We used to spend every Christmas day with
her. She was my grandmother not by blood, but by love. She showed me
the meaning of family and the true meaning of Christmas and the holiday
season. Grandma knew what it was to help others that are not as fortunate
as us. The unconditional love she showed was a representation of her open
heart. I am better and so extremely lucky for having had her in my life."

Let Walt Disney, Tyra Banks, George Zimmer, Ma, and all of our
great featured leaders inspire you to create a customer-centric culture by
sprinkling the real pixie dust—love.

Do not question "love," just take 27 actions!

## Actions to Take

### Twenty-Seven Ways to Unleash
### Love in Your Organization

1. Live the Golden Rule. Think about all the times you
   received horrible customer service. What specific
   behaviors contributed to that experience? Next, think
   about all the times you received fabulous customer
   service. What specific behaviors contributed to that
   experience? If you commit to practicing the behaviors
   of your "fabulous" experiences and eliminating the
   behaviors of your "horrible" experiences, your customers
   are bound to feel the love!

2. Take care of YOU. Your first love affair begins with yourself! If you feel inadequate, unworthy, or victimized, you have no power to truly give love to another.

3. Remember Stephen Covey's Fifth Habit: "Seek first to understand, then to be understood."

4. Demonstrate love without conditions . . . the joy is in giving.

5. Take accountability; if you are having a lousy day, don't blame others.

6. Forgive and forget. Oh, yes, there's a song for this: "Let It Go!"

7. Be visible to your team members and customers. Do not hide in your office.

8. Share your hopes and dreams with your team members.

9. Trust your team members to use their best judgment to solve problems even when you disagree with their decisions.

10. "Plus" ideas, don't criticize. Provide feedback that is timely, specific, and in private. Focus on the positives in others, and never slide the "dig" into the compliment.

11. Say "please" and "thank you."

12. Send handwritten thank-you notes.

13. Practice transparency and candor with members of your entire organization. When people are left in the dark, they often fill in the "blanks" with negative interpretations of situations.

14. Conduct a weekly meeting during which all team members share their biggest learning experience of the week.

15. Buy donuts or cookies for your team for no reason (or fresh fruit for those who are more health conscious).

16. Throw a party for your team. Don't forget Valentine's Day!

17. Take your team out for an unexpected outing such as the latest Disney animated feature film.

18. Mentor new team members. Don't forget that the best teachers always want their students to excel.

19. Do everything possible to help a fellow coworker in need, especially those outside your department.

20. Do not pass up a chance to send unique holiday or celebratory cards to your team members and customers. Try to send a fun-filled card every month (recognizing Groundhog Day, "half" birthdays, or team members' anniversary dates with your organization are unexpected, but they can be fun and are often appreciated).

21. Keep legends alive. Our hopes and dreams elevate us with the possibility of tomorrow. Legends add an element of wonder to our lives and give us something to look up to and strive for. There is an old Indian saying, "When legends die, the dreams end; when dreams end, there is no more greatness."

22. Never pass up an opportunity to sincerely engage others: hellos and questions such as "May I help you?" and "How are you?" are the beginning of meaningful relationships.

23. Solve your customers' biggest and smallest problems, and they will love you forever. In other words, customers love problem solvers!

24. Find significance in your work. Ask yourself, "How am I impacting the lives of my customers and team members?"

25. Schedule "cultural appreciation" days. Choose a culture and celebrate with food, dress, music, and so on.

26. Never compromise your values. Remember the words of Roy Disney: "When values are clear, decisions are easy."

27. If you don't feel the love for your work, your product, your customers, and your team members, consider looking for other employment opportunities!

**Chapter Chats with Bill: http://capojac.com/disneyway/12/**

# Putting It Together

# Chapter 13

# Ottawa County, Michigan: Disney's Success Credo Transforms County Government

*The city of tomorrow ought to be a city that caters to the people as a service function.*

Walt Disney

Over the past three years, we have had the extraordinary privilege of assisting Al Vanderberg, Ottawa County Michigan Administrator, and his team transform their culture through a comprehensive adoption of *The Disney Way* principles. The Ottawa County employees named their new culture the Ottawa Way.

Al proclaimed, "The results have been nothing short of amazing as preconceived notions of limitations of the applicability of customer service to local government services have been shattered!" The real kudos go to Al and his esteemed leadership team that represents numerous distinctly different areas of county government and a supportive Board of Commissioners. And unlike some who make decisions weighted to short-term political benefit, the board dares to innovate and has made long-term investments in the organization. As Bill assured Al, "We may have provided you with a roadmap; however; you, your leadership team, and your Board of Commissioners did the heavy lifting of paving the way."

We have met plenty of people who wonder why a customer-centric culture is needed in any government entity. At least in the private sector, competitive forces provide an incentive to emulate outstanding customer service icons like Disney, Starbucks, or Four Seasons Hotels and Resorts. Surely, counties already have a monopoly on their services, many of which are regulatory in nature, and Ottawa County is no exception.

Given its assets, why should the county be concerned with customer service? Responding to this question, a county official noted that this specific county has earned its reputation largely due to the people who live, visit, and do business with it. As such, it owes great service to visitors, residents, and employees. Besides, it's just good business.

For example, when a new business locates within a region, the effect on employment is threefold. First, it has a direct impact on the jobs provided by the business itself. Second, it causes an indirect impact if the business buys production materials and services locally. Third, it creates an induced impact or multiplier effect from the flow of wages spent by new employees, which may provide new jobs in other businesses, and in turn, the spending of those wages.

The Michigan Multiplier 2013 (Montgomery Consulting, spring 2013) reported that Ottawa County's employment multiplier was 2.12. This meant that if a business located within the county and provided 100 new jobs, 212 additional jobs would be created to support the new business.

If a visiting executive who is searching for a new location within a county has a good customer service experience, it certainly may help his or her decision to locate there. A terrible customer service experience, however, could result in a search for another location.

We believe that when you read the following story of unwavering passion to accomplish Ottawa County's customer-centric transformation, and the testimonials that speak to the dramatic results, you will understand that indeed, government should and can establish a Disneyesque customer-centric culture. But without inspired and dedicated leadership, none of this would have been possible.

Within the broad scope of the implementation, the Ottawa Way represents undertakings that began prior to our involvement with the organization as well as those that are a direct result of *The Disney Way* experience in which the entire workforce participated.

## Make Everyone's Dreams Come True: Al Vanderberg Leads the Way

Ottawa County consists of 33 administrative departments, elected offices, courts, and agencies. The Board of Commissioners maintains total budget control, which weaves a supportive web throughout this fractured political and administrative power structure. As County Administrator, Al has budgetary control over all 33 departments, yet only 15 report directly to him.

Throughout Al's career, he has witnessed and studied examples of both poor and outstanding customer service experiences. Al related, "I realize that we did not have the customer service vision for the entire organization. We left it up to each of the 33 areas, and in many cases it was further left up to the individual employees regarding the level and quality of customer service."

Several years ago, Al read that Disney seeks to "startle and amaze" each Guest at least once or twice per visit. In government, those actions are uncommon and hence, the bar is set really low in terms of extending great customer service to the public. Al wondered, "What would it really take to 'startle and amaze' citizens and businesses in Ottawa County? What if every county employee shared the passion and vision for providing amazing, startling, and outstanding customer service to each person he or she assisted?"

After reading *The Disney Way*, Al called Bill to discuss our approach to working with his large and highly compartmentalized organization. As a first step, we formed a Steering Team that included Al and the heads of all 33 areas of the county. Their first task was to develop a shared customer service vision, story, and Codes of Conduct.

## You Better Believe It: Corporation Counsel Greg Rappleye Brings the County's Story to Life

As we previously mentioned, people tend to remember a story 22 times more than a series of facts and figures. An excerpt from the short version of the Ottawa County story is presented in Chapter 3; however, because of the complexity of the county functions, the Steering Team, which is made up of leaders from Ottawa County who directed the entire implementation, determined that a long version of the story would be beneficial. They were fortunate to have an award-winning poet and writer as one of their members, Greg Rappleye. Greg is Ottawa County's Corporation Counsel, and he also teaches creative writing at a local college.

Greg related, "Many of the employees in the county, working different shifts in different locations, do not know one another. It occurred to me that any story about Ottawa County ought to feature some of the diversity of our work experiences." And, residents oftentimes do not realize that local government is a full-time job. Greg continued, "I thought the story that I call *Daybook* [represents Ottawa County] should move through time, roughly a 24-hour day. Perhaps because we were in the middle of a difficult winter when we began planning *The Disney Way* training, the story occurs throughout the day and night of the fall snowstorm.

Most citizens of Ottawa County do not care about or even comprehend their county's complex organizational structure. They simply desire and expect access to services in the shortest amount of time at the least possible cost. *Daybook* is an excellent way for all employees to not only appreciate the complexity of the county but also embrace a single vision for providing outstanding customer service. At the end of this chapter is an Internet link to the *Ottawa County Daybook* story.

## Never a Customer, Always a Guest: Environmental Health Changes Its Tune

A recent case study published in *Food Control* focused on small and medium-sized food establishments, and it revealed that 83 percent of respondents (restaurant owners and others) demonstrated an "active" lack of trust in the inspectors and the regulations. Lisa Stefanovsky, Ottawa County Health Officer, confirmed this truth: "Historically, the food establishments within Ottawa County have demonstrated a lack of trust in inspectors and the regulations, and that distrust was clearly expressed in surveys that were conducted."

Ottawa County leaders instilled a systematic process to better understand the causes of the strained relationship between county officials and restaurant owners. They learned that Environmental Health leaders had communicated a set of expectations to staff and had positioned them as enforcers of the "code." Consequently, the attitudes of those staff members were commensurate with a regimented and impersonal environment.

Initial steps for improvement included changes to staffing within Environmental Health; an active shift toward positive customer interactions; a focus on building a foundation of trust; and increased efforts to collect data on perceptions of restaurant owners and managers. Lisa said, "*The Disney Way* training provided a foundation of cultural values that Ottawa County was building upon as an organization and instilled confidence in staff that they would be supported in their efforts to change the practices within Environmental Health."

Not only does a fear-based climate impede the development of trust bonds between internal team members but it also can have a negative effect on one's customer base. Several food establishment representatives provided testimonials regarding the positive "new" culture that has been established in recent years. These are some of the things they had to say:

- "Overall, Ottawa County has come a long way from the past fear that was instilled in people when they would hear, 'The Health Department is here.'"
- "Our health inspections have gone from fear and terror to pleasant anticipation."
- "I no longer worry about their coming to visit me. And when something isn't up to code, they are very helpful and don't treat me or my staff poorly."
- "I have lost the scary, breathtaking, pulse-racing anxiety that had previously accompanied our inspections."

In the years leading up to the culture change, high-risk violation rates for each of the food establishments averaged 3.54 per year. In the years subsequent to the program interventions, the rates declined to the mid 2s, a 22 percent reduction in the number of high-risk violations cited in Ottawa County.

Lisa concluded, "This data justifies the time and expense of the customer service–related initiatives at Ottawa County. It highlights the importance of developing collaborative relationships built on mutual respect to improve trust in the regulated community. Open lines of communication are imperative to share information, and feelings of distrust can greatly impair efforts to educate. Finally, it demonstrates that re-aligning program goals to achieve customer service improvements can have a positive impact on public health."

Walt Disney said, "Get a good idea and stay with it. Dog it, and work at it until it's done right." Lisa and her staff not only believe in the "ideas" that created Disney's legendary service standards but they have also worked at making them "right" for the Ottawa County Health Department.

## All for One, and One for All: Sheriffs Create a Foundation of Mutual Respect

A positive perception of law enforcement is critical to the well-being of any community. As Ottawa County Sheriff Gary Rosema so eloquently stated, "In this day and age, public perception of customer service, at least from our perspective in law enforcement, is really important. As we know, there are many cases right now in which the public perceives cops as not being the best thing for communities. So any time that we can show them that we are part of the community, and that we are providing a service that they understand and respect, is really important."

The success of modern-day law enforcement hinges on the ability to recruit, develop, and lead officers who not only understand their role as highly visible government authorities but also realize an equal responsibility to provide community service. Ottawa County Undersheriff Steve Kempker said, "I think customer service doesn't necessarily have to be something big that they bring to our attention that one of their staff did. . . . It is as much as somebody gave a person a ride to get a gallon of gas. . . . You need to figure out how you are going to help that person while you are there. I think we do a lot better job of that than we used to do." In the same vein, remember that Walt Disney told his security officers, "You are never to consider yourselves cops. You are here to help people."

A few years ago, Steve responded to the high-speed pursuit of a bank robber on a motorcycle. Steve blocked the street with his car, giving the robber a chance to end the pursuit. Steve related, "He was too busy looking behind him, and he hit my car. I thought he was dead. I got out of my car and walked up to him to see him throw his arms over his head and say, 'I give up, and I'm sorry.' I said to him, 'Look, you've screwed up, but right now your medical issues are more important to us.'" During this whole ordeal, the bank robber couldn't believe how well Steve and his officers were treating him. One of the officers turned to Steve and said, "It's the Ottawa Way."

Sheriff Gary shared his perspective: "There are a lot of good people who come through the 'back door' of the county jail. They get out, they go into the communities, become our neighbors and our friends, go to our churches, and have kids in the same school as your kids. So how they are treated in here becomes really important. I really do think our staff that has been through this training, *The Disney Way* process, has a lot better understanding of that." Gary, Steve, and the officers of the Ottawa County Sheriff's Department are making Disney-style customer service a very real aspect of their lives, each and every day.

## Share the Spotlight: Michigan State University Extension—An Enduring Partner Stays Strong by Hard Work and a Commitment to Excellence

Betty Blase, District Coordinator, Michigan State University (MSU) Extension, proudly stated, "The partnership between Ottawa County and MSU

Extension is one that has lasted for nearly a hundred years. In many ways, this partnership epitomizes *The Disney Way* principles of Dream, Believe, Dare, Do."

In 1914, Senator Hoke Smith of Georgia and Representative A. F. Lever of South Carolina created the Smith-Lever Act, taking vocational education from universities to the homes of those in remote rural areas. This act enabled land-grant universities to oversee the extension programs in every county across the nation.

Ottawa County and MSU Extension continue this long-standing partnership today, and they share responsibility for extension education and research programs in the community. MSU Extension is critical to the success of agriculture and tourism, two of the leading industries in Ottawa County that are directly related to the goals of the community. Betty stated, "MSU Extension helps people improve their lives through an educational process that applies knowledge to critical issues, needs, and opportunities. This partnership is kept strong through hard work and commitment to excellence by the Ottawa County Board of Commissioners, the County Administrator, and the MSU Extension educator staff and administration."

Walt Disney said, "No one can have a well-rounded education without some knowledge of what goes on in the physical world around us." The MSU Extension and Ottawa County partnership is an excellent long-term example of bringing the knowledge of the physical world to county residents.

## Dare to Dare: The Great Lakes Ag-Tech Business Incubator Facilitates Business Success

Developed by Ottawa County, the Great Lakes Ag-Tech Business Incubator (GLATBI) specializes in helping farmers and entrepreneurs turn their ag-tech machines, equipment, or software ideas and inventions into successful businesses. Both the incubator's operating model and client service delivery model are unique in the industry. Unlike most incubators, GLATBI does not own or operate a large physical building where clients rent cost-subsidized space. Operating in this fashion allows the incubator staff to focus solely on providing services that develop businesses rather than raising money to maintain and operate a building. The GLATBI invests all of its resources into staff who provide specialized assistance designed to propel start-up companies through their business hurdles.

Mark Knudsen, Director of the Ottawa County Planning and Performance Improvement Department, acknowledged, "The unique aspects of GLATBI developed by staff were opposed by some other economic development agencies, some management-level county employees, and a renowned consultant who created the Market Needs Assessment and Feasibility Study for the incubator. The consultant refused to back off from his recommendation that we build a 20,000-square-foot facility that would cost $2.5 million to construct while operating a traditional incubator that provided traditional services. Although there were times when elected officials questioned our endeavor due to this opposition, the county administration continued to support our efforts and provided the time needed to complete the project."

The funding for the incubator will be subsidized for three to four years, after which time it will be self-sufficient. This is also unique for incubators because typically, they are funded by large, annual appropriations or grants from government. In the GLATBI model, clients pledge 2 percent of their gross revenue to the incubator. An incubator may help an entrepreneur create a profitable business that may become self-sustaining, but if this does not happen, both may fail. It is a pure, performance-driven initiative for both the client and the incubator.

Mark stated, "We have been fortunate to have a culture of leaders who will listen to and consider new ideas, provide funding and staff to substantiate the concept, and patiently wait without interfering while an innovative initiative materializes."

Walt Disney said, "Courage is the main quality of leadership, in my opinion, no matter where it is exercised. Usually it implies some risk—especially new undertakings. Courage to initiate something and keep it going—pioneering an adventurous spirit to blaze new ways, often, in our land of opportunity." Ottawa County has demonstrated the courage to "blaze new ways in Ottawa County . . . a land of opportunity."

## Practice, Practice, Practice: Immersing All Employees in the Ottawa Way Culture

Training has always been an important part of the Ottawa County culture. Keith Van Beek, Deputy County Administrator, explained, "Human Resources has developed and continues to refine the Growth Opportunities in Learning and Development (GOLD) Training Program for Ottawa County employees." The department offers a comprehensive list of programs, from leadership certification to compliance training. A tuition reimbursement program was temporarily discontinued during the 2008 Great Recession, but it has since been reinstated. County Administrator Al Vanderberg recalled, "We implemented GOLD as the Great Recession struck. GOLD had the promise of reaching all employees, and indeed we have had more than 1,200 different employees receive some GOLD training, and more than 250 received the internal degree."

During 2013 and 2014, monthly three-day Customer-Centric Culture: *The Disney Way* training sessions were conducted for all employees of Ottawa County. Stephanie Roelofs, an administrative secretary who assisted with most of the training sessions, commented, "The training took our employees from a skeptical mood to one of contagious excitement of possibilities. We really can influence our own work culture, both imparting value to others while feeling the value within ourselves."

During the afternoon of the second day of the training sessions, participants experienced the Hot Seat, a panel of three Steering Team (department head) members. Participants are permitted to ask the panel any questions pertaining to the implementation efforts or organizational operations. The purpose of the Hot Seat is twofold: (1) Senior leaders are available to participants, and those leaders display candor and demonstrate support. (2) The importance of trust and open communication between management and the workforce is reinforced.

Al said, "We frequently were asked about what would happen if employees didn't buy in. Our response was that all employees would be given ample opportunity to get on board with this cultural improvement, but if they did not, they likely would be seeking other employment opportunities."

The Hot Seat experience was as important to the leaders as it was to the participants. The following are comments from some of the Hot Seat leaders who participated:

- Lisa Stefanovsky, Public Health Department Director, said, "A common leadership challenge is understanding the customer service barriers faced by staff. The Hot Seat provided a great opportunity to listen, gain understanding, and provide supportive feedback on how organizationally, we can work together toward improved customer service."
- Kevin Bowling, Circuit and Probate Court Administrator, related, "The Hot Seat was truly a test for leadership. Employees can smell a phony response immediately so the questions were as much a test

of the buy-in of the top leadership as it was a test of participants' comfort in asking top leadership truly difficult questions."

- Steve Kempker, Undersheriff, said, "You always go into the Hot Seat session with the nervous thought of, 'What am I going to be asked this time around?' . . . Being open and honest with the answers is important. It reflects upon us as management to show who we are."

Walt Disney communicated the following message to the very first orientation class for Disneyland Cast Members: "To make the dream of Disneyland come true took the combined talents of artisans, carpenters, engineers, scientists, and planners. The dream they built now becomes your heritage. It is you who will make Disneyland truly a Magic Kingdom and a happy place for the millions of Guests who will visit us now and in future years. In creating happiness for our Guests, I hope that you will find happiness in your work and in being an important part of Disneyland."

In true Disney style, Ottawa County employees have parlayed their own dream of a customer-centric culture into their Ottawa Way heritage.

## Make Your Elephant Fly—Plan: Facilities Take a Commonsense Approach

Rick VandeKerkhoff, Facilities Director, remarked, "I inherited great people, and when you ask people to follow you, they really want to know that you have a plan. That is our responsibility to have a plan in place, and people are counting on you to tell them where we are going and what we have to accomplish, and they will follow you."

In many facilities departments, the work order is "king." Everything is scheduled to the nanosecond. Typically, workers are given specific project instructions and a deadline for completion. As a result, these maintenance departments might be cost-effective and efficient, but they lack a focus on the customer. Rick's management philosophy is quite the opposite: "We hire good people. They all have common sense. I tell them, 'Here's what I want.' I want them to get the month's work orders. There might be 30 work orders there and you are smart enough to figure out what needs to be done first and what you can accomplish. Because the customer service extends to your employees too."

As a result of *The Disney Way* training, Rick's staff members have expressed to him that they feel enabled and trusted to use common sense to serve their internal customers. And a heightened level of engagement has contributed to the reduced number of calls from customers. Since Rick and his team have inspired trust, customers also feel free to request assistance from any maintenance staff member on a less formal basis, often during a chance meeting in their buildings. Rick affirmed, "They [staff] don't have to ask permission. If they can't fix it now, they know how to say, 'I can't do it today, but if you put a work order in, then I will get that reminder.' So we are also training our customers to submit work orders."

Walt Disney said, "Keep the place as clean as you can keep it. Keep it friendly and a fun place to be." What a fitting mantra for Rick and his Ottawa County Facilities Department!

## Capture the Magic with Storyboards: An Organizational Game-Changer

### A Champion Pulls It All Together

There's an old saying, "Behind every great man, there's a great woman." In Ottawa County Administrator Al Vanderberg's case (at least in his business life), she is Misty Cunningham, his administrative assistant whom he chose to be the champion of the Ottawa Way initiative.

On a side note, most leaders would not dream of diluting the amount of time their administrative assistants spend catering to their needs. But Al is in a category of "best," not "most," leaders. He realized that the Ottawa Way provided a timely and unparalleled growth opportunity for Misty. During the first two years of the initiative, Misty was "burning the candle at both ends." Her role was continuing to change and expand to match the growth in the department and to accommodate the responsibilities associated with managing the complexities of a customer-centric organization. Reflecting on the initiative, Misty admitted, "I wasn't sure if county employees would take this . . . and accept it, or how they would feel about it. But now you can see the culture shift. You can see people engage with one another. I'm not even sure that employees realize that it [the training] has done that. It has definitely changed the culture of Ottawa County."

Over the course of the initiative, 90 percent of Ottawa County's employees participated in the multi-day *The Disney Way* training during which they learned the storyboarding technique (see Chapter 10). Storyboarding was a tremendous way for all employees to share their customer service concerns or "barriers"; ideas to remove the barriers; and ideas for ensuring a successful implementation. The employees produced an amazing total of 480 storyboards!

Al stated, "I realized that we were about to delve deeply into what W. Edwards Deming described as the 80/20 principle, where most employees give their organization 20 percent of their full capacity and a major role of management is to motivate employees to enthusiastically give as much of the remaining 80 percent as possible. Employees were saying loudly and clearly [through storyboards] that accountability, encouragement, setting clear expectations, and basically, living the Golden Rule would be great areas for improvement."

Misty assisted in every single training session and recorded most of the storyboard data. Misty shared, "There was a lot of information captured from all the storyboards. What is amazing to me is the messages are very similar in all of them. Even though there are different people doing the storyboards in each session, what comes up is always the same. So it is easy to know what the county needs to work on."

Among Misty's new responsibilities is leading the Customer Service Team. Prior to the team's launch in September 2013, all county employees were invited to volunteer for the team. Misty said, "The application was simple. We asked what customer service meant to them and why they wanted to be on the team. The applications were from various departments and various levels. They did have to get supervisor approval because it does take time away from their work. It's a really great team with some great people. I am so happy to be part of it."

The Customer Service Team has gathered a wealth of information from the 480 storyboards. As an initial undertaking, the team tackled "recognition." They implemented a quarterly customer service award. Internal (fellow employees) or external (county residents) customers may nominate county employees for providing outstanding service. To date, the number of nominations has averaged 50 to 90 per quarter. At the end of this chapter, we have included several of the inspiring stories associated with customer service award winners.

Based on the storyboards, the Customer Service Team continues to address issues such as communication, management buy-in, resources, and tools.

One of the team's stellar accomplishments is the implementation of the Ambassador Program. Misty explained, "When new employees are hired, they can be assigned an Ambassador, and that Ambassador will meet them right at orientation or on their first day, show them around, tell them where the lunchroom is, where the workout facilities and locker room are . . . just be there to answer any questions that they have." The Ambassador Program was also designed to be a resource for all county employees. Misty continued, "If you just have a question about a specific department, you don't know whom to call. So we created a directory of Ambassadors with pictures, phone numbers, and email addresses. You can pick up your phone and call an Ambassador, and you know you will get a happy person on the other end of the line because they have signed up for this program." The county currently has 79 trained Ambassadors.

## Great Leaders Seek Feedback from Their Teams

In all of *The Disney Way* customer-centric implementations, we challenge top management to be open and transparent with all employees, and we also encourage them to solicit feedback from their direct reports on a regular basis.

As the top leader at Ottawa County, Al initiated the organization's Leadership Storyboard (see Chapter 10) process by scheduling a session with his own staff. Al greeted everyone and encouraged them to be open and honest, and then he left the room to ensure group anonymity. The staff members created and posted storyboard cards that defined "behaviors of an ideal leader"; then they each ranked the cards accordingly with priority color-coded Dots: "Most important," "Al does best," "Al could improve." Al confessed, "Although I had worked continuously in local government management for 30 years, and in the top role as County Administrator or City Manager for 20 years, I was still a little nervous as the group storyboarded me for over an hour. The results were not surprising, and they were valuable. Beyond the positives, my staff identified four areas of improvement that I took to heart and began working on right away."

Continuing in Al's footsteps, many of the other county leaders invited their teams to provide feedback through the Leadership Storyboard process. Two of the leaders gave the following feedback on the process.

*County Treasurer Brad Slagh:* "The Leadership Storyboard is definitely not for the faint of heart. It provides an honest assessment by your team members who see you day in and day out. If done well, you will come away with a valuable understanding of both your strengths and growth areas, and an understanding of the impact you are having on your workplace. Then your decision is, 'What am I going to do about what I now know?'"

*Thom Lattig, Assistant Juvenile Service Director:* "Leadership Storyboarding is instrumental in developing trust and truth between the leadership and employees."

Walt Disney said, "Of all our inventions for mass communication, pictures still speak the most universally understood language." Storyboarding creates a "word picture," or what we frequently refer to as an "idea landscape." Certainly, throughout their entire customer-centric initiative, Ottawa County has created a vast idea landscape through storyboarding!

## Give Details Top Billing: The Courts Simplify a Complicated System and Inspire Trust

In the words of Kevin Bowling, Circuit and Probate Court Administrator: "Michigan trial courts are all about justice, but we are also all about the details. We have to understand and pay attention to constitutional requirements, statutory requirements, court rules, administrative orders, case law. . . . Our mission is: To administer justice and restore wholeness in a manner that inspires public trust."

The Ottawa County courts have one of the most diverse customer bases in the county. Their customers include parents who seek support for their children; victims of crime who seek restitution; businesses that require payment for services or contract clarification; families or friends who seek guardians for loved ones who can no longer care for themselves; and criminals who seek assistance navigating a complicated court system. These customers, along with attorneys, law enforcement personnel, jurors, witnesses, and the general public deserve excellence in service as they navigate the intricacies of the judicial system.

Kevin remarked, "Training to see customers as guests; using storyboards for capturing our practices and ideas for improvement; considering ways to empower and reward employees; and aligning our strategic vision with execution—all have helped the courts improve and provide excellent service. Ultimately, *The Disney Way* can help the courts serve others in a manner that inspires public trust."

Walt Disney said, "We must reflect on how completely dependent we are upon one another in our social and commercial life. The more diversified our labors and interests have become in the modern world, the more surely we need to integrate our efforts to justify our individual selves and our civilization." Kevin and the Ottawa County courts have truly integrated their efforts to effectively serve their citizens in a manner that inspires trust, the Ottawa Way.

## The Real Pixie Dust—Love: A Christmas Surprise

In the depths of the Great Recession, Ottawa County had to eliminate all pay increases to make their budget balance. Al Vanderberg told us, "Everyone pulled together and did not fight the lack of increases." By year's end, they realized better than projected results and right before Christmas, they surprised everyone by paying out year-end increases. Al continued, "We didn't have to do that and no one would have known or faulted us if we didn't. We did this to be fair with resources and because we care about our employees and their families."

Walt Disney said, "Whatever we accomplish belongs to our entire group, a tribute to our combined effort." Like Walt, Al recognizes his team, even in hard times. That's really living The Golden Rule.

## Parting Thoughts

One of our favorite Walt Disney quotes is reminiscent of Al Vanderberg's approach to blazing the trail for the Ottawa Way: "Disneyland is like a piece of clay: If there is something I don't like, I'm not stuck with it. I can reshape and revamp it." That's exactly what Al did in Ottawa County. It's true that Al is a gifted leader, but transforming a government entity is perhaps the most challenging leadership endeavor we have ever witnessed. And yet, he accomplished his Dream. Let Al and his wonderfully talented and dedicated workforce inspire your own Dream of a customer-centric culture!

In the next chapter, we share a roadmap for your journey.

## Examples of Outstanding
## Customer Service Award Winners

Deputy Benjamin Terpstra from the Ottawa County Sheriff's Office works the security detail at the Ottawa County's 58th District Court building in Holland, Michigan. The security of judicial buildings is, not surprisingly, a complex job. It involves the operation of metal detectors, the explanation and execution of county security policies, and, of course, the eye-to-eye evaluation of the needs and threat potential of each visitor to the facility. In the increasingly violent world in which we live, court-house security is also a high-stress way to make a living.

A particular problem of working in a courthouse is the fact that so few customers of the courts are happy to walk through the courthouse doors, a problem Deputy Terpstra readily acknowledged: "Many of our visitors are facing criminal charges, others are victims, some have trials that day, some are there to resolve traffic tickets. Many don't understand precisely why they are there. My job [as Court Security Officer] is to treat everyone with empathy and concern. I try to make it so that the customers feel that I am interested in them—that I am paying attention to them and am con-cerned about their problems."

His coworkers at the 58th District Court recognize the importance of Deputy Terpstra's interpersonal skills, and they nominated him for the Ottawa County Customer Service Award. They wrote the following about him:

Ben always has a great attitude. He always has a smile on his face and is kind and courteous to all staff and customers. He goes above and beyond to make sure that the customers coming into the court know where they are going, and he makes them feel as comfortable as pos-sible in what could be a stressful situation. He is also quick to help out in any situation and handles everything in a calm, professional manner. Ben is fabulous to work with!

Also noted in the nominations were some very particular actions by Ben Terpstra—how, on a snowy, blustery day, he had helped a visitor to the court properly secure her toddler in a car seat. Also cited in the nomination were Ben's successful efforts to reunite a lost child with his parents during a major annual festival in downtown Holland.

"I really believe in the Golden Rule," Deputy Terpstra told us, "and I believe that the Golden Rule is at the heart of *The Disney Way*. Yes, we employees talk about doing things *The Disney Way* on a regular basis."

Mary Beth Rokisky is from the Ottawa County Clerk and Register of Deeds Office. The specific reason Mary Beth received the award was her careful and patient work with an employee of a title insurance company who had attempted (unsuccessfully) to record affidavits and other legal documents necessary to record a complex property transaction. The parties were waiting for the recorded documents. Time was of the essence, and Mary Beth worked with the customer to be certain that all of the technical filing requirements were met and that all of the necessary fees were paid, and she went out of her way to work with the Treasurer's Office to assure payment of the appropriate transfer taxes.

Mary Beth's coworkers in the Register of Deeds Office supported Mary Beth's nomination:

Mary Beth Rokisky treats each call in our office as if it is the first call of the day. She painstakingly answers each question with concern and clarity and often goes the extra mile. Customers enjoy her calming voice and professional attitude. When they come in with their document to record, they often hope to meet Mary Beth because they feel as though she became their friend over the phone. Mary Beth does not like to be in the limelight, but I just have to nominate her. She is a great asset to our department and to the face (and voice) of Ottawa County.

Mary Beth is the definition of helpfulness. She said, "When I am on the phone, I always try to put a smile on my face. I hope that it comes across to the customer." When asked if *The Disney Way* training had been useful to her, she replied, "Yes," and she said it with enthusiasm. "I was taught how to treat people by my mother—to treat everyone with kindness and respect. *The Disney Way* program was a great reminder of this, of how important it is to listen to the customer with empathy and to always be nice."

Kristen Caron is a relatively new employee of Ottawa County. She works as a Probation and Community Corrections Officer with the 58th District Court in Grand Haven, Michigan. Kristen received the Ottawa County Outstanding Customer Service Award as a result of her work with a probationer found to be in crisis during a middle-of-the-night sobriety check. The customer was despondent, and she said that she was thinking of harming herself. Once Kristen was assured that her customer did not present an immediate threat of harming herself, and after Kristen contacted her client's social worker, Kristen went out of her way to find an open store and purchased a journal and some pens. She then returned to the customer's home and recommended that her customer try journaling when she was feeling overwhelmed.

The person who nominated Kristen for her award wrote this:

When I heard about this from a coworker, I was extremely impressed with the level of care and thoughtfulness Kristen demonstrated in her actions. She went above and beyond by reaching out to the individual to ask what was wrong and then taking the additional steps well outside of what is required of her to prevent the individual from harm. Not only did Kristen prevent harmful behavior but she also provided a healthy outlet for the individual to express her feelings in similar future situations. Kristen has been involved in her current position for less than a year, and although she is relatively new to field supervision, she demonstrated concern and compassion that perfectly exemplifies the standards the 58th District Court hopes to set for customer service and community outreach.

Kristen had not yet participated in Ottawa County's *The Disney Way* training, but she was looking forward to doing so. She did say *The Disney Way* had become a continuing subject of discussion among her coworkers, and she was certain that the training had a positive impact upon her coworkers' relationships with their customers.

Kristen noted that because much of her work involved night-time sobriety checks, her customers were not always happy to see her. She said, "Under those circumstances, my attitude is so important. I try to be friendly, and I try to be supportive. But I have a job to do, and it isn't an easy one. Because my customers are often not talkative, I rely a lot upon body language to assess their condition. I want to be certain that my presence is not contributing unnecessarily to that stress. Treating the customer well doesn't simply make my job easier; it allows me to do a better job."

Deputy Rachel McDuffee of the Ottawa County Sheriff's Office was recommended for the Outstanding Customer Service Award by a woman to whom she had presented a traffic ticket!

The individual who nominated Rachel wrote this:

Deputy McDuffee stopped a vehicle for a vision obstruction (windows covered with snow). Deputy McDuffee scraped all the windows of the vehicle before letting the driver proceed. At the informal [court] hearing, the driver expressed her sincere gratitude to Deputy McDuffee for providing this service and complimented the Deputy for treating her with respect even in spite of giving her a citation.

Rachel is a graduate of *The Disney Way* training, and she is enthusiastic about its benefits. She told us, "The people I work most closely with are law enforcement officers, and there was some skepticism among the Deputies about the idea of *The Disney Way* training; a few Mickey Mouse jokes."

She found, however, that her fellow Deputies' attitudes began to change during the course of the training. She said, "*The Disney Way* is a different way for a law enforcement officer to think. Once my fellow Deputies and I became comfortable working together and problem solving, on the question of customer service, everyone became much more open to different approaches and different solutions."

She also liked the fact that the training gave her an opportunity to work with Ottawa County employees who were not involved in law enforcement. Rachel reflected, "It was great to problem solve with employees from the Clerk's Office or the Health Department and to learn about their perspectives on customer service. Some of our thoughts about the customer were very similar, others were quite different."

Rachel has been assigned by the Sheriff as a school resource officer for Zeeland Public Schools, a large school district located in south-central Ottawa County with a district small-town feel to it. She loves working with students. She said, "I know so many of these kids. I know their families, and I know their friends. As a school officer, not only do I need the different skills that are taught by *The Disney Way* training but I want to use those skills in helping to make my community a better place to live and grow."

Mark Bos is a Magistrate at the 58th District Court. Like many other Ottawa County employees, he performs his duties (traffic hearings, resolving small claims, authorizing warrant requests) at several locations around the county. A former police officer, Mark's dedication to good customer service is legendary.

His fellow employees (note the plural!) who nominated Mark wrote the following:

Mark provides excellent customer service by going "above and beyond" on a regular basis. His knowledge of law enforcement is very useful in his position here at the court, and he shares that knowledge willingly. He is so helpful to his coworkers, and his willingness to serve is much appreciated. He is thoughtful and patient and is a great example for Ottawa County.

Mark is always very willing to help out in any way. He takes the initiative to ask coworkers if he can help them. When asked to research an issue, he consistently responds very quickly. If an issue arises, he tries to find a solution. He does this with a positive attitude and a smile.

Mark is a true team player. He will go above and beyond to help each and every one of his coworkers in the court. If a question arises and he is unsure of the answer, he will follow through and get back to you. He is flexible to change his schedule to cover in areas where needed. He treats others with great respect and is a true example of how to live out the Golden Rule.

Mark was an early participant in *The Disney Way* training. He said, "My reaction to *The Disney Way* training was that it conveyed a clear and concise message using very practical applications that we can use every day."

**Chapter Chats with Bill: http://capojac.com/disneyway/13/**

**Ottawa County Daybook Story:**
**http://capojac.com/disneyway/13story/**

# Chapter 14

# Producing a Customer-Centric Culture: An Implementation Strategy

*The way to get started is to quit talking and begin doing.*

Walt Disney

Over the course of our consulting careers, we have worked in a cross-section of industries, both nationally and internationally, with differing internal structures as well as varying numbers of locations and workforce populations. In the majority of these cases, the organizational leaders understood that establishing and sustaining a customer-centric culture required a long-term commitment and that every phase of the process must be well planned and well executed.

What is disturbing, however, is the number of leaders we meet who are on a mission to develop new "policies" and "procedures," not to produce a customer-centric culture. Some fly off to a management retreat location where they create a list of objectives to be executed by their frontline supervisors. While their intentions may be understandable, an unintended consequence is that supervisors often internalize management's mandates as "I am responsible for fixing the problem." Frontline supervisors are also the first to witness decreases in employee morale, customer service, and market share.

After several months of unacceptable results, sometimes under a useless umbrella term or slogan, organizations resort to hiring consultants to evaluate their futile efforts. Through the years, we have evaluated a variety of such unsuccessful attempts at "change," a few of which we believe were for the sake of "change" alone. We have listened to countless leaders explain that they were hoping to improve customer service but that "it isn't working." Recently, the most prevalent excuses we have heard are these: "We can't afford to pay for 'good people,'" and "This generation doesn't have the same work ethic as we do."

Think about some of the most recognizable service providers in the United States. Of course, Disney is number one in our lives, but there is also a string of others including Starbucks, Zappos, and Nordstrom. They *all* rely on entry-level, low- or minimum-wage earners to deliver their stellar service. What sets these outstanding companies apart from the rest is that they are *totally* committed to establishing and sustaining customer-centric cultures.

Now you may be thinking, "What company is *not* committed to providing great customer service?" While we can't imagine any leaders or business owners *claiming* they aren't committed to their customers, but are they *really*?

Consider the definition of *commitment*: "being bound intellectually and emotionally to a course of action." It is easy to commit to providing legendary customer service *intellectually*, but committing oneself *emotionally* is difficult and requires hard work. While many organizations experience short-term results, true cultural transformation may take several years. There is no instant pudding!

## Factors to Consider Before Embarking Upon a Journey to Produce a Customer-Centric Culture

1. **Readiness of the organization.** The organization must be ready and capable of accepting a new set of values. If there is upheaval in the organization due to mergers or acquisitions, major product changes, significant stock devaluations, pending bankruptcy, or other serious issues, the time may not be right to begin a cultural transformation.

2. **Steering Team.** Leadership from all areas of the organization should be represented on the Steering Team. They will be responsible for reinforcing the new values and implementation efforts at every opportunity.

3. **Customer-Centric Culture Champion.** One staff member should be the go-to person who will be in charge of managing the various phases and details of the implementation effort. This can be an employee at any level of the organization and someone who exhibits great facilitation and organizational skills.

4. **Training.** Top leaders must commit to immersing each and every employee in a multi-day customer-centric culture experience.

5. **Resources.** The funding and employee time commitment needed for the implementation effort must be available.

6. **Communication.** A formal communication plan must be drafted to reinforce the customer-centric cultural implementation.

Once these six requirements are in place, an implementation for establishing a customer-centric culture can begin.

## Planning: The Steering Team

The first step of the journey is the Steering Team Workshop. The participants will be immersed in Creating a Customer-Centric Culture: *The Disney Way*, as shown in the model (Figure 14-1). The model depicts the organization's principles of Dream ( may incorporate a vision, mission, and/or story) and Believe (values). These are the inputs, or drivers, to produce the culture. The Dare principle represents the leap of faith required for employees to embrace the organization's story and values. The Do principle brings the Dream to reality. Now let's look at the outputs of show, cast, and review. Each and every department and/or team of an organization will produce their own unique show and train their cast or employees to perform their roles or responsibilities accordingly. Last, a review process is established to track and measure results.

The Steering Team Workshop actions include the following:

- Develop preliminary Dream (vision, mission, and/or story).*
- Develop preliminary values.
- Develop preliminary Codes of Conduct.
- Storyboard potential barriers and potential solutions to the implementation.
- Plan roadmap for implementation.

*Tip: Remember in Chapter 3, we explained that "a visionary story is for 'Main Street'" and "a mission or vision statement is for 'Wall Street.'" Every culture is different, and you must define the Dream in your own way!

**Figure 14-1.** Customer-Centric Culture Model

## Preparation (Frontline Leadership Buy-In)

The next step in the journey is the multi-day Frontline Leadership Workshop. All frontline leaders should attend this workshop.

**Tip:** Organizations with greater than 100 managers may require several three-day workshop experiences.

Frontline Leadership Workshop actions include the following:

● Finalize Dream.
● Finalize values.
● Finalize Codes of Conduct.
● Storyboard potential barriers and potential solutions to the barriers.
● Understand the roadmap for implementation.
● Embrace the Dream, Believe, Dare, Do principles.

## Realization (Employee Buy-In)

Upon completion of the Frontline Leadership Workshop, a multi-day Customer-Centric Culture: *The Disney Way* experience for all employees begins.

You may be wondering, "Why does this experience require a commitment of several days? Couldn't the principles required for any new culture be communicated in less than a day?" If it were that simple, countless organizations would be as magical as Disney! Years ago, we invited two University of Illinois organizational development professors to attend and evaluate the customary three-day experience. We had tried several different training agendas previously such as one day a week over three weeks and several half-day sessions. But we discovered that those formats were not nearly as effective as the three-day format.

We asked the professors for a rationale as to why the three-consecutive-day format was so successful. They told us that on day one of the training, employees arrive with their own set of values that has been ingrained in them over time. During the workshop, the employees will be learning, and invited to embrace, a new set of values. Through a series of experiential exercises, discussions, and presentations, they begin to realize that some of their old values will no longer be applicable in the new culture. For most, a multi-day process allows time for old values to be challenged and new ones to take root.

The Customer-Centric Culture: *The Disney Way* Experience actions include the following:

- Storyboard potential barriers and potential solutions to the barriers.
- Embrace the Dream, Believe, Dare, Do principles.

## Top Management Hot Seat

During the afternoon of the second day of the Customer-Centric Culture: *The Disney Way* Experience, the Hot Seat occurs (See Chapter 13, Ottawa County Example). Two or three of the Steering Team members or department heads make up the Hot Seat panel. Participants are invited to ask the panel any questions pertaining to the implementation efforts or organizational operations.

The purpose of the Hot Seat is twofold:

1. Senior leaders are available, and they display candor and demonstrate support.
2. The importance of trust and open communications between management and the workforce is reinforced.

## Storyboard Treasure Trove

Something extraordinarily beneficial results from the Customer-Centric Culture: *The Disney Way* Experience: storyboarding. Storyboarding is an activity that involves everyone in the organization, and it provides a wealth of information about what employees think. The completed storyboard "landscape" often includes feedback that pertains to management and leadership as well as suggestions for improvements in the culture. Remember to refer back to Chapter 10 for more detail on the types of storyboarding, their applications, and their processes.

## Support: The Brain Trust Follow-up

A successful customer-centric culture is dependent upon a true commitment from each frontline supervisor. In many organizations, the frontline supervisor is the conduit between the employees and middle management. They are the "first responders" to customer complaints, and they perform the roles of trainer, mentor, disciplinarian, and cheerleader for their team members. They also become the "implementer" of company policy and the "eyes" and "ears" of upper management.

For years, we have held the belief that frontline supervisors have the toughest role within an organization. They are constantly trying to solve problems while balancing the needs of multiple stakeholders. For example, solving a customer complaint about poor service may upset an employee who feels unjustly blamed; and solving an employee overtime issue might violate a management policy to limit overtime costs.

The Brain Trust is a way to help frontline supervisors cope with a variety of leadership issues. Ed Catmull, Co-founder of Pixar Animation Studios and President of Walt Disney and Pixar Animation Studios, said, "A hallmark of a healthy creative culture is that its people feel free to share ideas." One of the best ways to produce this type of environment is by establishing a Brain Trust.

A Brain Trust is a group of people who assist, advise, and support one another, but they do not have authority to make decisions for one another's teams or departments. A key benefit of the process is the opportunity for members to help one another become more effective leaders.

Typically, a Brain Trust is composed of 15 to 20 leaders and one facilitator. Within the structure, each leader completes a self-assessment Customer-Centric Culture Implementation Questionnaire by rating their teams in the following categories:

- Constancy of purpose and improvements in the customer service process
- Training in Codes of Conduct, customer service values, and quality
- Elements of the show or customer experience
- Elimination of fear
- Breakdown of barriers between departments
- Removal of barriers to pride of workmanship
- Elimination of numerical quotas

Brain Trust members should meet multiple times per year to discuss the progress of the implementation, barriers that need to be removed, and corresponding potential solutions. The Brain Trust process may be established for leaders at all levels of an organization.

## Customer-Centric Improvement Team

A cross-functional Customer-Centric Improvement Team consists of members from most departments and is led by the Customer-Centric Culture Champion.

The Customer-Centric Improvement Team actions may include the following:

- Evaluate, provide, and schedule ongoing and future training for the entire culture.
- Assess the Customer-Centric Culture: *The Disney Way* Experience storyboards and sponsor improvement efforts.
- Promote cross-functional Process Evaluation Teams.
- Evaluate customer service best practices.
- Establish and monitor a multi-day new employee orientation process.

## Implementation Checklist

### Vision and Values

1. Complete preliminary Dream and values.
2. Complete preliminary Codes of Conduct.
3. Review and finalize the Dream, values, and Codes of Conduct with management team.
4. Prepare a Communications Plan that includes the Dream, values, and Codes of Conduct for all stakeholders.

5. Reinforce the Dream and values on a regular basis.

6. Make customer-centric culture implementation a strategic line item.

## Show

Create a "show business" mentality.

Identify key products and/or services, and produce your own show:

### Story

- What mood are you setting for your customers and employees?
- How do you engage your customers from their first Moments of Truth?

### Setting

- Does your setting positively contribute to the mood of your story?
- Examine the setting through the eyes of your customers and employees.

**Tip:** Remember that the setting includes your office, showroom, parking lot, warehouse, website, and service vehicles.

### Roles

- Are team members trained in their roles?
- Do they know how their roles relate to the entire show?
- Do they know how they interact or complement other roles in the show?

### Backstage

- Is the infrastructure in place to ensure a good show?
- Challenge your backstage processes in terms of your customers' ease in conducting business with you.

## Cast

1. Hire people who match your culture.

2. Require multiple interviews in addition to human resources screening.

3. Consider using personality instruments such as the Myers-Briggs Type Indicator to promote better communication and understanding between individuals and teams.

4. Plan for all employees to attend the three-day Customer-Centric Culture: *The Disney Way* Experience.
5. Build a multi-day orientation process focusing on the company's Dream, values, and culture.
6. Create a new employee mentoring or onboarding process.
7. Replace traditional performance appraisals with development plans.
8. Hire people who demonstrate a desire to work with fellow team members to design solutions to problems. Desirable traits of all new hires (inspired by Pixar) include the following:
   - **Depth.** Mastery of their expertise
   - **Breadth.** Insights from many different perspectives
   - **Communications.** Verbal, written, and most importantly, listening skills
   - **Collaboration.** Working together to accomplish a common goal
9. Create, support, and mentor the Brain Trust process.
10. Create, support, and mentor cross-functional improvement teams.

## Reviews

1. Identify key products and services.
2. Conduct Customer Feedback Storyboard sessions.
3. Establish measurements for items important to the customer or areas in which the organization needs to improve.
4. Once a year, conduct organization-wide Barriers Storyboards.

● ● ●

As we explained earlier, large-scale cultural change initiatives are often developed by a few top leaders in a retreat setting. Many of them fail to realize that if they expect employees to embrace a new culture, they must engage people at *all* levels of the organization too. In the Dream section of this book (Part 1), we described the power of an organization's story. Similarly, management must also be able to communicate a compelling story that can both explain the need for a culture change and motivate employees to adopt new values and behaviors.

It is little wonder why so many cultural initiatives fail. Many show a lack of passion, lack of understanding of what it takes to make serious improvements in customer service, and most of all, lack of commitment to the long term. Becoming customer centric is not an activity to be "checked off" during annual strategic planning sessions or meaningless performance review sessions. Instead, top management must drive an organization-wide customer-centric cultural initiative, while also inspiring their frontline leaders to take ownership in its development and results.

**Chapter Chats with Bill: http://capojac.com/disneyway/14/**

# Epilogue

## The Magic Continues

*After 40 some odd years in the business, my greatest reward, I
think, is that I've been able to build this wonderful organization, . . .
also to have the public appreciate and accept what I've done all
these years—that is a great reward.*

Walt Disney

From a young boy's doodling to a worldwide empire with a host of
magical characters that are instantly recognizable by both children
and adults—this is The Walt Disney Company's legend and legacy.

Would Walt recognize his brainchild as it is today? Of course, since
Walt's time, the physical plant has changed dramatically. In 2001, his
beloved Disneyland expanded to include California Adventure, and the
Company continues to revamp the Park again and again. Walt Disney
World, which hadn't yet opened at the time of Walt's death, is now composed of four separate parks. Furthermore, Disneyland Paris, Walt Disney
Studios Park, Tokyo Disneyland, Tokyo DisneySea, Hong Kong Disneyland, and the newest park, Disneyland Shanghai illustrate the Company's
international reach. Last, at the time of this writing, Disney Cruise Line,
Disney Vacation Club, ABC, and Broadway stage shows exemplify the
variety of business activities that make up The Walt Disney Company.

Yet chances are that Walt would feel right at home because the culture
and traditions he established—his dreams, his beliefs, his goals, and his style of
managing the business—provided the direction that makes The Walt Disney

Company one of the most admired companies in the world. The "good show" mentality, which dictates pulling out all the stops to exceed Guests' expectations and which demands superior performance from everyone, holds as much sway now as it did when Walt Disney first decreed it.

The fact that The Walt Disney Company manages continually to top itself and delight the world with its magic year after year, decade after decade, is a tribute to its leadership, both past and present. Part of Walt Disney's greatness was that he laid down a solid foundation of beliefs and values, including a standard of performance excellence and a mechanism (Disney University) for inculcating his Cast Members with these values.

We believe that one of the greatest gifts from CEO and Chairman Bob Iger to the Company is that he recognizes the value of Walt's legacy, and he has fearlessly protected the traditions that Walt and Roy instituted in the 1920s.

## Committed to Beliefs

The spectacle, the excitement, the breadth of product—all of these things contribute to the legend. Yet if there is one thing that keeps people coming back, it is the consistency of the experience. The Walt Disney Company is the master at creating controlled environments that never disappoint. Because the Company goes to great lengths to communicate its beliefs and traditions to every Cast Member, the Disney product offers people a comforting familiarity that is hard to duplicate in today's fast-paced world. That's not to say that there are no surprises. Instead, it's merely that all the surprises are on the upside.

Disney's insistence that customers be treated like Guests continues to be of paramount importance in providing that always-positive, expectation-exceeding experience. Thus a visitor to any of the Theme Parks will find that a question is answered as pleasantly today as it would have been in the Disneyland of the 1950s and 1960s. Cast Members are never too busy to stop and chat with Guests; crowd control is performed with a smile; and lost children are pampered with small pleasures. The human touch is still very much in evidence.

Yet without a corresponding belief in and commitment to Cast Members, the Guest philosophy would soon flounder. The two go together, as the song says, like a horse and carriage, and you can't have one without the other.

Maintaining the Company's focus amid enormous growth (the number of Cast Members has more than tripled since 1984) requires that the Company be ever more vigilant about recognizing the significant role that each Cast Member plays, and then emphasizing that all the pieces are needed to ensure the success of the entire team. By making Cast Members feel that their input makes a difference, the Company inspires further contributions.

# The History of Leadership at the Walt Disney Company

## The Walt and Roy Years: 1923 to 1966

This 40-year span saw the likes of Oswald the Rabbit, Mickey Mouse, Minnie Mouse, Donald Duck, Goofy, and Pluto. Walt and Roy reinvented the cartoon industry, created a new art form (animated feature films), and changed the look and experience of amusement parks forever. Interestingly, even though Walt was the creative leader, he never was an official officer of the Company. In fact, he attended board meetings only when Roy insisted!

## The Lonely Years for Roy: 1966 to 1971

Roy was in the midst of planning his retirement when Walt suddenly became ill with lung cancer and subsequently died in December 1966. Then, to honor his brother's final dream to complete Disney World (the "Florida Project," as it was known prior to Walt's death), Roy postponed his retirement and officially changed the name of the Park to Walt Disney World. Two months after the opening of Walt Disney World in 1971, Roy died of a cerebral hemorrhage.

## The "What Would Walt Do?" Years: 1971 to 1984

During this period, the Disney organization went through several CEOs: Donn Tatum, Card Walker, and Raymond Watson. None of them are credited with taking creative risks as Walt would have done. Walt's "dreams" and "values" still ruled, but everyone lost the ability to Dare or to take risks to make new dreams come true. Despite minor successes, the Company was unable to compete with other studios. In 1984, American cartoonist and illustrator Saul Steinberg launched a hostile takeover bid for The Walt Disney Company.

## The Eisner and Wells Years: 1984 to 1994

To fight off the hostile takeover and reinstill the Dare principle, Sid Bass and Roy E. Disney (Walt's brother Roy O.'s son) hired Michael Eisner as the CEO and Chairman and Frank Wells as President. For 10 years, Michael and Frank breathed new life into the "sleeping giant" with such blockbuster hits as *The Little Mermaid, Beauty and the Beast*, and *The Lion King*. Michael and Frank functioned well as a team, much the same as Walt and his big brother Roy had done for decades. Michael, like Walt, was the creative genius, and Frank, like Roy, was the business genius.

Michael and Frank brought risk taking back to the Disney organization, a piece of Walt's success credo that had been missing for many years prior to their arrival. Sadly, on Easter Sunday in 1994, Frank Wells was tragically killed in a helicopter crash. The partnership that was responsible for increasing Disney's stock by 1,400 percent (the S&P 500 had increased 184 percent during the same period) had ended.

## The Dark Eisner Years: 1994 to 2005

For reasons that perhaps only Michael Eisner knows for sure, he lost sight of many of the values that Walt had spread throughout his organization—quality, creativity, long-term goals, and mutual respect and trust. During this period, the Company's stock performed only a little better than the S&P 500, 220 versus 153 percent, respectively. Once again, Walt's nephew, Roy E., stepped in to "save the day." He resigned his board position as the Company's Vice Chairman and accused Eisner of turning The Walt Disney Company into a "rapacious, soul-less company."

Roy began a "Save Disney" campaign to remove Eisner. At the March 2004 annual stockholders meeting, 43 percent of the Company's stockholders withheld their vote to reelect Eisner to the board of directors. He was not removed from the board, but he was replaced as Chairman. In March 2005, one year before his contract expired, Michael announced he would step down as CEO.

## Bringing Back the Magic in the Iger Years: 2005 to the Present

On July 8, 2005, Roy E. Disney returned to the board of directors of The Walt Disney Company. On October 1 of that year, Bob Iger replaced Michael Eisner as the CEO.

Bob is known to be quite a "shopper." Just a few short months after taking the reins as CEO, he purchased Pixar in January 2006. In 2009, he purchased Marvel, and in 2012 he bought Lucasfilm. The result: $15 billion spent on acquisitions that would strengthen the Disney brand. Priceless! Most importantly, Bob brought values and beliefs back to the Disney organization, critical elements in Walt's success credo.

Bob is a big-picture executive who believes the best decisions are made at the lowest possible levels of the organization. The culmination of Bob's team-oriented philosophy is the 2013 blockbuster cinematic hit *Frozen*—the highest-grossing animated feature film of all time. Prior to Bob's leadership, many of the decisions for animated feature films were made at the executive level. After purchasing Pixar, Bob realized that the best decisions regarding a film should be made by the people making the film, not the executives.

With the help of Ed Catmull (Co-founder of Pixar Animation Studios and current President of Walt Disney and Pixar Animation Studios) and John Lasseter (current Chief Creative Officer of Pixar, Walt Disney Animation Studios, and DisneyToon Studios), Bob began to produce a supportive and collaborative culture, not only in Disney's Animation Studios but throughout the organization. Bob has not only brought back the magic to the Company but he has also protected its founder's legacy. Sadly, during Bob's tenure, Roy E. Disney—the man who actually saved the Company twice by bringing in new leadership—passed away.

## In Tune with the Nation

The Walt Disney Company thrives on the business of making magic. Success of the magnitude the Company has achieved always brings out the critics and the fearmongers, those who cry that the Company is too powerful and wields too much influence in our society. But investors don't share the angst; they have driven the price of the Company's stock to ever-higher levels, and its stock continues to substantially beat the S&P 500 performance. The investors sense that The Walt Disney Company has its finger firmly on the pulse of the nation—indeed, the world.

There may be some disagreement as to whether the public's blood is pumping with longing for a return to the old-fashioned values of family, hard work, and excellence that Disney symbolizes, or whether a public preference for escapism is at the heart of Disney's popularity. (No one, by the way, disputes that the escapes the Company constructs are anything short of magnificent.) In any event, the crowds that flock to virtually every venue would seem to bear out the assessment that the Company surely has the Midas touch, whatever its source.

Walt Disney's legacy, then, flourishes at the astonishing institution called The Walt Disney Company. Like our nation, it is a restless enterprise, always seeking new and better ways to entertain its audiences, to put on the good show.

What's more, every dream continues to be achieved with a management style that remains true to Disney's original vision: a firm belief in core values backed up by hard work from a well-trained and dedicated team that relentlessly strives for perfection. The Company today is a vital, living monument to the enduring power of *Walt's Way*.

We have examined the practices that make up the Disney management style in separate chapters for the sake of our book's organization, but it is their integration and interplay that work to foster change. As you envision their implementation in your organization, think in terms of a holistic integration, and imagine the benefits to be derived. For example, giving employees a chance to dream and to express their creativity not only reinforces their value as people but also inspires them to bring forth innovative ideas from which the organization can draw. By the same token, a firm set of cultural beliefs not only ensures consistency in operations but also encourages all parties (coworkers, partners, suppliers) to work cooperatively to further those beliefs.

Unshakable convictions, in turn, nourish the self-assurance and confidence in one's instincts that are needed to overcome a fear of risk taking. Daring to take risks encourages still further creativity and maintains the vibrancy of an organization. It creates a sense of fun and adventure that motivates individuals and teams to reach higher and work harder. And in the end, the factors that make it possible to follow through and turn the dreams into reality—that is, training, planning, communicating, and attention to detail—all double back to promote more creativity, more concern for customers, and more commitment to teamwork.

We see the cycle as one that constantly reinforces itself, and we believe that by incorporating the basic elements of the Disney success credo, every organization can lift itself out of the ranks of the ordinary.

We believe that the real pixie dust is love—love for your fellow team members, your customers, your product, and for yourself. Great leaders love their employees and inspire them to embrace heartfelt values and codes of conduct, not policies and rules. Walt led with his heart, and he loved his Cast Members. And he was loved in return.

After a long day of making dreams come true, Walt would often retire to his private apartment above the Firehouse at Disneyland, a retreat that he enjoyed by himself and sometimes with his family. The first Disneyland Cast Member to arrive each morning would always look to see if the light was on in the apartment and if so, would pass the word out that Walt was on the property. On the morning of December 16, 1966, the day after Walt's passing, a Cast Member went into the apartment and turned on the light. To this day, the light continues to shine . . . a loving reminder that one man's dream made a difference in the lives of so many.

Don't ever let your light go out. Keep Dreaming, keep Believing, keep Daring, and keep Doing!

---

**Chapter Chats with Bill:** http://capojac.com/disneyway/epilogue/

# Acknowledgments

A heartfelt thank you to Mary Glenn, our former Executive Editor at McGraw-Hill, who asked us to write the third edition of *The Disney Way*. After working with Mary on five book projects, we were sad to see her leave McGraw-Hill; however, we are grateful that she championed our dream to continue sharing examples of leaders and their teams who are masterfully applying *The Disney Way* principles in their organizations. We wish to thank Donya Dickerson, our new Editorial Director, and Cheryl Ringer, our Associate Editor, who worked tirelessly to help us navigate through all of the details to bring this book to life!

A warm thank you to Charlie Wissig, our friend and renowned artist, who designed the book cover.

We thank the many organizations, associations, and chambers of commerce who have invited us to bring the Dream, Believe, Dare, Do principles to their employees and audiences through Dream Retreats, seminars, keynote presentations and customer-centric cultural implementations. We would also like to thank the many clients who helped make the second edition of *The Disney Way* so successful in many languages.

We also thank John Christensen, our friend and *FISH!* guru, for his heartfelt and well-penned foreword. We have appreciated our friendship with John, which spans over two decades.

A special thanks to Don Johnson, City Manager, and Kayla Barber-Perrotta, Customer Service Champion, from the city of Royal Oak, Michigan, for leading and facilitating the city's customer-centric cultural implementation; and also to Roberto Jara of Holland, Michigan, for introducing storyboarding to the Holland community.

We are in awe of the following leaders and their staffs associated with our current featured organizations:

**zTailors.** George Zimmer, Founder and CEO

**ACTS Retirement-Life Communities.** Mark Vanderbeck, CEO; Jerry Grant, President and COO; Charlie Coxson, Senior Vice President of Community Operations; Bill Mead, Chaplain; and the many residents who shared their experiences

**Flanagin's Bulk Mail Service.** Donna Flanagin, Owner and Chief Excitement Officer

**Grand Lake, Colorado.** DiAnn Butler, Economic Development Coordinator; Ed Moyer, Assistant County Manager and Director of Community Development; Judy Burke, Mayor; Jim White, Town Manager; and Jackie and Mike Tompkins, Co-owners of Western Riviera Motel

**TYRA** *Beauty.* Tyra Banks, Founder and CEO; Anita Krpata, General Manager; Kim Giannini, Director of Beautytainer Experience; and Elana Weiss, Co-founder and Publicist

**Rainbow Babies & Children's Hospital, University Hospitals Case Medical Center.** Claudia Hoyen, MD, Director of Innovation; and Stephen Behm, Director of Technology Management

**California State University Channel Islands.** Dr. Wm. Gregory Sawyer, Vice President of Student Affairs; Dr. Jennifer Miller, former Director of Student Affairs Assessment, Research and Staff Development; Gary C. Gordon II, Coordinator of Residential Education; Michael McCormack, Coordinator of Community Programs; Motoko Kitazumi, Coordinator of Intercultural Services; Dr. Amanda Carpenter, Assistant Director of Career Development; Henry "Hank" L. Lacayo Institute Internship Program; and Dorothy Ayer, Special Assistant to the Vice President of Student Affairs

**Joe C. Davis YMCA Outdoor Center/Camp Widjiwagan.** Jeff Merhige, Executive Director of the YMCA Outdoor Center; and Bob Knestrick, COO of the YMCA of Middle Tennessee

**McLean County, Illinois, Unit (School) District No. 5.** Dr. Mark Daniel, Superintendent

**Science Center of Iowa.** Curt Simmons, President and CEO; Renee Harmon, Vice President of Science Learning; Allison Schwanebeck, Director of Exhibits; and Jennifer Koska, Visitor Experience Manager

**Ottawa County, Michigan.** Al Vanderberg, Administrator; Keith Van Beek, Deputy County Administrator; Misty Cunningham, Administrative Assistant and Champion of the Ottawa Way; Stephanie Roelofs, Administrative Assistant; Greg Rappleye, Corporation Counsel; Gary Rosema, Sheriff; Steve Kempker, Undersheriff; Lisa Stefanovsky, Health Officer; Betty Blase, District Coordinator, Michigan State University Extension; Mark Knudsen, Director of Planning and Performance Improvement Department; Kevin Bowling, Circuit/Probate Court Administrator; Rick VandeKerkoff, Facilities Director; Brad Slagh, County Treasurer; Thom Lattig, Assistant Juvenile Service Director; the Ottawa County Board of Commissioners; and the hundreds of county employees who make the county special

Your stories will surely inspire others to bring Walt Disney's success credo to their own organizations. Thank you for inspiring us!

Bill Capodagli and Lynn Jackson

# Index

Note: page numbers in *italics* refer to illustrations.

Aaker, Jennifer, 40
ABC network, 129, 263
Achievement recognition, 149–150
ACTS Retirement Communities, 46–50
Advertising, 207, 218
Aetna, 88
Aflac duck, 41
Albrecht, Karl, 3
Allen, Thomas J., Jr., 87
Amazon.com, 92
Ambassador Program, Ottawa County, Michigan, 244–245
American Airlines, 219
Animal Kingdom park, 110–111
Animation. *See also specific films*
  innovation and, 6–7
  perfection and, 204
  planning and, 163–164
  rerelease policy, 35
  story and, 15
  storyboarding and, 179, 180–181
Apple, 112, 221
Aristotle, 151
Attitude, 151, *152*
Auerbach, Red, 89
*Avatar*, 110–111
Awards, 149–150
Ayer, Dorothy, 161

Backstage processes, 58, 80, 260
Baird, Sharon, 158
*Bambi* (film), 37, 53, 215
Banks, Tyra, 114–121
Barber-Perrotta, Kayla, 56
Barriers Storyboard, 152, 193
Bass, Sid, 266
*Beauty and the Beast* (film), 53, 266
*Beauty and the Beast* stage play, 135–136
Behm, Stephen, 138–139
Believe principle. *See also* Guests and Guest
    service; Partnerships; Teams and
    teamwork
  ACTS Retirement Communities example,
    46–50
  The Company's commitment to, 264–265
  core values and, 32–34, 35
  employee buy-in and, 40–42
  family values and, 31
  innovation and, 36–40
  long-term mentality and, 35–36
  Ottawa County, Michigan, story,
    234–235
  training and, 34–35
  vision alignment, 42–44, *43, 45*
"Bibbidi-Bobbidi-Boo" (song), 18
*Big Hero 6* (film), 38–39
Bishop, Rebecca, 169
Blake, Catherine, 135
Blase, Betty, 238–239
Blizzard Beach, 18–19

Blue Sky process, 165, 168
BoardWalk, 80–81
Boatwright, Peter, 215, 221
Bonuses, 150
Bowling, Kevin, 241–242, 246–247
Box, Mark, 252
Brainstorming, 181
Brain Trust process, 93, 258–259
Brand loyalty, 60
Bristol-Myers Squibb, 83–84
Broken Squares exercise, 172–173
Brown, Hubie, 89
Brown, Stuart, 134
Buddha, 223
Budweiser Clydesdales, 218
*Built to Love* (Boatwright and Cagan), 215, 221
"Bump the lamp," 210–211
Burke, Judy, 96
Buscaglia, Leo, 220, 227
Butler, DiAnn, 97–98
Byfuglin, Max, 109–110

Cagan, Jonathan, 215, 221
California Institute of the Arts, 16
California State University Channel Islands, 158–161
Cameron, James, 110–111
Candland, Paul, 108–109
Capodagli, "Ma," 224–227
Carlzon, Jan, 68–69
Caron, Kristen, 250–251
Carpenter, Amanda, 161
Carpenter, Loren, 38
Carroll, Dave, 61–62
Case studies versus stories, 41
Cast Excellence Survey, 157
Castillo, Tony, 90–91
Casting Centers, 132
Cast Members. *See* Employees or Cast Members
Catmull, Ed, 17, 38–39, 93, 111, 112, 126, 258
Catmull, John, 17
Chapek, Bob, 169
The Cheesecake Factory, 109–110
Chief Technology Officers (CTOs), 77–78
Chouinard Art Institute, 144

Christensen, John, 135
Christmas Parade, Disneyland, 221–222
Chrysler, 88
*Cinderella* (film), 18
Cinderella's Castle, 206
ClearPoint Credit Counseling Solutions, 191
Closed attractions, 212–213
Close out stage, 166
Coca-Cola, 105
Codes of Conduct, 56–58, 133
Collaboration. *See* Partnerships; Teams and teamwork
Colocating, 87–89, 172
Communication
  colocating and, 87–88
  customer-centric culture implementation and, 255
  formal plans for, 188–189
  informational diversity, 113
  partnerships and, 104
  planning centers and, 194
  storyboarding and, 189–190
Communications Storyboard, 198
Compensation reviews, 156
Competition, 89
Concept development, 165
Continuous learning, 154. *See also* Training, practice, and professional development
Contract documents, 166
Cook, Rob, 38
Core values, 32–34, 35, 208
Corporate partnerships. *See* Partnerships
Corporate strategy, redefining, 40–42
Covey, Steven, 112
Coxson, Charlie, 48, 50
Craig, Jim, 191
Creativity
  Dream Retreats and, 20–22
  Google and, 133
  informational diversity and, 113
  managed, 164–166
  storyboarding and, 193, 198
  **TYRA** *Beauty* and, 118
  Walt on sticking with an idea, 237
Crofton, Meg, 151
Cross, William, 65, 209, 210

Crowther, Bosley, 107

Culture, organizational, 8, 24–25, 37, 128, 144, 146, 150–153, 261–262. *See also* Implementation of customer-centric culture

Cunningham, Misty, 243–245

Customer-Centric Culture: *The Disney Way* Experience, 255–261. *See also* Implementation of customer-centric culture

Customer Feedback Storyboard, 194–196, *196*

Customer service. *See* Guests and Guest service

Cynicism, 44

Dalai Lama, 218

Daniel, Mark, 199–200

Darden Restaurants, 109–110

Dare principle (risk and risk taking)
  The Company leadership and, 265–266
  courage and, 240
  Disneyland and, 125–126
  Disney Theatrical Productions and, 135–136
  forms of risk, 130–132
  Great Lakes Ag-Tech Business Incubator (GLATBI), 239–240
  human resources (HR), rethinking, 132–134
  Pixar and, 38
  play and making it fun, 134–135
  premier players and, 125
  Rainbow Babies and Children's Hospital and, 137–139
  short-term mentality, avoiding, 128–130
  solid fundamentals to support, 126–128
  Walt and, 125–127, 128–129

Da Vinci, Leonardo, 211

Day, Jake, 37

Deming, W. Edwards, 133–134, 154, 173, 244

Design objectives, planning, 166

Destinations West, 97

Detail Cards for storyboarding, 183–185, *184*

Details. *See* Perfection and attention to details

Development planning, 155–158

Digital Immersive Showroom, 23

The Dish, 23

Disney, Roy E. (nephew), 103, 266, 267

Disney, Roy O. (brother), 4, 6, 31, 86–87, 112–113, 126, 149, 206–207, 221–222, 265

Disney, Walt
  *Bambi* and, 37
  on Cast growth and development, 143–144
  Cast Member participation and, 21
  on city of tomorrow, 233
  on cleanliness, 243
  company culture and, 34
  on courage, 125, 240
  death of, 265
  Disneyland Christmas Parade and, 221–222
  on doing, 253
  Dream, Believe, Dare, Do principles and, 1–2
  as dreamer, 5–7
  early life and career of, 1, 3–5, 31
  on education, 239
  "entertainment" test of, 127
  at first Disneyland orientation (1955), 71, 242
  on Guests, 53, 66, 70–71
  hiring process and, 133
  humility of, 222
  Imagineering and, 18, 23
  innovation and, 36–37
  on interdependence, 246–247
  "it was all started by a mouse," 1
  on joy, 223–224
  leadership, definition of, 77
  legacy of, 268
  long-term mentality of, 35–36
  love and, 215, 217, 220, 222
  on new projects, 163
  partnerships and, 101, 105–106
  as penny pincher, 207
  perfectionism of, 8, 203, 204–206
  as pioneer, 125
  planning and, 164
  planning centers and, 194
  private apartment at Disneyland, 269

Walt Disney (*Cont.*)
  on reshaping Disneyland, 247
  on reward, 263
  risk taking and, 125–127, 128–129
  Roy, relationship with, 86–87, 101–102,
    265
  on sticking with an idea, 237
  story and, 15–16
  storyboarding and, 179, 180–181, 193,
    246
  teamwork and, 75, 79, 84, 247
  Tyra Banks on, 114–115
  values and, 31–34, 44
Disney Brothers Cartoon Studio, 4,
    101–104
Disney Cruise Line, 263
Disney Interactive, 108
Disneyland
  author's experience with, 2
  the castle, 15–16, *16*
  Christmas Parade, 221–222
  colors in, 205
  construction of, 7–8
  corporate partnerships, 105–106
  expansion of, 263
  first Cast Member orientation (1955),
    71, 242
  Haunted Mansion, 84–85
  Jungle Cruise, 33
  love and passion for, 220
  Main Street railroad station, 167
  monorail, 167
  opening of, 53
  real estate and, 36
  as reshapable, 247
  as risky concept, 125–126
  Star Wars Land, 169
  story and, 15–16
  success of, 10
  Tom Sawyer casting story, 145–146
  Walt's private apartment in, 269
  "weenies" (landmarks), 167
Disneyland Paris, 66, 263
Disney Springs, 20
Disney Theatrical Productions, 135–136
Disney University (Disney U), 34–35, 66,
    112, 144, 206

Disney Vacation Club, 221, 263
*The Disney Way Fieldbook* (Capodagli and
    Jackson), 86, 172
Disney World. *See* Walt Disney World
Diversity, 113, 147, 189–190
Docter, Pete, 76, 134
Do principle. *See* Implementation of
    customer-centric culture; Planning;
    Training, practice, and professional
    development
Dowagiac Union Schools, Michigan,
    199–200
Dream, Believe, Dare, Do principles, 1–2,
    9–10, 255, *256. See also specific*
    *principles*
Dream principle
  cultural transformation and, 24–25
  Dream Retreats and, 20–22
  Imagineers and, 18–20
  Jiminy Cricket's definition of dream, 15
  love and, 220
  storytelling, dreams coming alive through,
    17–18
  tracking good ideas, 22–23
  turning dreams into reality, 7–8, 170
  values-based approach and, 25
  Walt as dreamer, 5–7
  zTailors example, 25–27
Dream Retreats, 20–22, 57, 174, 190,
    194–195, 208
Dreyer, R. S., 83
Drucker, Peter, 94
Dugan, Michelle, 191
*Dumbo* (film), 163–164

80/20 principle, 244
Eisner, Michael, 22, 37, 106, 135–136,
    211
Emerson, Ralph Waldo, 226–227
Emotional needs, 216
Employees or Cast Members. *See also*
    Training, practice, and professional
    development
  balancing Guests, Cast, and business
    practice, 208
  buy-in by, 40–42, 256–257
  Disney Casting Centers, 132

diverse talent base, 147
employee handbooks, 133–134
engagement of, 60–61
Gong Show event, 22–23
human resources and hiring, rethinking
of, 132–134, 261
love for, 215–217
number of Disney Cast Members,
265
"outside help," problem of, 34
participation of, 7–8, 21
roles, not jobs, 57–58
storytelling and, 15
street cleaners at Walt Disney World,
206
turning into guests, 59
turnover rates, 21
Engagement, 60–61, 218–219
Environments inferior vs. enriched, 199
Epcot, 106, 146, 207
Ernst & Young, 39
Euro-Disney, 66
Excellence, 6, 33–34, 35, 50, 146, 151,
174, 200. *See also* Perfection and
attention to details

*Fantasia* (film), 22, 107–108
Feasibility planning, 165
Feedback, 67–69, 194–196, *196*
Fields, Mark, 127
Finances
licensing, 106–107, 207–208
partnerships and, 105–106, 110
planning and, 164
profits, 10, 17
stock performance, 1, 10
*FISH!* (Lundin and Christensen),
135
Flanagin, Donna, 72–73
Flanagin's Bulk Mail Service and
"Flanagin's Fairies," 71–73
Ford, 127–128
Four Seasons Hotels and Resorts, 59,
62–64, 78–79
Frankl, Viktor, 151
Fred Astaire Dance Studios, 190
Frito-Lay, 105

Frontline Leadership Workshop, 256
*Frozen* (film), 18

Gallup Customer Engagement Score (CES),
218–219
General Mills, 88
Generation Tux, 27
Generation X, 89
Giannini, Kim, 116, 118, 120
Giuliani, Rudy, 136
Golden Rule, 78–79, 217–218, 244, 247,
248, 252
GOLD Training Program, Ottawa County,
Michigan, 240–242
Gong Show event, 22–23, 32
"Good show" mentality, 4, 33, 57–58,
109–110, 144, 204, 207, 264
Google, 133
Gordon, Gary C., III, 160
Gracey, Yale, 84–85
Graham, Don, 144
Grand Lake, Colorado, 96–98
Grant, Jerry, 46
Great Lakes Ag-Tech Business Incubator
(GLATBI), 239–240
Great Service Fanatic cards, 149
Green, Paul, Jr., 94–95
Grump, Rolly, 84–85
Guests and Guest service (customers and
customer service)
customer engagement, 60
employee engagement and, 60–61
feedback and, 67–69
Flanagin's Bulk Mail Service example,
71–73
getting your company on track,
66–71
good versus poor service, 54–58
innovation and extraordinary service,
39–40
motif of Guests in Disney films, 53
MyMagic+ as innovation for, 58–59
Ottawa County, Michigan, Health
Department and, 236–237
perception, power of, 69–70
problem solving and, 61–64, 67

Guests and Guest service (*Cont.*)
  process and, 64–66
  returning Guests, 10, 17
  turning employees into Guests, 59
  **TYRA** *Beauty* and, 117
  values and, 33
  Walt on, 53, 66, 70–71
Gunn, George R., Jr., 47

Habits, *150*, 150–153
Hamel, Gary, 94
Harmon, Renee, 212
Haunted Mansion, Disneyland, 84–85
Header Cards for storyboarding, *184*,
    184–186
Heiskell, Marian, 136
Hench, John, 205
Hendrickson, Andy, 38
*Hercules* (film), 23, 32
Hiring processes, 132–133
Holidays for Your Home collections, 168
Holistic approach, 172–173, 210
Holland High School, Michigan, 191–193
Hollywood Studios park, 169
Holmes, Phil, 157–158
*Holocracy* (Robertson), 92
Honenberger, Christopher, 191
Hong Kong Disneyland, 129–130, 263
Hot Seat, 241–242, 257
Hoyen, Claudia, 137, 139
Hsieh, Tony, 92–93
Human resources, rethinking, 132–134,
    144
*The Hunchback of Notre Dame* (film), 32
Hundredth monkey story, 23–24
Hyperion, 38–39

Ideas Storyboard, 193
Iger, Bob, 23, 36–37, 58, 77–78, 102, 110,
    111–112, 130, 266–267
Illinois Power, 188
Imagination, 5, 23
Imagineers and Imagineering, 18–20, 23,
    110–111, 130, 167–169, 205. *See also*
    Planning
Implementation of customer-centric culture
  Brain Trust process, 258–259
  checklist, 259–261

cultural change, commitment to,
    253–254, 261–262
Customer-Centric Improvement Team,
    259
factors to consider beforehand, 254–255
Frontline Leadership Workshop, 256
Hot Seat, 257
realization (employee buy-in), 256–257
Steering Team, 254, 255
storyboarding, 258
Improvement Team, Customer-Centric,
    259
Indian River Estates, Vero Beach, Florida,
    49
Infinity, 108
Informational diversity, 113
*Innovate the Pixar Way* (Capodagli and
    Jackson), 17, 77, 111
Innovation, 5, 6–7, 36–40, 117, 128,
    137–139
International Flower and Garden Festival,
    Epcot, 207
ITunes store, 111–112
Iwerks, Ub, 103–104

Jara, Roberto ("Bert"), 191–193
Jeep, 218
Jiminy Cricket, 6, 15, 206
Jobs, Steve, 89, 111–112
Joe C. Davis YMCA Outdoor Center/
    Camp Widjiwagan, Nashville,
    173–176
Johnson, David, 89
Johnson, Don, 56
Johnson, Roger, 89
Jungle Cruise, 33

Katzenberg, Jeffery, 77
Kempker, Steve, 238, 242
Kennedy, John F., 9
Kennedy, Natalie, 168
Kimball, Ward, 6, 16
King, Martin Luther, Jr., 223
Knestrick, Bob, 175
Knudsen, Mark, 239–240
Kodak, 106
Koestler, Arthur, 92
Kohn, Alfie, 89

Koska, Jennifer, 213
Krpata, Anita, 115, 117, 118, 119, 120

Ladouceur, Bob, 225
Lady (dog), 166–167
Lakeshore Youth Leaders, 192
Lakhiani, Vishen, 88
Lasseter, John, 16–17, 38, 76–77, 93, 103,
    134, 179, 267
Latin Americans United for Progress
    (LAUP), 191–193
Lattig, Thom, 246
Leadership
    courage and, 240
    customer service and failures in, 54
    innovation and, 37
    *most* individuals as leaders, 147
    Ottawa County, Michigan, and, 234–235
    teams and, 77–79, 81–84
    training and, 147
    **TYRA** *Beauty* and, 118–121
    Walt's definition of, 77, 118–120
Leadership Storyboard, 196–197, *197*,
    245–246
*Leading at the Speed of Change* (Capodagli
    and Jackson), 120
Learning, continuous, 154. *See also*
    Training, practice, and professional
    development
"Let It Go" (song), 18
Lever, A. F., 239
Licensing, 106–107, 207–208
Line company, 108–109
Linkletter, Art, 105–106
*The Lion King* (film), 266
*The Little Mermaid* (film), 171, 266
Long-term mentality, 35–36, 105, 110–
    111, 119–120, 128–130
Love
    Boatwright and Cagan's *Built to Love*,
        215, 221
    for customers, 217–220
    for employees, 215–217
    Ma Capodagli and Village Toy Center,
        Bensenville, Illinois, example,
        224–227
    for oneself, 222–224
    for product, 220–222

*Loyalty Rules!* (Reichheld), 54
LRN, 94

Macy's, 27
MagicBands, 58
Main Street railroad station, 167
Market knowledge, 65–66
*Mary Poppins* (film), 53
Más Adelante program (Holland High
    School, Michigan), 192–193
Mathews, Fred L., 200
McCormack, Michael, 160
McDonald's, 90–91
McDuffee, Rachel, 251
McKuen, Rod, 25
McLean County, Illinois, Unit (School)
    District No. 5, 199–200
Mead, Bill, 49
Mead Johnson Nutrition, 65, 209,
    210
Measurement of details, 208–210
Mello Smello, 109
Men's Wearhouse, 26, 27
Menzel, Idena, 18
Merhige, Jeff, 174–176
Merryweather Pleasure, 19–20
Michaels, Al, 102
Michigan State University Extension,
    238–239
Mickey Mouse, 1, 4, 32, 102 103,
    106–107, 222
*Mickey Mouse Book*, 105
Mickey Mouse watches, 106
Micromanagement, avoidance of, 171
Mies van der Rohe, Ludwig, 203
Millennial generation, 88–89, 147–148
Millennium Celebration, Walt Disney
    World, 200
Miller, Diane Disney, 102
Miller, Jennifer, 159–160, 161
Mindvalley, 88
Miner, Jon, 109
Miner, Leah, 109
Mintz, Charles, 102–103
Mission statements, 79
"Moments of truth," 68
Monkeys story, 24–25
Monorail, 167

Monroe County, Michigan, Chamber of
    Commerce, 191
Morning Star, 94–95
Mousecar award, 149
Moyer, Ed, 97
Mulally, Alan, 127–128
Munansangu, Evita, 57
Music and storytelling, 18
My Disney Experience, 58–59
Myers-Briggs Type Indicator, 85–86,
    261
MyMagic+, 58–59

Naisbit, John, 135
National Institute for Play, 134
Neilsen, Kay, 171
Net Promoter Score (NPS), 68
Neuschwanstein Castle, Bavaria, *16*
*No Contest* (Kohn), 89
Nordstrom, 57
Nunis, Dick, 33

Oliveri, Concetta "Connie," 80
Oliveri, Domenico "Chef Dom,"
    80–81
Oswald the Rabbit, 102
Ottawa County, Michigan
    Christmas surprise, 247
    County Administrator, 234–235
    County Clerk and Register of Deeds
        Office, 249
    courts, 246–247, 251–252
    customer-centric culture, need for,
        233–234
    Customer Service Award winners,
        247–252
    Customer Service Team and Ambassador
        Program, 244–245
    *Daybook* story, 41–42, 235–236
    Facilities Department, 242–243
    Great Lakes Ag-Tech Business Incubator
        (GLATBI), 239–240
    Growth Opportunities in Learning and
        Development (GOLD) Training
        Program, 240–242
    Health Department, 236–237
    Michigan State University Extension,
        238–239

Probation and Community Corrections,
    249–250
Sheriff's Office, 237–238, 247–248,
    250–251
storyboarding and, 243–246
Overton, David, 109, 110
Overton, Evelyn, 109

Pandora, 110–111
Parks and Resorts division, 8, 17, 33–34,
    111. *See also specific parks and resorts*
Partnerships
    Disney Brothers Studio and, 101–104
    essential elements of "Share the Spotlight"
        strategy, 104–105
    expanding horizons with, 106–109
    good show experiences through, 109–110
    as long-term investments, 110–111
    Ottawa County, Michigan, and Michigan
        State University Extension, 238–239
    Pixar, Apple, and Disney, 111–112
    prosperity and, 105–106
    **TYRA** *Beauty* example, 114–121
    values, reflecting, 112–113
Patton, George, 173
Peanuts comic strip, 132
Perception, power of, 69–70
Perfection and attention to details
    balance of, 206–208
    big picture and, 203
    "Bump the lamp," 210–211
    excellence and, 203
    "good show" and, 204
    Ma Capodagli and, 226
    measurement and, 208–210
    Ottawa County, Michigan, courts and,
        246–247
    relentless search for perfection,
        204–206
    Science Center of Iowa (SCI) example,
        211–214
    Walt and, 8, 203, 204–206
Performance appraisals, 153–156
Performance Learning Cycle, *148*,
    148–150
*Peter Pan* (film), 2
Peters, Tom, 54–55
Photography, 206–207

Pike Place Fish Market, Seattle, 135
*Pinocchio* (film), 6, 16, 33, 206
Pirates of the Caribbean (ride), 8
Pitaro, Jimmy, 108
Pixar Animation Studios, 17, 38–39, 76–77, 89, 93, 111–112, 134, 267
Planning
  animation and, 163–164
  development planning, 155–158
  holistic approach and, 172–173
  ideas, testing, 167–171
  Joe C. Davis YMCA Outdoor Center/ Camp Widjiwagan example, 173–176
  managed creativity and the planning process, 164–166, *165*
  monorail and, 167
  Ottawa County, Michigan, Facilities Department, 242–243
  planning centers, 87, 171–172, 194
  "weenies" (landmarks), introducing, 166–167
Planning Storyboard, 190–191, 194
Play, value of, 134
Pleasure Island, 19–20, 43–44, *45*
Plumbing & Industrial Supply, 70, 152–153
"Plus-ing," 204, 221–222
Post-it notes, 64
*The Practice of Management* (Drucker), 94
PricewaterhouseCoopers (PwC), 88–89, 147
Priority Voting Dots for storyboarding, *184*, 185
Process improvements, 157
Production stage of planning, 166
Professional development. *See* Training, practice, and professional development
Project planning. *See* Planning
Purcell, Theresa, 219

Quality measurement, 208–210
Quarterly pulse checks (QPCs), 175

Radio frequency identification (RFID) wristbands, 58
Rainbow Babies and Children's Hospital, Cleveland, 137–139
Ranft, Joe, 76

R&D Divisions, 37
Reagan, Nancy, 63
Real estate, 36
Recognition, 149–150, 247
Redenbacher, Orville, 72
Reichheld, Frederick F., 54, 68
*Reinventing the Corporation* (Naisbit), 135
Reward systems, 89–91
Risk taking. *See* Dare principle
Robertson, Brian, 92
Roelofs, Stephanie, 241
*Roger Rabbit* (film), 210
Rokisky, Mary Beth, 249
Rosema, Gary, 237–238
Rothweiler, Jack, 190
Royal Oak, Michigan, Codes of Conduct, 56–58
Rush, Richard R., 159

Saint-Exupéry, Antoine de, 223
Sales Protocol International, 135
San Jose State University, 69
Sawyer, Gregory, 159, 161
Scandinavian Airlines (SAS), 68 69
Schematic planning, 165
Schneider, Peter, 22, 32
Schofield, John, 217
Schulz, Charles, 132
Schwanebeck, Allison, 212
Science Center of Iowa (SCI), 57, 211–214
Security officers, Walt's advice to, 34, 238
Self-management, 91–95
Semco, 91–92
Semler, Ricardo, 91–92
Senn, Larry, 119
*Service America* (Albrecht and Zemke), 3
Seven Dwarfs Mine Train, 168–169, 205
"The Seven Trends Impacting Today's Workplace," 83
Shah, Niki, 227
Shanghai Disneyland, 23, 110, 130, 263
Sharing the spotlight. *See* Partnerships
Sharp, Isadore (Issy), 44, 78–79
Short-term mentality, avoiding, 128–130. *See also* Long-term mentality
Simmons, Curt, 212, 214
Skees, Theron, 20
Sklar, Marty, 203

Slagh, Brad, 245–246
Smith, Hoke, 239
*Snow White and the Seven Dwarfs* (film), 3,
    5, 6–7, 53, 76, 125, 205
Soarin', 168
*Song of the South* (film), 171
*The Sorcerer's Apprentice*, 107
Southwest Airlines, 219–220
Spock, Benjamin, 137
Staggs, Tom, 58–59, 110, 146–147
Stanton, Andrew, 76
Star Wars Land, 169
*Steamboat Willie* (film), 4, 103
Steering Team, 254, 255
Stefanovsky, Lisa, 236–237, 241
Steinberg, Saul, 265
Stokowski, Leopold, 107–108
Storyboarding
    acceptance of, 186–188
    for animation, 179, 180–181
    Barriers Storyboard, 152, 193
    birth of the technique, 180–182
    communications dilemma, solving,
        188–190
    Communications Storyboard, 198
    creative and critical thinking, role in,
        198–199
    customer-centric culture implementation
        and, 258
    customer feedback and, 68
    Customer Feedback Storyboard,
        194–196, *196*
    for enriched environments, 199
    facilitator, role of, 186
    Holland High School, Michigan,
        example, 191–193
    Ideas Storyboard, 193
    Leadership Storyboard, 196–197, *197*,
        245–246
    for *The Little Mermaid*, 171
    logical progression, 182, 187
    McLean County, Illinois, Unit District
        No. 5 example, 199–200
    Ottawa County, Michigan, and, 243–246
    Planning Storyboard, 190–191, 194
    preparation for, 183
    procedure, 183–186, *184*

Rainbow Babies and Children's Hospital
    and, 138
supplies for, 182
teamwork and, 88
uses of, 179–180
Storytelling
    animation and, 15, 16
    authenticity and, 205
    brand storyteller, secrets from, 41
    culture transmitted to employees through,
        34–35
    customer-centric culture implementation
        and, 260
    Disneyland and, 15–16
    dreams coming alive through, 17–18
    employees and, 40–41
    music and, 18
    show experience and, 58
    teamwork and, 79–81
    Walt and, 15–16
Strategic thinking, 40–42
Stravinsky, Igor, 107
Sumner, Mark, 168
Supplier Diversity Outreach statement,
    113

Tatum, Donn, 265
Teams and teamwork
    "Be our Guest" philosophy and, 75
    colocating, advantages of, 87–89
    Disneyland construction and, 7–8
    Dream Retreats and, 20–22
    feature animation and, 75–76
    Ford and, 127
    Grand Lake, Colorado, example, 96–98
    leadership and, 77–79, 81–84
    multinational, 21
    Ottawa County Sheriff's Office and,
        237–238
    Pixar and, 76–77
    reward systems and, 89–91
    role and potential uses of, 95
    self-management and, 91–95
    sports and, 75–76
    story and, 79–81
    structure for, 81–84
    success factors in team building, 84–87

Technicolor, 105, 125
Technological advances, 125, 128–129
Television, emergence of, 129
Terpstra, Benjamin, 248–249
Thompkins, Jackie, 98
Thompkins, Mike, 97–98
Thompson, Ruthie, 134
Thoreau, Henry David, 96
3M, 64, 109
*Thriving on Chaos* (Peters), 54–55
TINYpulse, 83
Tokyo Disneyland and DisneySea, 263
Tom Sawyer casting story, 145–146
Topiaries, 33–34, 207
Topic Cards for storyboarding, 183, *184*,
     185
"Touch points," 68
*Toy Story* (film), 76–77, 93, 111, 134
Traditions training program, 34–35, 145–
     146, 158
Training, practice, and professional
     development
  California State University Channel
     Islands example, 158–161
  development planning, 155–158
  Disney University, 34–35, 66, 112, 144
  first Disneyland orientation (1955), 71,
     242
  habits for customer-centric culture, *150*,
     150–153
  importance of, 143–144
  leadership, values-based culture, and,
     147–148
  Ottawa County, Michigan, GOLD
     Program, 240–242
  performance appraisals, problem with,
     153–155
  Performance Learning Cycle, *148*,
     148–150
  recognition and awards, 149–150,
     247–252
  responsibility for, 145–147
  sink-or-swim mentality, 146
  traditional programs, 67
  Traditions program, 34–35, 145–146,
     158
  **TYRA** *Beauty* and, 118

Walt on, 143
  wholesome behaviors, love for self, and,
     223
Transformation, cultural, 24–25
Trattoria al Forno (BoardWalk), 80–81
Tsum Tsum toys, 108–109
Turnover rates, 21
**TYRA** *Beauty* company, 114–121

Uber Technologies, 26
Uhale, Peggy, 219
Uncle Robert, 1
"Under the Sea" (song), 171
United Airlines, 61–62
Universal Studios, Orlando, 18
University Hospitals (UH) Rainbow Babies
     and Children's Hospital, Cleveland,
     137–139
Unkrich, Lee, 76

Values-based approach
  ACTS Retirement-Life Community and,
     46
  alignment with, 42–44
  core values, 32–34, 35, 208
  cultural transformation and, 25
  customer-centric culture implementation
     and, 259–260
  family values, 31
  long-term mentality and, 35–36
  partnerships and, 112–113
  safety, courtesy, good show, and
     efficiency, in priority order,
     32–33
  training and, 147
  Walt and, 31–34, 44
  The Walt Disney Company and, 5
Van Beek, Keith, 240
Van Beusekom, Ben, 205
Vance, Michael, 112–113
VandeKerkhoff, Rick, 242–243
Vanderbeck, Mark, 48–49, 50
Vanderberg, Al, 233, 234–235, 241,
     243–244, 245, 247
Village Toy Center, Bensenville, Illinois,
     224–227
Vision, alignment with, 42–44

Vision Align tool, 42, *43*, *45*, 65
Visitor Experience Team (VET), Science
    Center of Iowa, 211–214

Walker, Card, 265
The Walt Disney Company. *See also specific*
    *topics*
  Believe principle and, 31–32, 264–265
  Disney Brothers Cartoon Studio, 4,
    101–104
  excellence and, 3–5
  growth of, 9–10, 263
  leadership history, 265–267
  legend and legacy of, 263–264, 268–269
  Pixar, purchase of, 111–112, 267
  planning centers, early use of, 194
  as service provider, 53, 56
  stock performance, 1, 10, 266, 267
  Supplier Diversity Outreach statement,
    113
  in tune with the nation, 267–269
  values of, 5
Walt Disney Legacy Award, 149–150
Walt Disney Studios, 103–104
Walt Disney World
  Blizzard Beach, 18–19
  carousel and photography in, 206–207
  Cast input at Magic Kingdom Park,
    157–158
  Cinderella's Castle, Magic Kingdom, 206
  construction of, 112–113
  corporate partnerships for Epcot, 106
  Disney's Old Key West, 221
  Disney Springs, 20
  Epcot's Discovery Day, 146
  expansion of, 263
  Guest problems and complaints, attention
    to, 56
  International Flower and Garden Festival,
    Epcot, 207

Millennium Celebration, 200
MyMagic+, 58–59
Pandora, Animal Kingdom, 110–111
Partners Plaque, Magic Kingdom,
    101
Pleasure Island, 19–20, 43–44, *45*
real estate acreage, 36
Seven Dwarfs Mine Train, Magic
    Kingdom, 168–169, 205
Star Wars Land, Hollywood Studios,
    169
street cleaners at, 206
success of, 10
*Walt's Way*, importance of, 3
Watson, Raymond, 265
"Weenies," 166–167
Weiss, Al, 148
Wells, Frank, 106, 266
West Point Military Academy, 217
"What Is Success?" (Emerson), 226–227
Whirlpool Corporation, 39, 90, 172,
    189–190
White, Jim, 98
WillowBrooke Court, 48
Winkler, Margaret, 102
*The Wonderful World of Disney* (TV),
    2–3

Xerox Corporation, 36

YMCA Camp Kern, Ohio, 174
YMCA Camp Widjiwagan, Nashville,
    173–176
Young, John, 59

Zappos, 92–93
Zemke, Ron, 3
Zimmer, George, 25–27
"Zip-A-Dee-Doo-Dah" (song), 171
zTailors, 25–27

# About the Authors

Bill Capodagli and Lynn Jackson cofounded Capodagli Jackson Consulting in 1993. The Capodagli Jackson Consulting Dream is the following:

> Imagine an organization where employees are enabled to use their good judgment to fulfill customer dreams . . . an organization where the values of mutual respect and trust abound . . . an organization where the individual's uniqueness, as well as the team's synergy, enriches the customer experience . . . a place where the creative talents and abilities of all are developed with great care . . . a place where workers are encouraged to take risks and learn from their mistakes . . . an organization where long-term goals and values guide all decision making . . . a culture where fun is encouraged for employees and customers alike.

Capodagli Jackson is dedicated to assisting organizations realize this Dream through keynote presentations; executive and team coaching and training; leadership, customer service, and creativity workshops; and customer-centric cultural implementations.

## Bill Capodagli: Dreamer, Castle Builder, Storyteller, Playground Wizard

With over three decades of dominion cogitating (a.k.a. management consulting, keynoting, facilitating), Bill Capodagli (pronounced "Cap'-o-die") has opined with many of the largest corporate kingdoms in the world as well as some of the smallest local serfdoms. Bill's renowned storytelling talent was acknowledged when his first book (coauthored with Lynn Jackson), *The Disney Way: Harnessing the Management Secrets of Disney in Your Company*, was recognized by *Fortune* magazine as a "best business book."

## Lynn Jackson: Playground Coach, Head Scribe, Chief Promulgation Centurion

Lynn holds degrees in psychology and counseling from Ball State University and organizational development and instructional systems technology from Indiana University. For over 20 years, Lynn has been leading corporate play-ground activities (a.k.a. coaching and counseling) and inspiring teams to adopt the Disney/Pixar principles.

● ● ●

Bill and Lynn have also coauthored *The Disney Way Fieldbook: How to Implement Walt Disney's Vision of "Dream, Believe, Dare, Do" in Your Company; Leading at the Speed of Change;* and *Innovate the Pixar Way: Business Lessons from the World's Most Creative Corporate Playground*.

To request a keynote presentation, workshop, or consulting engagement, contact Capodagli Jackson Consulting at dreamovations@aol.com or 317-547-5390. Visit their website at www.capojac.com.

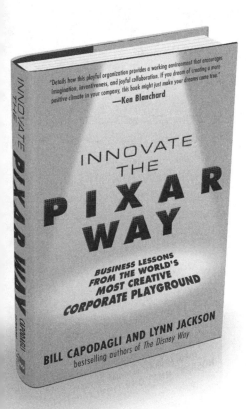
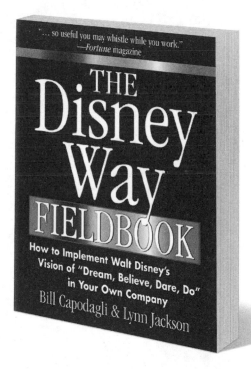